TO BUILD A BLACK FUTURE

TO
BUILD A
BLACK
FUTURE

THE RADICAL POLITICS
OF JOY, PAIN, AND CARE

CHRISTOPHER PAUL HARRIS

PRINCETON UNIVERSITY PRESS

PRINCETON AND OXFORD

Published by Princeton University Press
41 William Street, Princeton, New Jersey 08540
99 Banbury Road, Oxford OX2 6JX

press.princeton.edu

All Rights Reserved

ISBN 978-0-691-21906-6
ISBN (e-book) 978-0-691-21905-9

British Library Cataloging-in-Publication Data is available

Editorial: Bridget Flannery-McCoy and Alena Chekanov
Production Editorial: Jill Harris
Text Design: Karl Spurzem
Jacket Design: Katie Osborne
Production: Erin Suydam
Publicity: Kate Hensley and Kathryn Stevens

This book has been composed in Arno Pro with FK Screamer Black and Widescreen

Printed on acid-free paper. ∞

Printed in the United States of America

10 9 8 7 6 5 4 3 2 1

The uprisings in 2020
sprang from deep roots.
Roots that spread and burst
through soil and concrete casings.
For centuries
on and on, until.
Here follows
a fragment of that branch.
The wretched blooms of late.

CONTENTS

PART I

CHAPTER 1. We're Not Going to Stand for This   3

CHAPTER 2. New Forms/Known Rivers   41

PART II

CHAPTER 3. Regarding Black Pain   83

CHAPTER 4. A Joyful Rebellion   121

CHAPTER 5. The Operation(s) of Care   159

CODA. Politics in (and of) the Wake   200

Acknowledgments   207
Notes   213
Bibliography   237
Index   247

ONE

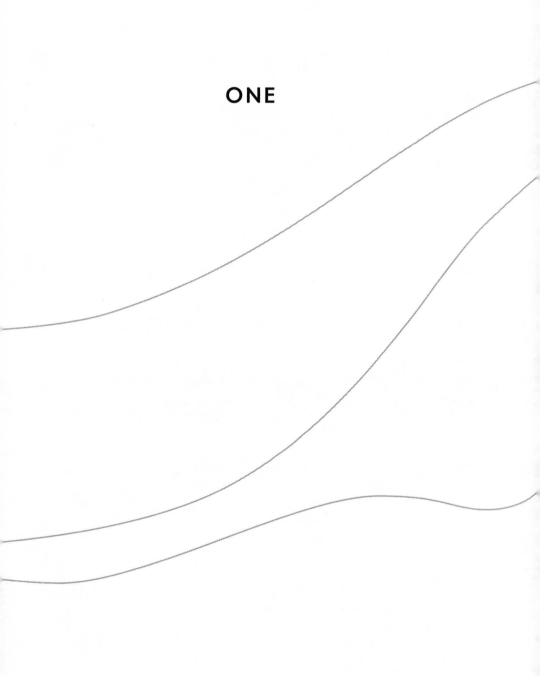

CHAPTER 1

We're Not Going to Stand for This

The mandate for Black people in this time,
is to avenge the suffering of our ancestors,
earn the respect of future generations,
and be willing to be transformed in the service of the work.

—MARY HOOKS

Every generation confronts the task of choosing its past. Inheritances
are chosen as much as they are passed on. The past depends less on
"what happened then" than on the desires and discontents of the
present. Strivings and failures shape the stories we tell. What we recall
has as much to do with the terrible things we hope to avoid as with the
good life for which we yearn.

—SAIDIYA HARTMAN

On a cold Saturday afternoon in December 2014, I joined tens of thousands of people on the streets of New York City to protest the killings
of Michael Brown, Eric Garner, and Akai Gurley while carrying the
names of countless victims of state-sanctioned violence against Black
and other people of color.[1] The march began near the iconic arch in
Washington Square Park and, fittingly, culminated at One Police Plaza:
the headquarters of the New York City Police Department. Throughout
the day, marchers from what seemed like every corner of the city bran-
dished now-familiar signs and shouted now-familiar chants. Each echoed

different iterations of a phrase that has since helped shift the terms of debate about anti-Blackness and its convergence with gender, sexuality, and class on a global scale: "Black Lives Matter."

Similar protests took place in other cities that afternoon, coordinated by loosely affiliated networks of support, leveraging social media. United in the spirit of a long-practiced tradition of public dissent, to "take it to the streets," people from across the country came together to publicly amplify the open wound of an anti-Black past whose shadow has yet to subside—a shadow, then and now, most viscerally present in the form of dead Black bodies.

With Black death center stage, the demonstration—labeled the "Millions March" by a self-described "multiracial grassroots collective of organizers committed to building [and] strengthening the movement for Black lives in NYC"—was a locally pitched call to arms. But their appeal to action and the magnitude of the response didn't arrive in a vacuum. The march came on the heels of smaller-scale protests sparked in the immediate aftermath of the acquittal of Daniel Pantaleo, the police officer responsible for choking Garner to death on Staten Island. It also took place less than six months after Brown's murder in Ferguson, Missouri—aided by the repressive tactics used by a heavily militarized Ferguson police department in its wake—ignited a highly visible tide of righteous rebellion, the effects of which similarly rippled across the country. The uprising in Ferguson was itself widely viewed as a turning point for Black people in that city and beyond. It marked a moment in the making since George Zimmerman was deemed to be "standing his ground" when he murdered Trayvon Martin the year before, the hour when many young Black people realized something must be done and that they were the ones to do it.[2]

Against this backdrop, the Millions March sought to harness and direct the outrage that, by the end of 2014, had all but boiled over. As twenty-three-year-old lead organizer Synead (Cyd) Nichols put it: "We want people to shut down their cities for justice. We are continuing where the freedom fighters of the Civil Rights movement left off. We are a new generation of young multiracial activists willing to take up the torch and we're not going to stand for this anymore."[3]

Continuity was essential to how these organizers understood their mandate. Nichols's words, along with the broader description of the collective's aims, suggested an ambition that surpassed the spectacle of a single march or the potential catharsis of staging a "day of anger."[4] In her tone, her reference to "freedom fighters" and the civil rights movement, and her stated willingness to "take up the torch," Nichols pointed to a prolonged and slower-moving process linked to centuries of Black political struggle and striving, a theater of battle they were now preparing to enter.

The history of this struggle and striving represents the narrative arc of Black politics, thought, and culture—its political development—fueled by generational trauma and the creativity that emerges from everyday survival, connected across political time and geographical space. It's not by chance that around the day of the march, a group of organizers, many of whom played central roles in sustaining the Ferguson uprising, gathered elsewhere in New York City. With the rebellion at an end, their goal was to discuss ways to continue working together and develop a more cohesive front to challenge anti-Blackness and its far too often deadly effects.[5] Something was brewing. To quote the widely used description of Black protest at that juncture: Nichols and these Black organizers were talking about a "movement not a moment."[6] How, why, and on what terms the movement would assert itself—what forms, in which domains, and with which lessons from the past—is the subject of this book.

~~~

When #BlackLivesMatter emerged in 2013, few anticipated the seismic role it would play in giving form and coherence to the most consequential and wide-reaching Black-led mobilization the United States has seen in decades, to say nothing of the many mobilizations that have taken place around the world. Since then, the hashtag-turned-rallying cry has helped solidify and spread a renewed, insurgent orientation toward Black politics, protest, and political thought, chiefly but not exclusively among younger Black folks.[7] *To Build a Black Future* examines the character and consequence of this insurgency, a political-cultural formation anchored by the assertion that *all* Black lives should and do matter, despite centuries of systematic devaluation and erasure—a dynamic and multimodal movement that operates from a threefold premise, underscoring its political culture: we must regard Black pain, champion Black joy, and practice a radically inclusive ethics of care.

But where to begin? The question is less obvious than it may seem. We know that movements don't emerge out of nowhere, even if they sometimes take us by surprise. Instead, movements are made, and their making, to borrow from Michel-Rolph Trouillot, is often "a story within a story—so slippery at the edges that one wonders when and where it started and whether it will ever end."[8] This slipperiness is particularly true of Black-led movements and for Black people more broadly, given the uneasy balance we often strike between a violent past that remains present and a present that, by definition, must in some way escape the past. Terror, or the potential for it, defies temporality. The racially motivated slaying of eleven people—ten of whom were Black—by a white supremacist teenager at a grocery store in a predominantly Black neighborhood in Buffalo, New York, could have as easily occurred in 1922 as when it happened: May 14, 2022—a hundred years later.

We would do well to bear the familiar warning in mind as we wander this mortal coil: objects in the mirror are closer than they appear. This message of caution captures what it means to live "in the wake" of slavery and colonialism, what it means to inhabit an anti-Black world—a story within a story, one that is now, before, and not yet, wherein Black and other marginalized people, those repeatedly faced with the sometimes brutal and other times subtle shank of subjection, are forced to wonder whether it will ever end.[9]

Despite the indeterminate nature of "living while Black," suspended between the past and present with the looming specter of Black pain serving as the connective thread, there is still one thing we can say for certain. Contingent circumstances, colored if not constrained by the gradual accumulation of history, condition political and social life in significant ways. To take one example, most of us did not choose to live under a system predicated on "growth" rather than "need," where the cost of living, what it takes to feed your family (however defined), what it takes to pay your rent or mortgage, fluctuates based on factors that have little to do with the way we live our lives and everything to do with logics we inherited but did not consent to. And this conditioning shapes how we interpret and move through the world at any given moment: the actions we pursue and what we think is possible. When approached through the prism of Black struggle, the converging ideological drifts that determine how Black people narrate the ending to our story within a story—how we escape the shadow of Black death and lead a life worthy of the term—have a concrete material basis, inseparable from the political, economic, and cultural paradigms that present certain pathways as legitimate and shade others with disdain. Taking stock of these contingencies by attending to what Anthony Reed has called the "Black Situation," meaning, "a total perspective" that links "the experience of time with historical analysis," helps illuminate the interplay between Black living, Black thought, and Black movement that concerns this book; it offers a place to begin.[10]

In a broader sense, the total perspective provided by the Black Situation, imagined here as a series of branches on the Black Diaspora's family tree, and a chronicle of the wretched of the earth, opens upon a larger, more overtly political aim: to employ histories of the Black present to speak to what might await us just beyond the horizon, an outlook on the other side of struggle, tempered in no small part by what such a horizon might call for, what it might demand if, when the dust settles and the embers have waned, "the last shall be first."[11] Just as Karl Marx remarked in reference to his own time, social revolution in the twenty-first century will require us to "create [our] poetry from the future, not from the past," even as the past still haunts and cannot be erased or forgotten if we are to make use of its lessons without succumbing to its weight.[12]

Attuned to the delicacy of this dance—as well as its necessity—I refer to the ideas, practices, and political culture that have come to define the current moment in Black rebellion as the "time of #BlackLivesMatter." Distinctive of this time is a radical praxis informed by the force of Black feminism and crystallized within and against a general atmosphere of political disillusionment. This disillusionment is rooted in a critique of Black politics and thought, particularly as advanced in the political and cultural mainstream following the Black Power era, those heady days when radicals had room to nurture meaningful alternatives and were both willing and able to make system-altering demands along the lines of what the Black Panther Party outlined in their Ten-Point Program in 1966. It's also closely tied to events that took place on the Continent, namely, the decline of African liberation's utopian promise, a juncture of diasporic hope that was, as Saidiya Hartman writes, "ambushed by the West and bankrupted by African dictators and kleptocrats" who, together, "made a travesty of independence."[13] This coincided with, in a manner of years, the advent of what Wendy Brown calls "neoliberal rationality," the "principles, policies, practices, and forms of governing reason" that have shaped the geopolitical landscape for the last forty-plus years.[14]

But this atmosphere of fading faith is also a reflection of—and in conversation with—a broader political current: the decade of global unrest challenging our prevailing political and economic structures and institutions. Following the financial collapse of 2007 and 2008, the unrest arguably began in 2011 with the Arab uprisings in the Middle East and Occupy Wall Street in the United States, subsequently stretching onward to where we find ourselves today, barreling toward an uncertain resolution whose prospects the astute observer would be forgiven for calling bleak, though not without opportunities. In other words, the Black Lives Matter Movement, now commonly referred to as the Movement for Black Lives (M4BL), is inseparable from what Neil Faulkner describes as a "wider crisis of world capitalism."[15]

~~~

What are the most salient characteristics of the current crisis of world capitalism? We can point to growing inequality and the social consequences of injustice, both of which were tragically evident in the disproportionate death toll of the Covid-19 pandemic among Black and Brown communities in the United States and in the unequal distribution of vaccines between the Global North and the Global South. The world we inhabit is layered by inequities that not only contain local, regional, and national dimensions but exist on a transnational scale, which means they will require the development of transnational solidarities. And we can just as easily point to the reemergence of fascist tendencies among both insurgent and more established right-wing movements, animated, to a large degree, by the swell of racial resentment and grievance politics that helped propel the presidency of Donald Trump and mainstream the formerly fringe "great replacement" theory that infected the mind of the Buffalo gunman.[16]

We might similarly note the war-caused displacement of millions of people across the "underdeveloped" world, often either spearheaded or supported by U.S. imperialism, not to mention the vigilant supply of American-produced arms and military aid to conflicts around the globe. Then there's the erosion of democratic norms and civil liberties if not "democracy" as such, to the extent that that word really applies in the American context, owed to this country's many, purposefully undemocratic national institutions—the Senate, the Supreme Court, and the Electoral College. Perhaps most menacingly of all, we face the planetary threat of ecological disaster resulting from climate change, made worse by the inertia of ruling-class political elites, with their perverse fidelity to capital accumulation, and the outsized political sway of predatory multinational corporations, whose origins, lest we forget, came by way of colonial pillage and exploitation.[17]

All of this suggests that addressing these interconnected crises, including the one that has engulfed Black politics and thought over the last several decades, necessitates a systemic critique that recognizes the particular in relation to the whole, an insight that Black feminists have been making for years. To borrow from the now famous words of the Combahee River Collective, a radical Black feminist organization founded in the mid-1970s, "the major systems of oppression are interlocking" and therefore demand "the development of integrated analysis and practice."[18] M4BL's political culture, carved from the crucible of the "morbid symptoms" associated with societal decline, and building on the critical foundation laid by Black feminist praxis, provides exactly that: an integrated analysis and practice.[19]

~~~

The wave of protests that swept across the country and world in the aftermath of George Floyd's lynching in 2020 was a reminder that the historical record of this latest iteration of the Black liberation struggle is still being written.[20] Nevertheless, the scale, composition, and geographical scope of the protests were a testament to the political and cultural imprint the movement has already established, an unambiguous register of rage and grief. Between late May 2020, when Floyd was killed, up until the end of April 2021—amid the deadly and poorly handled pandemic—there were over 11,000 demonstrations connected to #BlackLivesMatter across almost 3,000 cities and towns in all 50 states and Washington, D.C., many promoting the clear and uncompromising demand to defund the police. One of the largest and most powerful of these protests occurred on a Sunday afternoon in mid-June in Brooklyn, where more than 10,000 people gathered to rally and march for Black trans lives. The size of the crowd was an indication that many of us are now refusing to allow the subjection of some (e.g., Black cis heterosexual men) to carry more weight than everyone else. Globally, the number of #BlackLivesMatter demonstrations was just as impressive, with nearly 9,000 taking place in 74 different countries,[21] which only goes to show that racialized police violence—and resistance to it—knows no borders.

The burning of the Third Police Precinct in Minneapolis, "an enemy outpost," as Geo Maher poignantly described it, just three days after Floyd perished under the pressure of Derek Chauvin's knee, set the tone for the weeks to come.[22] As the summer unfolded, burned-out police cars, broken storefront windows, and toppled monuments that previously stood as tributes to white supremacy and colonialism all became militant markers of a growing consensus, a line in the sand, and a way forward. The uprisings reflected the disillusionment of the era, which is why it's notable that many of the sites of collective discontent during the rebellion also featured prominent displays of Black joy, a joy we might think of as an embodied practice, theory, and vision of the future performed in the present, in this case enacted through the countermodalities of Black culture.

Over the course of the summer, the streets brimmed with music and movement: protesters singing together to classic R&B songs like Bill Withers's "Lean on Me" in the nation's capital and dancing to modern remakes of familiar favorites like Beyoncé's take on the Frankie and Maze hit "Before I Let Go" in George Floyd's city. The transgressive interventions of hip-hop were just as prominent, such as when songs by the rappers BeatKing, Missy Elliott, and Chief Keef elevated a protest turned block party as the evening waned in Chicago. More than a somber procession or an expression of collective anger chorused by the dispossessed, Black culture and performance—an unapologetic Black joy—were centered at and central to the aesthetics of the uprisings. They were key parts of what made the demonstrations "rehearsals of revolution," as the Marxist art critic and novelist John Berger once put it, transforming the streets into a "temporary stage" to "dramatize the power [Black people] still lack" while simultaneously "confirming [our] potential."[23]

The uprisings were by no means a Black-only affair. Commentators have pointed out that, in an appreciable change from previous rebellions connected to the movement—Ferguson in 2014 and Baltimore in 2015, for example—the charge against anti-Black racism was often multiracial, taking place in both major cities and small towns located in areas thought to be more racially homogeneous (e.g., white) and conservative.[24] Consequently, many of the cell-phone videos capturing the character-defining jubilance—and destructive defiance—of these protests show Black people in song and step with non-Blacks, unequally harmed but nevertheless impacted by the violence of our shared social order.

If only temporarily, then, the 2020 rebellions offered a glimpse of what a multiracial and cross-class coalition could consist of, the analytic glue that, if taken seriously, will hold it together. The poet and theorist Fred Moten explains the dynamic well. True coalition among Black and non-Black people "emerges out of [the] recognition that it's fucked up for you, in the same way that we've already recognized that it's fucked up for us."[25] The message for Moten is as assertive as it is clear. Rather than try to "help" Black people in the life-or-death battle for liberation, we need to "recognize that this shit is killing you, too, however much more softly, you stupid motherfucker, you know?"[26] Coalition requires acknowledging that Black liberation is not an outcome solely reserved for Black people; it means liberation for all, regardless of color, class, or creed.

It is no accident that M4BL has demonstrated a global, multiracial reach. Nor can it be reduced to the unique convergence of circumstances that colored the uprisings. One of the critical features of the contemporary moment in Black movement, the time of #BlackLivesMatter, is how capacious the definitions of Blackness and, with it, Black radicalism have become.[27] Included in this constellation are the variety of spaces in which these definitions are hashed out and the types of actions they manifest. To approach M4BL as a social movement whose presumed viability gets measured by traditional organizational structures, campaign wins, or mass mobilization alone is to turn a blind eye to the full extent of its impact. The movement is much more expansive, its potential, much more profound, at least in so far as it maintains a political and cultural praxis that avoids not seeing the forest for the trees or, as Sylvia Wynter cautions, mistaking the map for the territory.[28]

While dramatic street protests and disruptive direct actions like those seen during the rebellion were hallmarks of the movement's early, hashtag-driven phase, M4BL has quietly and self-consciously evolved into a sophisticated network of activists, organizations, and cultural workers whose broad aim—abolition—has, for many, come to mean not just the end of policing, prisons, and the carceral state. It names the pursuit of another world altogether, one free from the institutions that structure and dominate our lives, systems that discipline and punish in the name of a racialized and gendered social cartography whose primary function is to maintain the territorial hegemony of capitalist social relations. In parallel fashion, the movement has also proven to be a powerful, borderless political and cultural zeitgeist with a shared language, aesthetic, and critique challenging the death-wielding mandates of anti-Blackness and white supremacy. This critique loudly and unabashedly confronts, and most importantly celebrates, different aspects of the Black experience as a key component of what it means to get free. I understand the movement's *cultural* dimensions to be fundamentally interlinked with the proliferation of institutions and collectives organizing on the ground. Black culture and Black politics are inseparable from one another.

To read M4BL in this way is to attempt to account for its influence over, connection to, and reliance on arenas often placed adjacent to the "political," if not beyond it altogether,[29] such as when social media platforms get treated as *ancillary to* social movements rather than a *constituent of* them. Similarly, the vast expanse of expressive culture and practice, especially in the popular realm, is often taken to be in conversation with but separate from political action. With M4BL, however, the distinction between what is and is not political is often blurred. So too are the domains in which political action does or does not take place. The blurring of these lines allows the movement to utilize and flourish from an expanded "repertoire of contention" that designates the tools we use to register dissent, assert our demands, and build bonds of solidarity.[30]

The political and cultural zeitgeist triggered by M4BL, organizationally, and across the assortment of spaces it appears, has helped facilitate a collective drive to unbind the meaning of Blackness from those who've sought to contain it and, in doing so, redefine justice—what it means to be with and for each other, regardless of differences and absent hierarchies. A desire to operate according to this kind of unity is another illustration of the movement's inheritance from radical Black feminist writers such as Audre Lorde, whose body of work is rightfully regarded as movement gospel. The following quote is demonstrative of her thinking and its relationship to M4BL's political culture, especially when it comes to dealing with difference and intramural conflict. "Black people," Lorde writes, "are not some standardly digestible quantity":

> In order to work together we do not have to become a mix of indistinguishable particles resembling a vat of homogenized chocolate milk. Unity implies the coming together of elements which are, to begin with, varied and diverse in their particular natures. Our persistence in examining the tensions within diversity encourages growth towards our common goal.[31]

Refusing to shed our differences, and accepting them in kind, encourages growth on both an individual and collective level. It is crucial to an ethics of care.

Settled atop these unruly grounds, the dialectical encounter between crisis and the creative complexities of Black radicalism, M4BL has mounted a compelling and sorely needed challenge to the logic and values that inform the modern world—racial capitalism, patriarchy, heteronormativity, carceral power, liberal democracy, the nation-state—exposing the impossibility of reform within existing structures and premised on current law. To put it another way, the movement maps a wayward route that leads beyond the colonial enclosures of "white sense," what Marisa Solomon and I have elsewhere defined as "the everyday language of law and order, civility, reform, and progress that shield . . . racial violence."[32] In articulating a total indictment of white sense, and the principles of capitalist modernity that comprise its core dictates, M4BL heralds a radically reimagined society and sense of collectivity premised on non-domination, inclusivity, and horizontal community control, a world that has been undone and remade—a Black future.

~~~

While the more transformative aspects of M4BL's political culture are clear to me now (its importance to our collective advance has risen to the level of common sense in my eyes), I was blind to much of it at the time of the Millions March. The movement itself was just beginning to evolve into what it has become, powerful enough to serve as the political and cultural backbone of a global uprising. In truth, my intellectual focus was elsewhere, at least in part.

As a graduate student, inspired by conversations I'd had with peers a few years prior while touring the country as a musician—a life-defining period I've to this day not fully processed—I imagined writing on the importance of generations and generational politics as defined and practiced by millennials, the generation I belong to and presently America's largest.[33] Broadly understood, generational politics refers to the political character—the ideas, modes of analysis, and methods of action—as varied as that may be, of one generation relative to, and often concerning, the generations that preceded it. Think, for instance, how people have made a habit of contrasting the attitudes of the "baby boomers" or "Generation X" with "Generation Z" and millennials on a host of issues. For example, it's become something of a talking point across the political spectrum that both millennials and Gen Z are significantly more supportive of socialism than were previous generations.

In that sense, generational politics is a temporally situated dialogue driving what David Scott calls the "constituting and orienting processes of the transmission of values, virtues, languages, practices, disciplines, and so on—the process that is usefully called tradition."[34] But a generation is more than a group of individuals born within a predefined range of dates. Generations are "social institutions of time" or, better still, a "community of experience," prompted by instances when historically contingent circumstances collude to create a broad, if heterogeneous, identity.[35] This identity takes on a political character when it openly and actively rejects aspects of society as it is in favor of how it could be, the search for a social order more closely resembling that particular generation's response to, and interpretation of, historical time. To put it somewhat differently, a *political generation* is a cohort that becomes aware of its distinct place in history, its "mission" to "fulfill or betray," to borrow from Frantz Fanon, and through that discovery works on some level to achieve political and social transformation.[36]

None of this is meant to suggest that a political generation is monolithic. It is often equally marked by both inter- and intragenerational conflict, competition over who controls and defines reality. No matter the case, be it conflict between or conflict within, a political generation aims to reconstruct the underlying values that animate the ideas, institutions, and social practices it has inherited. To speak concretely about generational politics, then, is to take seriously how a constellation of similarly situated people envision their future. It allows us to consider which version of the past, which truths and which mythologies, a generation authorizes to, following Scott, "inform their sense of what their present [demands] and how the present could be made into the futures they [hope] for."[37] In short, as Hartman writes, "inheritances are chosen as much as they are passed on."[38] Attending to these choices tells us a lot about who we are now, and even more about who we might become.

~~~

I happened to be in New York City during Occupy Wall Street, which followed the outbreak of revolutions in Tunisia, Libya, Egypt, Yemen, Syria, and Bahrain. Within two years, #BlackLivesMatter emerged. Taken together, in the early 2010s and proceeding ever since, there have been an array of opportunities to register, on a global level, millennial discontent toward and a willingness to mobilize against the ravages of the political and economic status quo as dictated by the capitalist world system. With a more locally focused orientation, my project's initial goal was to pursue the question of generational politics as evidenced by these prominent displays of generational rage across different political characteristics, such as race, gender, sexuality, and class. I began to do this by selecting multiple sites of engagement in New York. The Black Lives Matter movement, as it was then known, was only one such site.

As a participant in and observer of the Millions March, what stood out most vividly to me was the assertion of a generational identity, the fact that, according to Nichols and her comrades, the fight for racial justice was to be led by young Black and Brown folks inspired to pick up where their predecessors left off—a passing of the torch and changing of the guard. The suggestion of sustained organizing work, or the ideological basis upon which that work would be directed, was, at best, a secondary concern. That realization and understanding arrived much later, once I became actively involved in the NYC chapter of the Black Youth Project 100 (BYP100), one of the movement's leading organizations and my first real political home.

Rejection can occasion opportunities. When I reached out to the now defunct NYC chapter of the Black Lives Matter Global Network (BLMGN) and explained my project and intentions, they politely told me that BYP100 might be a better place to start. At the time, they were inundated with similar requests given the name recognition the organization garners. I'd never heard of BYP100, but after doing some due diligence, I realized they'd be a perfect fit since to become a member of the organization, you had to be both Black and between the ages of eighteen and thirty-five. As it had been with the Millions March, what excited me most was the explicitly generational dimensions of their mission.

I ended up writing a nearly verbatim message to BYP100 NYC as I had to BLMGN, outlining my research. They replied that if I met the membership requirements, I was welcome to attend an orientation and begin the process of joining the chapter, which I did in January 2016.[39] Ultimately, and apropos of the project's initial inflection, I was able to access the movement ecosystem generally and BYP100 in particular because I'm a Black millennial.

~

Given the goals Nichols laid out, and through the efforts of the coalition she helped assemble, the sheer number of people who took to the streets that day signaled an unambiguous announcement, an assertion of what was to come. A new and in many respects more radical generation was intent on being the principal agitators of a political agenda crafted on their terms, noting that those who came before had, returning to Fanon, "fought as best they could with the weapons they possessed at the time."[40] What they needed now was a different tableau, colored by the sentiments and grand design they believed best suited the moment, including the ability to rely on social media as both the primary means of disseminating information and a central mechanism for collective action and community-centered dialogue.

As Johnetta Elzie, one of the more prominent activists on the ground during the Ferguson uprisings, put it:

> The youth leading this movement is important because it is our time. For so long the elders have told us our generation doesn't fight for anything, or that we don't care about what goes on in the world. We have proved them wrong. Consciousness has been raised; people are waking up to take a stand against injustice. Thankfully for this generation, instead of waiting for a letter in the mail from Malcolm X, we have social media to drive this movement and get the truth out to millions of people, live.[41]

By the end of 2014, proof that it was "our time," that a millennial-led Black insurgency was taking shape, could be seen in cities across the country. And just as Elzie notes, a big part of what helped raise political consciousness among Black youth and moved them to mobilize was the ability to leverage social media—where Black people could get the "truth out" with the urgency the times required. Social media proved to be, to borrow Barbara Ransby's words, "the soapbox and *public square* of this generation, where many of the debates about strategy, tactics, and ideas are argued."[42] Consequently, M4BL has developed horizontally across various networks that are, as Manuel Castells puts it, "self-generated in content, self-directed in emission, and self-selected by many who communicate with many."[43]

Thinking of social media as this generation's "public square," the place where "debates" within the Black intramural take place, clarifies an additional point about the movement's rhizomatic nature. M4BL, in its earliest moments and since, participates in and has helped foster a rejuvenated version of what Michael Dawson has termed the "Black counterpublic."[44] As Dawson explains, the Black counterpublic constitutes the "discursive site" housing the "semi-autonomous" development and evolution of Black political thought, as well as the formation, dispersion, and "clash of ideologies which typifies public debate" among Black people.[45]

Unlike the Black counterpublic(s) of previous periods, however, Black culture and political thought are no longer situated, nor do they seek to situate themselves, at a peripheral distance from larger, more hegemonic domains of public debate; they no longer constitute a mostly subaltern space. The "counter" public narrative nevertheless remains relevant, in that it suggests a much-needed all- (or mostly) Black arena for external critiques of the capitalist world system and internal debates within the Black community, as well as a space for grief and healing in the aftermath of traumatic events, mostly stemming from Black death. Alicia Garza, one of the creators of #BlackLivesMatter, sums the point up well: "It is appropriate and necessary to have strategy and action centered around Blackness without other non-Black communities of color, or White folks for that matter, needing to find a place and a way to center themselves within it."[46] Nevertheless, the critiques and debates that help shape today's Black counterpublic do not sit on the outer edges of political discourse. Instead, they aim to create a different normativity altogether by attempting to tear down and replace the values and presuppositions that many of us have been socialized to accept, starting with the concept of Blackness itself.

As if aware of the potential limitations of an approach overly reliant on social media, in the early days of the movement, Black millennials were doing more than just getting the truth out and galvanizing people to take to the streets using the digitally driven Black counterpublic as a resource. They were also building national, regional, and locally focused organizations to coordinate action and, perhaps most significantly, sustain their efforts long after the heightened passions produced by the seeming impunity of anti-Black violence had subsided. In January 2015, during a gathering at the famed Riverside Church in New York City, organizer Asha Ransby-Sporn summed up the effort to build sustainable infrastructure with precision: "Organizations are longer-lasting than an action, longer-lasting than a campaign, longer-lasting than a moment. Organizations are where we can build structures that reflect our values and build communities that help us sustain ourselves in this work and sustain the work itself."[47]

Abdul Alkalimat and Saladin Muhammad call this the first "wave of mass struggle."[48] During the initial wave, the "action" stage, there is mass mobilization, often in response to violence. This mobilization is further galvanized by growing outrage and the development of slogans like #BlackLivesMatter that clarify and deepen an understanding of what that fight is about, what it's for, eventually leading to the emergence of organizations to maintain the movement's momentum.[49] The political institutions that emerged between 2012 and 2014, the movement's first phase, sought to build an army of Black and Brown millennial leaders who could then disseminate the skills they learned throughout the communities in which they lived. Even in the few instances in which this mandate was indirect, the majority of those who took up the call were nevertheless Black youth aspiring to build structures that reflect our values, as Ransby-Sporn put it—values that would consolidate into a political culture that is at once feminist in its frame and abolitionist in its core objectives.

~~~

The basic contours of the movement's early history are well-documented, a matter of "political legend," as Donna Murch termed it.[50] But they are nevertheless worth repeating with an eye toward M4BL's generational character and the seeds of its political culture, a constellation of pain, joy, and care.

Seventeen-year-old Trayvon Martin's murder in 2012 by the racist and predatory George Zimmerman, known at the time for his penchant for calling the police on Black boys, led to an eruption of protests around the country. The killing itself can be tracked directly to the surge in Stand Your Ground laws that, beginning with Florida in 2005, sanctioned the use of lethal force in the name of self-defense virtually anywhere a given person can claim the right to be, whether in their home or on the street.[51]

In New York City, the efforts to coordinate a response to Martin's death helped provide the foundation upon which the self-proclaimed multiracial organization Million Hoodies Movement for Justice (Million Hoodies) was formed, taking its name from the hoodie, a now iconic symbol of anti-Black terror, Martin was wearing at the time of his death. As Dante Barry, the organization's director, explained:

> Million Hoodies was founded in large part due to the failure of the media to adequately report on the murder of Trayvon Martin in 2012. It took a full month before it became national news. Local media didn't want to report it, and context around the details concerning Trayvon's death [wasn't] highlighted. Million Hoodies used social media to mobilize, amplify, and empower folks to take action. And we continue to use social media to bring attention to the police and vigilante violence cases that happen every twenty-eight hours.[52]

Central to the organization's founding, then, was the use of social media to create a counternarrative around Martin's death, subverting the media's silences and distortions, and galvanizing people to act. They wanted regard for Martin's pain.

With this as their beginning, Million Hoodies declared itself to be a "human rights membership, chapter-based organization building next generation leaders to end anti-black racism and systemic violence."[53] That they foregrounded "human rights" is not accidental, nor is the fact that they specifically linked anti-Blackness with systemic violence. Doing so points to a broader rhetorical shift—what some have called a "revival"—toward explicitly highlighting the different ways anti-Blackness reduces Black people to subhuman status as structural rather than incidental, much like the explicit assertion of Black humanity that would later anchor the phrase "Black Lives Matter."[54]

Through the lens of human rights, Million Hoodies sought to, in their words, "develop the leadership of young people of color to collectively challenge the defining issue of our time." Moreover, they hoped to become "a vibrant political home for youth of color activists shaping the country's narrative about safety and justice and effecting social change at the local level." So from their initial attempts to highlight the flagrant injustices surrounding Trayvon Martin's death until the organization shuttered several years later, the contribution Million Hoodies aimed to make in and for Black and Brown communities was to facilitate leadership training and provide a space to reframe how we speak about and address anti-Blackness.

Also in 2012, Dream Defenders, a "multiracial, multiethnic, multi-chapter organization of young people," likewise joined the movement fray. The initial spark for the organization came following a student-led march from Daytona Beach to Sanford, Florida—Trayvon Martin's hometown—to protest the fact that Zimmerman initially escaped charges in the case; he was charged shortly after the march.[55] In many respects, Dream Defenders pursued a similar mission to that of Million Hoodies. As the organization put it, they sought to "bring social change by training and organizing youth and students in nonviolent civil disobedience, civic engagement, and direct action while creating a sustainable network of youth and student leaders to take action and create real change in their communities."[56] Their statement identifies civil disobedience and direct action as touchpoints for training, which shows that, even at this early stage, the nascent movement planned to make disruptive tactics a significant part of their strategy, an attribute of all the radical instantiations of Black struggle and a mechanism to make people regard Black pain. To quote Dante Barry, disruptive tactics "provide a heartbeat," in that they "demonstrate the energy of this movement, and the constant pain black people are feeling. This movement is about transforming power structures."[57]

An attempt to transform power structures through direct action was on full display when, in 2013, Dream Defenders led a monthlong occupation of Florida governor Rick Scott's office to express outrage and demand action over Zimmerman's acquittal. Although the occupation did not succeed in shifting the priorities of the state government in Florida, it did illustrate that young Black folks were willing to shut things down to produce the changes they deemed necessary to inch closer to liberation. Through their intentional focus on the impact of racial injustice in their state, combined with a desire to address the criminalization of Black and Brown people more broadly, Dream Defenders joined Million Hoodies' effort to offer a space for and by young people, somewhere to "[build] a powerful, deep, local organization and movement for freedom and liberation in Florida." In an interview following the occupation, cofounder and former executive director Phillip Agnew put it this way: "Young people are getting to a place where they can no longer avoid pointing out the leaky roof, and rather than calling for others to fix it, they want to fix it themselves."[58] As the years progressed, it would become evident that the problem was more than just a leak that could be addressed by fixing the roof.

The murder of Trayvon Martin and subsequent acquittal of George Zimmerman similarly helped provoke the movement's namesake, #BlackLivesMatter, the hashtag initiated via social media by three Black women and veteran organizers: Garza, Opal Tometi, and Patrisse Cullors. From the start, as Garza explained in an oft-cited article, #BlackLivesMatter was a response to "the anti-Black racism that permeates our society and also, unfortunately, our movements."[59] The intention was to mount "an ideological and political intervention in a world where

Black lives are systematically and intentionally targeted for demise."[60] Her use of the word "intervention" is essential to the movement's developing agenda. It suggests that Garza recognized a gap that needed filling, that a new ideology was required to address the problem spaces of Blackness in the present. Just as importantly, for Garza, the hashtag was meant to be "an affirmation," a way to celebrate who we are and what we do despite oppression, Black joy in and as Black life.

While the founders of BLM did not explicitly name young people in their declaration, the ideological and political intervention they announced unquestionably helped give shape to the emerging spirit of insurgency among Black millennials. And it did so not only by providing a slogan that was easy for people to understand and identify with but by creating what they thought could be a "platform and organizing tool" others could use "to amplify anti-Black racism across the country, in all the ways it showed up."[61] Organizer and political strategist Ejeris Dixon summed up the meaning and potential impact of #BlackLivesMatter in a way that echoes that view:

> Framing the message as "Black Lives Matter" is brilliant. It's forward-looking, it's simple, it's aspirational. . . . When Black lives matter, we will not be free, but we will be on our way. That distinction is critical, so we don't confuse the message with the goal. The goal is the restructuring of our society. The goal is no longer needing police. The goal is no longer needing prisons. The goal is for people to have the tools and supports to live within their full dignity and humanity.[62]

In other words, before evolving into an organization in 2014 and later a global network that would prove to be a lightning rod for criticism among Black organizers, #BlackLivesMatter provided the discursive and ideational ground, the central "infrastructure," for young Black activists and organizers looking to politically assert themselves, often for the first time.[63]

This infrastructure was further cemented following Michael Brown's murder in Ferguson and the subsequent uprising that took place there. Cullors and the writer and activist Darnell Moore helped organize what they collectively called the Black Life Matters Ride, an homage to the

Freedom Rides initiated by the Congress of Racial Equality in 1961. As rebellion took over the streets, the twenty-first-century adaptation aimed to support the efforts of Black people protesting on the ground.[64] While long-standing collectives like the Organization for Black Struggle had been around for decades, many of the Ferguson area protestors were themselves Black millennials, including the founders of the two most prominent, locally based collectives to emerge during the rebellion: Millennial Activists United (MAU) and Hands Up United.[65] According to Zakiya Jemmont, one of MAU's original members, the group's origins were organic, if grounded in a shared sense of urgency first facilitated by social media:

> We are a gifted group of 20 and 30 something year old activists who were brought together by Twitter. We knew that we were passionate about bringing light to the injustices of police brutality in our communities and we dedicated ourselves to sustaining the movement. What began as making sandwiches for protesters and marching every night turned into us becoming street medics after being tear-gassed and shot at. After working together for weeks, we realized we needed a name. Today we operate as Millennial Activists United, a youth-led grassroots organization that focuses on educating and empowering our communities.[66]

Like Million Hoodies and Dream Defenders before them, MAU intentionally emphasized the fact that they are both "youth-led" and driven by community need. In addition, four of the five original members were Black women, three of whom—those most often connected to the group—identified as queer. Because of this, their organizing also sought to explore the intersections of racism and sexism. As Brittany Ferrell, perhaps the most visible of MAU's founders, put it: "I hope that we as a majority woman organization can empower women to not be afraid to confront all oppression, sexism included. This is a fight way greater than we can imagine but we are fully capable of [fighting] to the end and being heard."[67] Ferrell's hope for female empowerment would prove to be an early harbinger of where the growing movement was heading.

Some of the participants in the Black Life Matters Ride were or would soon be members of BYP100. Like #BlackLivesMatter and Dream Defenders, BYP100 emerged in the aftermath of Zimmerman's acquittal. The founders of BYP100 were initially brought together at a convening organized by political scientist Cathy Cohen called "Beyond November," which, as Barbara Ransby notes, was a direct reference to the November 2012 elections.[68] "Beyond," in this case, indicated a desire to act without relying solely on the promises of elected officials. It also underscored a desire to move forward in ways that were separate and distinct from previously established, Black-led organizations. For many, these organizations were, at best, out of touch with the political concerns of Black youth, if not altogether retrograde.

In this respect, the group of one hundred millennial Black activists and leaders from around the country had a straightforward but by no means simple mandate. They gathered to discuss what kinds of organizational formations by and for young Black people were possible and how such an organization could adequately attend to the vast expanse of the Black experience in America—particularly that of young Black folks. Once the announcement of Zimmerman's acquittal swarmed the airwaves and the sadness of the initial shock subsided, the discussions the convening brought to the fore took on greater urgency. That urgency inspired many of the participants to reconnect in Washington, D.C., a month later, during the fiftieth anniversary of the March on Washington, to draft what would become the political and philosophical basis of the new organization.

Given that history, it isn't surprising that BYP100 describes its mission in clear generational terms, owing to the composition of the original convening and a belief in the importance of maintaining a Black-only space for young Black people to lead:

BYP100 is a national, member-based organization of Black 18–35 year old activists and organizers, dedicated to creating justice and freedom for all Black people. We do this through building a network focused on transformative leadership development, direct action organizing, advocacy, and political education using a Black queer feminist lens [and aspire to create] a world where all Black people have economic, social, political, and educational freedom.[69]

According to cultural worker and former national director Charlene Carruthers, the Black queer feminist lens "is a political praxis . . . based in Black feminist and LGBTQ traditions and knowledge, through which people and groups see[k] to bring their full selves into the process of dismantling all systems of oppression."[70] Like the Combahee River Collective and other Black feminist thinkers before them, for many in BYP100, the power of a Black queer feminist lens is in its ability to name how "our identities make us vulnerable to multiple types of oppression" and to recognize that those identities and vulnerabilities may not always be the same. With an eye toward these differences in common cause with the threat of violence all Black people face, "liberation can only be realized by lifting up the voices and experiences of historically silenced and vulnerable groups within Black communities."[71] In other words, liberation requires a radically inclusive ethics of care.

BYP100's mission and lens, its intentional focus on gender and sexuality as laid out early in its formation, were additional signals that the time of #BlackLivesMatter was going to be about more than just state and vigilante violence perpetrated against cis Black men. As Garza powerfully explains:

> [Black Lives Matter] goes beyond the narrow nationalism that can be prevalent within some Black communities, which merely call on Black people to love Black, live Black and buy Black, keeping straight cis Black men in the front of the movement while our sisters, queer and trans and disabled folk take up roles in the background or not at all. Black Lives Matter affirms the lives of Black queer and trans folks, disabled folks, Black-undocumented folks, folks with records, women and all Black lives along the gender spectrum. It centers those that have been marginalized within Black liberation movements. It is a tactic to (re)build the Black liberation movement.[72]

Centering the historically marginalized is a practice that seeks to repair the destructive behaviors within Black movements, a "tactic to (re)build" intramural solidarity to create a more authentic, more representative, and therefore more powerful liberation struggle.

The proliferation of youth-centered, Black-led organizations from 2012 to 2014 helps situate the Millions March I attended within a broader trajectory of political action and thought adopted by Black millennials in the first phase of the movement, the originating wave in mass struggle and the production of a distinctive political culture. Together, they helped usher in what Alkalimat and Muhammad describe as the "second wave," called "cadre development."[73] Cadre development occurs when the institutions created in the first wave expand and become staffed (paid or unpaid) to ensure the movement doesn't stall. The cadre "engage[s] to win particular battles that help people understand their power while building the basis to transform the entire system."[74] In short, they become "infrastructure," which is perhaps the best way to think about M4BL's namesake umbrella organization. Since 2015, the organization has helped develop collective visioning and coordinating strategy across otherwise autonomous configurations within the ecosystem, complementing the independent circulation, across the Black counterpublic, of the movement's political and cultural zeitgeist.

In the years since, the persistence of viral images of Black death and suffering helped spawn the founding of even more young, Black-led organizations, expanding the movement's orbit on the ground. Just as before, many of these newer constellations center Black women, as well as queer, trans, and gender nonconforming folks. Some, such as Chicago-based Assata's Daughters, even claim to be abolitionist. This new crop of organizations, including the Black Visions Collective, which was founded in 2017 in Minneapolis and at the center of the 2020 uprisings, demonstrates the overlap and continuity between the first two waves of struggle, provoked by the hypervisibility of Black pain—the way Black youth continue to take up the torch on their own terms.[75]

The repetition of Black death, and the radical politics young Black people were crafting in response, made me reevaluate my project and my thinking. While there are obvious ways M4BL fits into a larger generational paradigm, the concept of "generation" itself was too broad to capture the specificity of the Black experience, the specificity of Black pain. Instead, I came to realize that generations and generational politics more usefully applies to the trajectory of Black politics, thought, and culture; it's a way to make sense of the Black Situation, to return once more to Reed's phrasing. This iteration of Black struggle, what we've witnessed in the time of #BlackLivesMatter, is an example of young Black people directly contesting the world system's more salient norms by creating new opportunities for understanding Blackness, Black politics, and Black thought. To put it another way, M4BL's political culture is based on an interpretation of the way previous generations of Black social movement fared in providing a blueprint for the liberation of all Black life, which is to say, how they chose to approach, wade through, and inhabit Blackness.

~~~

Though often violently suppressed, Black political thought and rebellion have consistently played a lead role in shaping discussions around freedom, justice, and equality on a global scale, if only because freedom, justice, and equality are all concepts whose realization we've been denied. In the United States, for example, as Manisha Sinha notes, "debates over Black freedom" have been central to the "conflict and contours of American democracy," such that it is, challenging the enduring disconnect between American ideals and American deeds.[76] Just as importantly, however (and Garza's statement alludes to this), Black thought and rebellion have also helped clarify and outline critical debates within the Black community itself—debates concerning "how we get free," what "free" living should look like, and who among us is deserving of it. In this regard, the political culture of M4BL is part of a continuum in Black politics that dates back to the Middle Passage. Over the course of the last decade, the movement has brought an expanded view of anti-Black racism and calls for racial justice back to the center of national consciousness, while simultaneously questioning staid beliefs about strategy, leadership, respectability, and inclusion, issues that have long troubled the internal dynamics of Black political and social life.

Black movements have always had a dual mode of address: one outward toward the world and the other inward toward the Black community.

As the women of the Combahee River Collective put it, "We struggle together with Black men against racism, while we also struggle with Black men against sexism."[77] The same is true regarding the treatment of Black trans and gender nonconforming members of the intramural. If we zoom out a bit, this parallel messaging is perhaps most recognizable when accounting for the different ways Black thinkers and cultural workers have tried to (re)construct a Black public image to combat anti-Blackness and affirm Black life, often through cultural expression. It's a tendency that began during slavery and colonialism, stretching forward from the "trope" of the New Negro in the late nineteenth and early twentieth centuries to the Negritude movement of Africa and the Caribbean in the 1930s, to the idea that Black is beautiful during the Black Power era, onward to pronouncements of Black joy today.

Consequently, the history of Black politics, thought, and culture throughout the Diaspora is also one of collective self-fashioning. This dual mode of address—and alongside it, the ways Black thinkers and cultural workers have crafted a Black public image they hoped would exceed and displace anti-Black characterizations—brings clarity to the form and substance of M4BL's political culture. The movement, and, more broadly, the "time of #BlackLivesMatter," is the manifestation of a conversation we have been having with ourselves for centuries and therefore emerges and departs from the past in a manner that is complex and nonlinear, setting the stage for a program well positioned to address the urgent necessities of the present moment, an abolitionist vision that is simultaneously now, before, and not yet.

The multitemporal nature of this narrative—a story within a story— usefully reveals what Margo Natalie Crawford describes as "the power of anticipation" in the Black radical tradition, facilitating a new correspondence between the Black present and the Black past, one attuned to historically grounded racial regimes and the specific political-cultural responses they produce, such that each generation advances a political position and aesthetic, a way of seeing and doing, that "anticipates" but can't fully actualize the approach their successors will take.[78] From this perspective, what we might imagine to be the shortcomings of those who preceded us (the perceived failures of, say, the civil rights and Black

Power eras) become preludes, limited, no doubt, by the tools they had on hand but that foretell opportunities for us to seize what they could not. Black radicalism's anticipatory power likewise brings into view the overall "undecidability" of Black politics—its "competing possibilities"—as Black people have, in various ways, debated how best to confront what Christina Sharpe calls the "total climate of anti-Blackness," an apt accounting of an environment awash in the violence brought about by the ravages of slavery, colonialism, and their aftermaths.[79]

With these competing possibilities in mind, the different ways Black people perceived how to get free, the pages to come make the case for recognizing and attending to the semi-autonomous trajectory of Black politics, thought, and culture, which is to say, I stake a claim on the crucial importance of analyzing the Black Situation on its own terms and for its own sake. I refer to this framework as *Black political development* to clearly name and properly trace the shifts in Black consciousness and expression that result from the collision between opposing social forces.

Following the Marxist methodological tradition championed by thinkers like Stuart Hall, Black political development is best imagined as a distinct form of "conjunctural analysis," intentionally tuned to the political, social, and cultural lives of Black people and the contradictions that exist within and beyond the Black community. Jeremy Gilbert helpfully defines a conjunctural analysis as the investigation of "convergent and divergent tendencies shaping the totality of power relations within a given social field during a particular period of time."[80] In short, to think about a conjuncture is to ask: What explains this moment? How did we get here? Where are we going?

Reading Black life in this way is critical not only for understanding the political and social dynamics, the "moments of rupture and settlement," as Hall might say, that facilitated the movement's emergence and gave rise to its form and character.[81] It also helps situate the force of M4BL's intervention in the context of what Vincent Harding once referred to as "The Great Tradition of Black Protest."[82] By charting the movement in this manner, I'm making the case for imagining Black political development as responsive rather than preordained, as circular rather than advancing in a straight line, bearing in mind the evolving technologies and techniques of anti-Black terror and captivity mobilized in the name of white supremacy, power, and property.[83] To put an even finer point on things, in its circulatory movement, its "back and forth . . . flow," Black politics, culture, and thought, just like the depictions of Blackness coursing through the history of our collective self-fashioning, build and repurpose rather than simply break away.[84]

~~~

From Trayvon Martin and Rekia Boyd to Breonna Taylor and Tony McDade, the movement's intervention is, first and foremost, an urgent response to the trauma and repetition of state and vigilante violence as experienced and witnessed by Black youth. The sheer volume of Black lives lost since M4BL began is staggering and continues to grow—the names too many to list. But death is not the only outcome worthy of mention. In late August 2020, for example, a white police officer shot and partially paralyzed Jacob Blake, a Black man just shy of thirty, in front of his children. A similarly violent police encounter took place in February 2022 when Jajuan R. Henderson, also a twenty-nine-year-old Black man, was shot and paralyzed from the chest down just after midnight in Trenton, New Jersey, by officers wearing plainclothes. Henderson was reaching for iced tea from a car parked outside his home. The driver-side window of the car he leaned into was smashed by one of the officers, and shortly thereafter, Henderson was shot four times by the alleged "protectors" of the community, including in the neck.[85]

There were no bystanders present to capture the moment Henderson's life was forever altered, his body forever changed, courtesy of the Trenton police department. The opposite was true of Blake's run-in with "the law," which was caught on camera and spread with the speed we've all become accustomed to. The shooting occurred in Kenosha, Wisconsin, several hundred miles from Minneapolis, the epicenter of the uprisings, and helped rekindle the flames of protest set ablaze back in May. But the narrative around the Kenosha rebellion and the illegitimate act of violence carried out by an illegitimate state-actor were overshadowed by a separate but related event, when the forces of armed, right-wing reaction descended on the city, ultimately leaving two (non-Black) people dead and another wounded.

In response to the Black-led protests that followed the shooting of Jacob Blake, a vigilante group called the Kenosha Guard, organized by a former city official, issued a directive to gather so they could help the police "guard" the community (i.e., private property) from the perceived mob's rath. The call, or "militia muster," is what prompted Kyle Rittenhouse, who, at the time, was only seventeen years old, to cross state lines with an AR-15 in tow. Following a confrontation with a protestor, Rittenhouse shot and killed Joseph Rosenbaum and Anthony Huber, after which a fleeing Rittenhouse wandered safely into the embrace of the police. Rittenhouse quickly became a "hero" and "patriot" in the eyes of the right and was later acquitted of all charges. That his victims were not Black didn't matter. After all, the "upstanding" young man had merely traveled with "his rifle to the scene of the rioting to help defend small business owners," according to a talking points memo issued by the Department of Homeland Security.[86]

What took place in Kenosha was by no means the only time movement-related actions were met with counterprotests, a matrix that includes the vitriol of pro-police organizations, militia presence, and the rage of individuals with murderous intentions. In 2017, a white, self-proclaimed neo-Nazi drove his car through a crowd of anti-racist protestors gathered to disrupt the "Unite the Right" rally in Charlottesville, Virginia. The attack, which was also captured on video, killed a thirty-two-year-old white activist named Heather Heyer and hospitalized eight others. His method, "car ramming," has since become a more common tactic wielded against movement protests, a weapon in a reactionary tool kit with a growing number of enthusiastic and increasingly emboldened proponents.[87] By one account, between early 2020, months before the uprisings, and April 2021, there have been well over seven hundred far-right counterdemonstrations, to say nothing of the overbearing, militaristic response by the police, a not infrequent collaborator.[88] The Kenosha example is nevertheless instructive. It gives further credence to Moten's previously referenced missive: anti-Blackness and white supremacy are absolutely "killing you, too, however much more softly." And in some instances, not more softly at all.

If anti-Black violence carried out by both state and non-state agents was and remains a primary catalyst, M4BL is likewise a response to the surveillance and militarized policing of Black communities, a trend that marks the early 1990s' turn to what Neil Smith calls the "social cleansing of public space" that has facilitated the gentrification process in city neighborhoods but had already been in motion decades prior in response to the Black rebellions of the 1960s and 1970s.[89] Observed through the lens of the economy—world capitalism's current crisis—the movement is also pitched against rising social and economic disparities that have long been hallmarks of racialized policymaking and geographies but have grown starker and more intense since the neoliberal turn in the 1970s, when Western societies generally, and the United States in particular, allowed market principles to overtake virtually all other considerations. Neoliberalism facilitated, among other things, a culture of hyperindividualism and the breakdown of a view of society premised on the common good that has hit Black and Brown communities the hardest.[90]

Lastly and in the broadest sense, the movement is responding to the historically rooted ways Blackness and Black life have been both criminalized and pathologized, aiding in the system-wide production and omnipresence of Black pain. We can trace this history to a genealogy of incarceration that is, as Dylan Rodriguez has put it, "a form of warfare against those (human) beings that embody the symbolic orders of death, pathology and unassimilability into the order of Civilization," initiated by enslavement, dispossession, and genocide.[91] The portrayal of Black deviance, in other words, our inherent criminality, our "backwardness," has been and continues to be essential to the construction and conservation of so called "civilization," even as there's an ever-growing number of "Black faces in high places."[92]

For these reasons, M4BL levels a structural critique against an unjust, anti-Black world that, from slavery and colonialism on to the present, by design, continues to make Black, Indigenous, and other marginalized people vulnerable. It is a world in which we all remain captive, and from which we all, in one way or another, are harmed. Consequently, it is a social order that must be torn down and built anew through a radical reimagining of who we are and who we might yet be, a freedom "yet to come."[93] Toward this reconstruction, M4BL also takes aim at the ways Black people have mirrored many of the world's injustices in their treatment of others within the Black community. That is, the movement pushes to the fore how Black folks themselves adopt hierarchies and enact violence (physical and otherwise) based on class, color, gender, and sex, in alignment with the dominant values of Western modernity.

The death of nineteen-year-old Black Lives Matter activist Oluwatoyin "Toyin" Salau is a case in point. Little more than a week after the 2020 uprisings began, mere days after protestors set fire to the Third Police Precinct, Salau, who organized in Tallahassee, Florida, went missing. Prior to her disappearance, she posted a Twitter thread recounting recent traumatic experiences with sexual assault.[94] Those experiences were unfortunately not her first, nor would they be her last. As a friend later tweeted, Salau had been trying to escape a "living situation where she was being sexually abused REPEATEDLY," which forced her to seek shelter from others in the community; "she wasn't safe at home."[95] Salau's killer was a forty-nine-year-old Black man named Aaron Glee Jr. Several days after she went missing, her body was found in Glee's home. Salau had been raped and then tied to a chair to suffocate her.[96] Vicky Sims, a white volunteer in her seventies, was found alongside her, dead and similarly strapped to a chair. Because Sims helped Glee out from time to time, he called her for a ride after meeting Salau at a local bus stop and offering her assistance.

There is no indication that Glee had anything to do with movement organizing or activism. He was just a member of the community, much like the cis Black men overwhelmingly responsible for the premature deaths of Black trans women and those who identify as gender nonconforming. But sexual assault and other gender-based violence also occur within movement spaces, past and present, to the detriment of our collective drive for liberation. As Fresco Steez, a "cultural engineer" and organizer responsible for crafting much of the movement's organizational aesthetic, put it in a tweet posted in May 2022: "Movement has a rape problem. A patriarchal violence problem. But particularly a sexual violence problem . . . AND. Each. And every. One. Of your favorite Black feminists. Have enabled an instance of sexual violence/harassment/ misconduct. It's a cultural crisis."[97]

Attending to intramural harm, a cultural crisis in and beyond the movement, as part of a larger project of social transformation, crystallizes the tensions and contradictions imbedded in the ways M4BL has attempted to elevate Black feminist praxis and shift the meaning and mode of Black politics and thought against the grain of the dominant ideologies, tactics, and leadership models that have defined the Black political-cultural formations of the past. This shift, of course, is especially true of the male-dominated, top-down leadership models that have characterized much of Black politics until now, from the Black conventions of the nineteenth century, through to the civil rights movement and the organizations associated with Black Power, onto Louis Farrakhan's "Millions Man" and "Millions More" marches in the 1990s and early 2000s, respectively. It is also true of the relative collapse of radical alternatives to the liberal status quo offered by Black activists and politicians in the post–Cold War era, pronounced most prominently by the Obama presidency and current Black political elites like Vice President Kamala Harris. Consequently, M4BL rejects outright strategies that have first or singularly sought accommodation through the state or that replicate the state's institutions and logic, choosing in its place community-centered practices of Black sociality toward a world undone. These divergences, though imperfectly executed at times, particularly in accounting for intramural harm and holding each other accountable when harm happens, are important because they point to the content of the paradigm shift, the recentering of priorities in Black politics and thought that define the time of #BlackLivesMatter. They help explain "why now?" just as they address "to what end?"

The movement's political culture and its advancement of an abolitionism, defined by the desire to create a new civilization unmoored by capitalist social relations, are perhaps best thought of as a philosophical *return to the source*. By that I mean we should align M4BL's radicalism, and its open-ended vision for the future, with the radicalism of Black folk culture and the plantation politics of the colonized and enslaved.[98] As Sylvia Wynter notes, slaves often attempted to imagine political and social transformation beyond the bounds of what was. They did so primarily by "constituting another self, another collective identity ... outside the framework of the dominant ideology."[99] The enslaved dreamed of something else, something more than the subjection that demarcated their existence, a "counterlife," to borrow Christopher Free-burg's phrasing.[100] Just as importantly, many of them knew it had to be taken, that it had to be snatched out of the grasping hands of the oppressor. Nothing less would do. Because freedom, as Hartman writes, "is the kind of thing that required you to leave your bones on the hills at Brimsbay, or to burn the cane fields, or to live in a garret for seven years, or to stage a general strike, or to create a new republic."[101]

For Wynter, to take stock of the prolonged and unabating struggle waged by the dispossessed against domination is not merely an account of events in the past but instead represents the theoretical basis for revolutionary action, a blueprint for our present.[102] By foregrounding the struggle of the dispossessed as the conceptual grounds for social revolution, Wynter invites us to recuperate and use the transformative political culture evident in and among the community of slaves, one that inhabits a space in excess of the enclosures of Western carceral power, the total eclipse of white sense. Following Hartman's lucid instruction, we must understand that "the demands of the slave on the present have everything to do with making good the promise of abolition, and this entails much more than the end of property in slaves. It requires the reconstruction of society, which is the only way to honor our debt to the dead."[103] This is, in effect, a call to reframe and center the figure of the Black slave as a revolutionary subject and along with them, I would argue, the historical terrain of the Black underclass, the multitude, those who pursued unknown elsewheres and crafted cultural practices to uphold Black life, a refusal of subjection, bondage, and racial rule. In other words, it is a recuperation of the roots of what Cedric Robinson has called the Black radical tradition, a radicalism unaligned with, though not untouched by, European political thought.[104] Accordingly, the Black radical tradition represents both a history of revolutionary politics and culture and a praxis upon which M4BL builds and has helped to reenter public discourse.

To Build a Black Future narrates and theorizes the political-cultural sea change, as well as its contradictions, evident in the movement's recovery of the Black radical tradition and the ascendance of Black feminist praxis through the prism of Black political development. It explores the social and political forces that have driven it, the conditions that sustain it, and, most importantly, what this political-cultural alteration in Black thought and culture tells us about the necessary steps we need to take if, returning again to Marx, we are to "create [our] poetry from the future, not from the past," a future where all people are permitted to live a life of dignity and fulfillment, a "buen vivir."[105] To do so, I draw on experiences indexed over the three years I spent organizing as a member of BYP100. The episodes sketched from my engagement with BYP100 function as entry points that shed light on themes observable within the broader movement ecosystem, characteristics that comprise the spirit of the moment. I read these examples alongside interviews and an analysis of multimedia texts, initiatives, and campaigns generated by young Black folks in the years following the movement's inception.

The ideas, practices, and political culture that distinguish the time of #BlackLivesMatter, as alluded to above, are both historically specific and part of a continuum. Mediated by social media, M4BL's response to—and regard for—the hypervisibility of Black pain has enabled and mobilized a self-conception that is "unapologetically Black." To be Black, unapologetically, is a militant appeal to the most expansive understanding of what Blackness can mean rather than one that seeks to police and control, which has been the case in earlier instances of Black struggle. It is also imbued with and arguably defined by the creative dynamism of Black joy as both a capacious embodiment of Black presence and a prefigurative politics forecasting a society free of anti-Blackness. The mobilization of an unapologetic Black joy directly confronts and regards the specter of Black pain as one of Western modernity's founding principles, the mirror through which the logic of white sense is reflected and confirmed. While doing so, the movement promotes a political culture premised on a radically inclusive ethics of care. Care, in this case, assumes the role of countercivilizational force, pushing us away from liberal and capitalist social relations toward what Ashon Crawley calls "otherwise possibilities."[106]

These otherwise possibilities will only take hold, at least in any complete sense, through the total abolition of the modern world system, which will require an unwavering rejection of its ideological foundations, not simply as something that exists "out there" but as something we also carry within. I refer to this complex cultural and political configuration— pain, joy, and care—as the *politics of the wake*, an emergent strategy marking the contours of the current conjuncture in Black political development, our story within a story.

In evoking "the wake" to describe M4BL's political culture and agenda, I build from and extend Christina Sharpe's provocative description, from her book *In the Wake: On Blackness and Being*, of the ways the rupture of slavery remains viscerally present as an attribute of the Black experience and is also, for many non-Black people, still hidden in plain sight. Therefore, for Sharpe, "being in the wake" is a form of consciousness. It is to knowingly inhabit the "total climate" of anti-Blackness to forge new ways of seeing and doing that inform and reconstitute our critical practices away from the historical trace of slavery and toward not just imagining but pursuing a world otherwise.

These new ways of seeing and doing, these critical practices, require first and foremost a refusal to look away from Black pain and precarity. It requires that we regard, embrace, and move against the structural and structuring fact of Black death in the afterlife of slavery, so we might fully recognize Black joy, the "largeness that is Black life," despite death.[107] This is to see Black life not merely for the sake of Black people but also as the foundation upon which we build a liberated society for all, one unbound by the subjugation and violence that define our present and past, an ethics of care. M4BL has created an ideological terrain for people to move according to this refusal and embrace, and simultaneously attends to the contradictions that underscore Black living, thought, and movement—Black life and premature death, pain and joy, mourning and healing, disposability and care—to mount its political culture and agenda, a politics in and of the wake.

~~~

As evidenced in the movement's early history, central to this politics is a demand to center the lives and experiences of those among us positioned furthest away from power: Black women, trans and gender nonconforming folks, immigrants, the poor, and the differently abled. Our path to a better world begins by listening to and learning from the historically marginalized—people whose interests have been dictated by others, whose concerns have been, at best, made secondary in previous, Black-led movements, and whose vulnerability has only increased in the decades following the turn toward neoliberal rationality. Foregrounding a "margins-to-center" approach based on experience rather than dictate, a debt to Black feminists like bell hooks, as the point of departure of M4BL's political analysis, informs the world-making necessity of abolition. It influences everything from the movement's outward-facing demands and direct actions to how notions of safety, justice, and community are articulated, practiced, and pursued within the M4BL ecosystem itself. Put otherwise, the recent hypervisibility of Black pain, and the fact that pain remains disregarded, has, for Black youth, brought about a radical critique aimed at abolishing the categories and structures of oppression that (re)produce all Black suffering.

At the same time, it has fed the creation of spaces to acknowledge, study, and heal from pain within a broader project of imagining what the world might look like without them, spaces where Black people can think, feel, and thrive without threat or fear of reprisal. This includes cultivating a sense of joy with and through other Black people, an unapologetic sense of Black love and celebration that rejects the hostility historically directed toward the Black body. As noted, these space-making practices extend well beyond traditional activist circles. From Instagram pages to podcasts, they help guide a digitally driven Black counterpublic that confronts and celebrates Blackness, often through the circulation of counterimages and discourses that highlight the resilience of Black life alongside the everyday heroism of Black survival.

More than a traditional political program or prefigurative vision of liberation that uses already existing (white European) models as a guide, the politics of the wake outlines an ethical commitment born from an awareness of, and regard for, Black subjugation and survival, past and present—everything Blackness has been and might yet be. In that sense, Blackness is not merely an "identity." Instead, it represents a mode of analysis, critique, and disruption toward a world undone. As a result, this book argues that the movement's power and promise are less about specific campaign wins or mobilizing people in the streets, though both are important. It resides in the political culture and agenda M4BL has created with and through the wake—the haunt of slavery and what we must do to overcome it—one that centers care, not ideological dictates, as its foundation.

~~

But before proceeding further into the time of #BlackLivesMatter, before we can fully engage the politics of the wake, we must first take stock of where Black politics and culture have been, the outline of our story within a story. Undertaking this journey is about understanding why it is necessary to "avenge the suffering of our ancestors," as Mary Hooks's mandate requires.[108] It's also about making sense of the past many Black people of this generation seem to have chosen, what Hartman describes as "the desires and discontents of the present,"[109] namely, the abolition of the capitalist world system, submerged in a fulsome embrace of Blackness, and all its possible futures, the tides of that known river.

CHAPTER 2

New Forms/Known Rivers

Men make their own history, but not of their own free will; not under circumstances they themselves have chosen but under the given and inherited circumstances with which they are directly confronted.

—KARL MARX

We must shed the habit of decrying the efforts of our forefathers or feigning incomprehension at their silence or passiveness. They fought as best they could with the weapons they possessed at the time.

—FRANTZ FANON

Black philosophy's savant is an Afrarealism that explores its contributions and contradictions. Through black radical, feminist-womanist, queer theories, Afrarealism confronts theoretical limitations and political practices in conceptualizing freedom. It has been operative in the "New World" for half a millennium. It is as old as black theory and philosophy's hunger for liberty. Although Afrarealism often seems relegated to the underground of resistance and to the shadow of formal concepts, its resilience allows for continuous agency.

—JOY JAMES

If nothing else, the 2020 uprisings made clear that, now two decades into the twenty-first century, the issues that have historically concerned Black communities and informed Black protest are (un)remarkably consistent. The Movement for Black Lives is a new form unfolding in a known river. That river is Blackness—a "held and errant pattern" traced to the mouth of the Atlantic and the wash that followed the slave ships from the shores of West Africa.[1] What we call Blackness is likewise flown from the break produced by colonial conquest in the New World and later, the Continent itself.

To say that the material conditions of Black life and premature death appear stable is not to imply that political and social causes rooted in the Black experience are entirely static or undifferentiated. On the contrary, continuity *despite* change makes explicit the depth of the problem—the story within a story. In that sense, the *new* is a coordinate to map the complex and contested arc of Black politics, thought, and culture—the shape of Black political and social life negotiated among Black people across Black publics in the seeming circulatory of Black time. Mapping this path requires reaching further back into the Black past, back centuries in fact, to allow for a more comprehensive view of the ideas, values, and underlying conditions that shaped Black protest and defined Black rebellion. As Steven Hahn notes, it is important to take seriously "how the relations and developments of one era [create] both limits and possibilities in the next."[2] Marking these limits and possibilities, the shifts in Black thought and expressive culture that emerge from what remains when opposing social forces collide, is the work of Black political development.

This chapter is about those shifts, what they reveal about where we are now and might soon be within and beyond the time of #BlackLives-Matter. But it is also about the things that have stayed the same. Black concerns—racial violence, perpetrated or tacitly endorsed by the state; political and social disenfranchisement; segregated neighborhoods; economic inequality—are, in the most immediate respects, a consequence of institutions and structures made to appear natural instead of what they truly are: ideologically constructed and politically motivated, all to preserve the hegemony of capitalist social relations for the benefit of the few in or close to power, the sordid maintenance of white sense.

From David Walker's 1829 *Appeal to the Coloured Citizens of the World* to M4BL's "Vision for Black Lives" statement not quite two centuries later, the animating question of Black political life has been how best to work through and move against these structures and institutions, to the extent that the issues were thought to be structural at all. This process has inevitably included attempts to understand and articulate who "we" are and what "we" (should) want as Black people. In that respect, what is contested and therefore shifts—what becomes new—is the nature and definition of Blackness itself: what "Black is" and "Black ain't," to riff off the filmmaker Marlon Riggs.

Of course, the way Black folks understand and approach Blackness greatly impacts how we engage other Black people, including ourselves, not to mention what we consider the aims of Black politics to be. The specificity of Black life and death as implied in contestations around (anti)Blackness and white supremacy makes Black political thought and culture a territory unto itself. As Robert Gooding-Williams has argued, the "preoccupations" of this distinctive "genre" include "the political and social organization of white supremacy, the nature and effect of racial ideology, and the possibilities of black emancipation."[3] What we are talking about, then, is a battle over what is meant when we say "freedom" and "liberation," what strategies and tactics might bring them about, and on what conceptual ground these approaches, these ways of seeing, are debated and taken up.

The creation of Black-led organizations and institutions that, taken together, represent the bedrock of Black social life—the Black counterpublic—has opened the door for intramural debates. In the past, these organizations and institutions have included familiar sites of Black sociality such as the Black church, clubs, lodges, schools, and the Black press. They also consist of, as Richard Iton reminds us, the cultural politics and political aesthetics of Black music, art, literature, film, and other expressive forms, which have long served as a primary outlet and "strategic option" for those within the Black intramural who were not "granted access" to the centers of Black political power and debate.[4] Since #BlackLivesMatter emerged, for example, the internet and social media have operated simultaneously as a locus from which a different collective experience of Black pain has taken place and where a collective and creative response—expressions of Black joy—has molded and circulated, largely without interference.

The idea of interference, and the ability to operate without it, is important, especially with regard to power dynamics *within* the Black community because implied in Iton's description of Black popular culture as a strategic option is another critical characteristic of Black politics and thought—the question of who gets to participate in the first place. Who has a seat at the table? Who acts on behalf of whom? Whose experiences (or interests) are privileged? And who makes these determinations? It is well known that Black politics and movements have long dealt with issues of inclusion, particularly as it pertains to class, gender, and sexuality.[5] Cathy Cohen calls these "boundaries" constructed within the Black community processes of "secondary marginalization," in which the (more) privileged members of a marginalized group take on a "policing" role. In this case, policing means the "regulation and management of the behavior, attitudes, and more importantly, the public image of the group."[6] The latter point, controlling the public image of the group, informs, at least in part, the utility in prioritizing Black culture and aesthetics to chart the development and circularity of Blackness and Black political thought. As figured (and contested) by Black thinkers and cultural workers, the Black image provides a window into the ways Black radicalism anticipates, through internal and external struggle and changes in material conditions, more expansive ways of viewing Blackness, unsaddled from the precepts of Western modernity, toward a philosophical return to the source.

That marginalization is a feature of Black politics is not absent an originating logic that is grounded in a concrete material reality. The tendency to define and police Blackness and the Black image is rooted in the division between the enslaved and the nominally free. As "representatives" of those confined to the plantation and aided by a burgeoning Black public sphere, Black elites, and others able to command authority in their communities, helped develop, steer, and consolidate a coherent (though by no means uniform) set of practices and positions for combating white supremacy while simultaneously crafting their own conception of a Black collective self. As the age of revolution dawned, it became a Black collective self, supported by a developing political culture, framed largely through the lens of citizenship and the quest to attain it, be that in America or in a nation of our own making.[7] From this, we might say that Black political thought has always centered the marginalized. But it has done so primarily in a paternalistic manner, reproducing their marginal status by adopting and transforming Western ideological frameworks that, ultimately, reinforce rather than correct.

To take a well-known example, uplift and respectability—the belief that education and self-help were routes to becoming recognized as worthy of citizenship—have consistently served as a mechanism to promote more restrictive ways of imagining and projecting what Blackness is and how Black people should act. Those with the capacity and means to debate and articulate a Black agenda were, for the most part, a select few acting on behalf of the many, especially when compared to the slave population. They were also largely, though not exclusively, male. This effectively created an enduring class of Black leaders (the would-be Black bourgeoisie), the basis for a masculinist Black politics, and the idea of the "backward Black masses." The ideological limits and possibilities of Black political thought reflect the blend of contradictory forces that defined the historical moment, one that also set in motion what would become a long-standing rift among Black thinkers about the appropriate uses of Black culture in the political realm. But this is a tale with two sides.

While defining dimensions of Black political thought were crafted by free Blacks largely living in the North, Black radicalism itself emerged out of the politics and culture of the slaves, which sought, at a minimum, to re-create the world anew.[8] The shared encounter of slavery's hardships and the major and minor rebellions it produced made possible a distinctive "plantation politics" and political culture in what we might describe as a "plantation public sphere," one that Gooding-Williams argues was "consent-and-affiliation based," fostering "collective projects" premised on "shared perceptions, understandings, and expectations."[9] In that sense, plantation politics made space for different and sometimes conflicting ways of understanding slavery and, through it, Blackness, rather than imposing meaning; it was horizontal and deliberative rather than hierarchical. Just as crucially, the plantation public sphere, such that it was, helped facilitate a distinctive cultural and aesthetic tradition that proved to be another vital form of world-making and a source of collective self-fashioning.[10] In its various dimensions, Black folk culture and aesthetics represented a powerful unwillingness to relinquish what remained and had been passed on after crossing the Atlantic. Its existence is likewise the result of a desire to (re)construct something of their own through songs, dance, rituals, and oral exchange to breach the brutal bounds of slavery, even if temporarily.[11]

Taken together, by employing the techniques of revolt and the modes of rebellion emanating from the embodied aesthetics of Black folk culture, enslaved Africans across the Atlantic world forged a sense of unity and a Black collective self out of the cloth of domination, wherein resistance and the will to survive were, in Cedric Robinson's words, "the antithetical core, the soul of Black life."[12] It was a process of "reinvention" that, as Katherine McKittrick writes, made it possible to "*live and construct* Black humanity within the context of racial violence" and against its deadly principles.[13] And it is this political culture—the "rebellion, invention, [and] groove" of the dispossessed—rather than the political thought of the Black elites that anchors a vision of Blackness most closely aligned with, though not always speaking to, everyday Black people and everyday Black life, just as it has attempted to harness Black culture and aesthetics as a full-frontal challenge to anti-Blackness and white supremacy.[14] In other words, rather than being a field apart, the sustenance provided by Black culture and aesthetics, its idioms, and modes of expression has consistently offered Black political thought additional avenues to explode what Blackness is and explore everything it might be, the essence of what another world might entail.

For Black people, slavery and colonialism are beginnings subject to both imposed and self-created narratives of (un)belonging. Black political and social identities—disputed as they often are—emerge from this absent-presence and survive across cycles of reconstruction, including attempts to fashion an image of Black humanity and a vision of Black life. These cycles of reconstruction, the content and character of how Black people image Black life, are informed by the conjunctures in which they emerge, moments in history that carry their own sets of questions to not only help "think the present" but craft "a horizon of possible futures," futures that, as Stuart Hall reminds us, represent "a distinctive formulation" of historical time.[15] The Black image, our collective self-fashioning as a distinctive formulation shaped by the social forces that comprise the total perspective of the Black Situation, helps us navigate and map the limits and possibilities of Black political thought and culture, a genealogy of our political development.[16]

In what follows, I divide this cycle of reconstruction into three historical conjunctures, set in motion by the originating cleave between the Black slave and the Black "would-be" citizen, the antecedents of the movement's political culture—pain, joy, and care—the politics of the wake. Following the Civil War, I travel through the contested paradigm of the New Negro, then move to the Black Power and Black Arts Movement era, and the notion of "Black Is Beautiful," before returning to the current cultural and political terrain: the time of #BlackLivesMatter.

Of Slaves and Would-Be Citizens

The history of Black political thought and culture is one of collective self-fashioning crafted within and against the totalizing and planetary regimes of anti-Blackness and white supremacy. It is a story that begins at sea, located in the ruptured worlds of captive human cargo bound together in the hold of the slave ship. Sterling Stuckey suggests imagining the Middle Passage as the initial site where slaves became "a single people," a process owed to the "common horror" of experiencing "unearthly moans and piercing shrieks, the smell of filth and the stench of death, all during the violent rhythms and quiet coursings of ships."[17] Paradoxically, to be trapped in the hold where, as C.L.R. James explains, "no place on earth . . . concentrated so much misery" conditioned the possibility of a collective Black self, at least for those souls for whom the absence of community and the acceptance of social death was a window better left closed.[18]

United in a grief powerful enough to render ethnic and cultural divides moot, if only for a time, the slave ship, Stuckey observed, in all its barbaric cruelty, fostered "resistance thousands of miles before the shores of the new land appeared on the horizon—before there was mention of natural rights in North America."[19] This cruelty ensnared African women in particular ways, setting them apart from male captives, namely through the pervasive threat of sexual violence and the capacity to reproduce commodities to be bought and sold. Consequently, the specificity of their subjection, as Jennifer Morgan writes, "produced an analytic perspective" unique to enslaved women, one that "enabled them to be conduits of information" and, now and again, the spark of insurrection, rather than merely "passive producers of enslavement."[20]

Black rebellion, then, begins with the slaves who, considering their "condition," refused bondage and its uncertain if not impossible future by rising against their captors. In revolt, some slaves would attempt to physically overpower the crew and take control of both ship and self by force. If the mutiny failed, or if desperation struck, many chose another route: to escape the known world altogether, sometimes through starvation but more frequently by jumping overboard, "uttering cries of triumph," according to James, toward a different kind of freedom, a spiritual return through the door offered by the ocean's depth.[21] Whatever the method, the goal was unmistakable: to regain possession of their bodies by any means necessary and to reject the fate the ship held for them as cultivators of the crops—sugar, tobacco, cotton—that would come to restructure the world economy.[22] These acts of defiance, the suicidal leap, the will for freedom of enslaved Africans, should make clear that the seeds of both Black radicalism and abolition as understood today were first planted on the decks of the slave ship.

In that sense, it is no stretch to say that Black radicalism has interwoven origins. It is a movement against captivity and the idea of human commodities while also and consequently a movement against racial capitalism, even if the latter is only a foreshadowing, an "imminent tendency," in the words of Eugene Genovese, whose day was still on the horizon.[23] Upon landfall, the force of this tradition, what W.E.B. Du Bois once called the "motive of revolt and revenge," was brought to full bloom.[24] To put it plainly, Black political development begins with and through rebellion against the burgeoning world system as such, launched by the life-and-death circumstances that force solidarities around a common cause: a freedom yet to come.

The experience of plantation life gave rise to a wider repertoire of refusals than what was available to those at sea. Still, these strategies, and the opportunity to use them, were dictated by the specificity of the physical landscape as much as what Stephanie Camp has termed the plantation's "geographies of containment."[25] In the fledgling United States, as elsewhere in the New World, location also defined a steadily expanding, though by no means uniform, legal system constructed to define and control the political and social life of property, a matrix that includes what would later become known as the police. Of the techniques of resistance used by slaves, escape was the first and one of the most common. Like those who favored the ocean floor over the hold, the dispossessed of the plantation knew there existed a world prior, or something other than their daily strife, and many went looking for it. The most successful and storied example of this, at least in the North American imaginary, is the Underground Railroad, a network anchored by the heroism of leaders like Harriet Tubman, who, as Robinson notes, was "small of stature" but nevertheless "a massive presence in the Black liberation struggle" before, during, and after the Civil War.[26]

In many instances, particularly in Brazil and the Caribbean but in North America as well, flight led to the establishment of independent collectivities of former slaves most frequently referred to as Maroons. From the tenuous safety of these settlements, the escaped could use their reclaimed agency to agitate and disrupt the sanctity of the plantation, occasionally waging guerrilla warfare. In some cases, they would do so as a means of survival by taking food and other supplies, including weapons. Today one might derisively refer to this practice as "looting"—a prominent political talking point during the 2020 uprisings, not to mention all the urban rebellions that preceded it—but is better understood as a rejection of the way liberalism and the corrupt nature of capitalist social relations privilege commodities over life, especially the lives of "we the people who are darker than blue," to borrow from Curtis Mayfield.[27]

On other occasions, willful Maroons attempted to free those still bonded and expand the community's number. With these attacks against slavery, particularly those that involved battles approximating war, "Maroon colonies," according to Genovese, "destroyed in a single stroke the more extravagant racist pretensions of the whites and provided a beacon to spirited slaves."[28] The very idea of escape, and the knowledge that others had successfully done so, became an important anchor in the political thought of the plantation, a lore that captures us still. It destabilized the notion of incapacity and inferiority as a rejoinder to white rule, a project that created and then relied on such characterizations for its survival.

The most radical form of flight was full-fledged insurrection, that is, conspiratorially organized violence and acts of destruction, such as the burning of houses, plantations, and other property with the explicit aim of bringing slavery to heel. The guiding light of this brand of struggle was the victory of slaves over the French, British, and Spanish during the Haitian Revolution, which lasted from 1791 until 1804.[29] The defeat of European colonial rule and the birth of the first Black state in the Americas provided lasting inspiration and instruction for Blacks both free and enslaved. In the U.S. context, perhaps the most famous example of Black-led revolutionary violence is the plot carried out by Nat Turner and those accompanying him in 1831. With a spirit not unlike the battle for San Domingo, Turner's insurrection, in league with the planned but ultimately betrayed attempts by a young slave named Gabriel Prosser in 1800, or by the free preacher Denmark Vesey in 1822, exceeded many of the more spontaneous acts of revolt that both preceded and followed the revolution these leaders hoped to bring to bear. It was not enough to flee from bondage while leaving the institution of slavery intact. In each case, they sought to abolish the political and social system in which they were ensnared by razing it to the ground. Slavery was not to be escaped; it needed to be destroyed.[30] The same necessity proceeds in its wake.

While flight and insurrection represented revolt in its most overt and revolutionary register, when this option was not available, or if political consciousness had not risen to the point of recognizing that, in Robinson's words, "the enveloping violence of conspiracies and rebellion . . .

provided the most profit of all," resistance was carried out on a smaller scale, often under the cloak of routine.[31] Acts of sabotage and subordination, such as work stoppages and slowdowns, breaking tools, stealing, pretending to be sick, ignoring commands, and secretly learning to read and write, along with a host of other strategies, represented accessible pathways to undermine the regulations Black slaves were forced to endure for the profit of their masters, particularly for enslaved women. They were core instruments of defiance.

Some thinkers have turned a critical eye toward these acts, either placing them outside of the political, calling into question their consequence, or, more poignantly, making clear they were inseparable from and thus defined by subjection, a demonstration of slavery's totalizing power.[32] There's some truth to this critique. They were not, in and of themselves, frontal attacks sufficient to dent "the machinery of control" that defined the plantation.[33] Even the potentially cathartic tactic of revenge—by arson, poison, suicide, self-mutilation, or the murder of one's own children—did not offer a systemic challenge to the "peculiar institution." We also cannot confidently claim they were meant to resemble anything of the sort; the archive doesn't allow for the discernment of a unified motivation to be applied to each and every instance. But their insufficiency to the task of total transformation does not make them any less important as a tactic. Nor does it make it any less essential to how we understand the development and continuity of Black radicalism. Everyday resistance aided in the production of an alternative political culture that provided the "collective spiritual life," as Genovese has put it, underpinning the more dramatic techniques of revolt.[34] If not for these acts, and the shared sense of community cohesion they engendered, the development of a Black revolutionary tradition might not have occurred; everyone plays a part. This is particularly true in the United States, where, to return once more to Genovese, "an organic master-slave relationship unfolded under objectively unfavorable military and political circumstances that compelled a different course."[35]

The material conditions and social relations surrounding the plantation made revolt in the U.S. South more difficult and dangerous than in other locations where slavery ruled. Nevertheless, acts of rebellion against forced objecthood did occur, and they constitute the spirit of "nondominated action" on and against the prerogatives of the plantation.[36] They are performances of freedom, even if at times partial, where freedom is defined in the classical republican sense: to be *free from* domination. Consequently, nondominated action sits at the center of a genealogy in Black politics that Gooding-Williams terms "politics without rule," fostering an atmosphere of community trust, solidarity, and purpose, not unlike the solidarities that arose in the hold of the slave ship.[37] The plantation politics that informed the worldview of the slaves, premised on a politics without rule, fostered a political culture that Nell Irvin Painter describes as "firmly egalitarian and marked by strong racial cohesion" to foster an "enduring communal identity," one in which it was possible to speak of "our race" without imposing meaning on precisely what that meant.[38]

Through an egalitarian and nonhierarchical infused politics without rule, the public sphere forged among the community of slaves also helped facilitate a distinctive "creolized" and embodied cultural and aesthetic tradition defined, in large part, by song and dance. For example, in recounting the "story and politics of . . . illicit parties" and "celebrations" attended by slaves on the outer peripheries of the plantation, Stephanie Camp has argued that the brutality inflicted on the slave body, in an inverse manner, made the body an "important site not only of suffering but also of resistance, enjoyment, and potentially, transcendence."[39] Camp insists we take seriously how attention to the body allows for a fuller consideration of the "roles of movement and pleasure in the culture of opposition developed by enslaved people."[40] This potential for transcendence, the not yet here and yet to come incumbent to Black "movement and pleasure," is crucial to understanding the ebb and flow of Black radicalism and its cultural and aesthetic traditions— the precursor to Black joy. Sterling Stuckey goes as far as to suggest that the roots of Black nationalism itself come from this folk culture, which is to say, Black nationalism was aesthetic and cultural before it took a more sociopolitical form.[41]

Through revolt, nondominated action, and the modes of resistance emanating from Black folk culture and aesthetics, enslaved Africans created a sense of unity and a collective self where none previously existed, a process of "reinvention" that strove to "construct Black humanity within the context of racial violence."[42] In that sense, Black "livingness," its political and cultural manifestations, was "engendered by the Middle Passage and plantation systems dynamically and simultaneously."[43] As McKittrick's reading of Wynter's *Black Metamorphoses* reminds us, "one cannot reinvent the human without rebellious inventions, and rebellious inventions require reinvented lives."[44] The culture of "rebellious inventions" that arose in opposition to "plantation and colonial capitalist structures and their attendant modes of knowing, continues *en force* with the Movement for Black Lives.[45] And the uprisings of 2020 affirm the continuity and specificity of this uniquely Black Grammar.[46] Burning police cars and precincts, toppling statues, breaking storefront glass, singing and dancing, chants and the call-and-response: all demonstrate the lasting influence of the Black radicalism and thought from the days of the slave ship and plantation—the cultural and aesthetic afterlives of slavery. If Black radicalism was invented by the enslaved, then M4BL has created a space to honor the long arc of the Black freedom struggle while returning to the source to help deliver us somewhere else.

But the culture and traditions of the antebellum South, rendered on and through the body, with and for each other, have constantly tangled with a different vision of Black politics and the proper construction of a Black image.

~~~

Free Blacks living in the North had the latitude to pursue other modes of protest and resistance in response to white domination, just as they had more expansive ways to develop a Black collective self. These two processes happened in tandem and began with the creation of independent churches, organizations, and newspapers, particularly after the War for Independence. They would later include local and national Black conventions. All would become central institutions in the Black counterpublic. Through this burgeoning forum an emerging class of Black elites, largely given to the types of reformism that tend to come with property and notions of civic virtue, began to craft the grounds that would define, though not completely contain, the ideological contours of Black political thought.[47]

Unlike the political culture of the plantation, in the North, collective consciousness was not driven by the same culture of invention or produced through a horizontal process of exchange afield from the impulses guiding capitalist social relations. Nor was it premised on any distinctive Black ethos connected to a shared, race-based sense of self. For the Black middle class, Black identity was premised on the acknowledgment of a common oppression mapped across vastly different material contexts and experiences. If on the plantation Black folk culture and plantation politics were markers of Black communal living, north of the Mason-Dixon line, collective self-fashioning was geared toward being and becoming "Men," which is to say, humans and fellow citizens in the eyes of the white republic. As a result, the central focus of Black politics and thought in the antebellum North concerned abolishing slavery and attaining equal rights in a redeemed United States, using what Patrick Rael artfully terms "the canvases and colors provided by an America bent on repressing them."[48]

Naturally, there were dissenters to this thesis, and free Black workers had their faith in the American project rattled much more quickly than their more well-to-do counterparts. Nevertheless, the objective conditions separating the enslaved from the nominally free, and the worker from the petite bourgeoisie, meant that for many free Black thinkers, abolition meant reform, not insurrection.[49]

Born out of the sweep of revolution, the language of rights and liberty was a key tool—the master's, Audre Lorde might say—in the effort to fulfill the purported "promise" of the Constitution and its "firm basis of opposition to slavery," as Frederick Douglass once proclaimed.[50] More than just a protest strategy, then, the choice of language also represented ideological commitments. It demonstrated Black belief in the universalism of the Enlightenment, the liberal and republican political traditions, and the young nation itself. Consequently, some Black leaders in the North understood anti-Black racism and white supremacy to be anomalies rather than structural; they believed America could be made to honor its ideals and that Black people could and should be integrated into the folds of its tapestry. Some two hundred years later, in the age of viral Black death, there are those within the intramural that still foster this misguided belief.

Petitions, pamphlets, clubs, and, later, the Black press and the National Convention movement served as vehicles for articulating Black demands and consolidating community dialogue. For these adherents, the route to equality involved pointing out both the horrors of slavery and the contradiction between slavery and the American ethos. In this effort, they were joined by white abolitionists, led most famously by William Lloyd Garrison, who garnered broad support among the Black population and whose Boston-based anti-slavery newspaper, *The Liberator*, circulated weekly from 1831 until the end of the Civil War in 1865. Garrison's newspaper would be the springboard that launched the career of the Black abolitionist and proto-feminist Maria Stewart, who is said to be the first Black woman to give politically oriented public lectures in the United States.[51]

While the appeals of both Black and white abolitionists did not do much to substantively improve the material circumstances of free Blacks—or, for that matter, the enslaved—they nevertheless signaled a Black voice in an increasingly antagonist public sphere, one in direct conversation with the social, political, and ideological discourses of the day. But in a country defined by a genocidal addiction to bloodshed, anti-Blackness is perhaps its most powerful drug. The idea that Black people were naturally inferior, unequal, and unworthy was a shared understanding even among some whites who were sympathetic to the cause of abolition. Take the structure of white-led abolitionist organizations themselves: many of them denied Black people membership.[52]

The "undercurrent of racist paternalism" among white abolitionists, to borrow Robinson's phrasing, was evidence of a difficult truth about the nature of antebellum solidarity, or the lack thereof. White abolitionists saw slavery as a social ill and opposed it on moral grounds, not because they believed Blacks were or should be viewed as socially equal. To combat this assumption, the Black middle class further fashioned a collective image to elevate the race to a footing that recognized our humanity, which meant not only projecting a "respectable" portrait of civilized Blacks into a white supremacist world but using that image to educate and "uplift" the Black masses—the free worker and the not yet free slave, Black struggle's dual mode of address.

Just as important to the arc of Black political development, alienation from white abolitionist organizations meant that Blacks were forced to form their own anti-slavery associations to grapple with "the contradictions of being free and Black," which facilitated approaches to the problem that differed from the program advocated by their "allies."[53]

With scant attention to the way the world wills Black people toward social death, white intransigence in the face of the demands of both Black and white abolitionists was fierce and grew increasingly violent. At the same time, laws like the Fugitive Slave Act of 1850, which mandated that escaped slaves must be delivered back to their owners, even if they were found in a "free" state, and Supreme Court rulings like the one handed down in the Dred Scott case, which held, among other things, that Black people were not and could not be citizens, further proved that the reformers' flights of fancy were not shared by America's representatives or its judiciary.[54]

The lack of progress produced an ideological splintering of sorts, and a further move toward militancy, as an increasing number of Black leaders began to view achieving equality in America as impossible without using force. As the abolitionist, writer, and physician Martin Delany put it, "I must admit, that I have no hope in this country—no confidence in the American people."[55] Nor should he have, and neither should we. It's in this orbit of lost hope that a more radical set of Black elites answered the question offered by Langston Hughes almost a century later: What happens to a dream deferred? The charge for Black sovereignty and self-governance gathered steam as did, even further to the left, a restive call for armed rebellion side by side with the slaves. Abolition as reform was a bullet that lacked a rifle. Black freedom required land and, for the boldest of the bunch, the "cleansing" cool of revolutionary violence.[56]

Neither idea was novel. Black emigration, the movement from a geography of confinement and suffering to one that, with any luck, would be less so, was always present, beginning with the Maroon communities across the New World that wrestled self-determination away from white rule. The 1850s gave this tradition renewed force among Black elites such that, just before the Civil War, many national leaders "paid deference to the twin concepts of emigration and Negro nationalism" that by then, as Robinson reminds us, were often coupled with concrete "ambitions for the economic development of the free Black community" and the desire to build a haven for the enslaved.[57]

Insurrection was no different. David Walker was as clear in words as Nat Turner would later be in bloody deed when, in 1829, he delivered the following warning to the American people:

> Remember Americans, that we must and shall be free and enlightened as you are, will you wait until we shall, under God, obtain our liberty by the crushing arm of power? Will it not be dreadful for you? I speak Americans for your good. We must and shall be free I say, in spite of you. You may do your best to keep us in wretchedness and misery, to enrich you and your children, but God will deliver us from under you. And wo, wo, will be to you if we have to obtain our freedom by fighting.[58]

In both respects, be it the tradition of Black separatism or Black rebellion, the radical edge of Black political thought tracks back to, and is inseparable from, the revolutionary Black slave. Consequently, it is imperative that we understand and embrace the slave as "Black philosophy's savant," to borrow from Joy James, offering future generations the ideological scaffolding to help address the conceptual contradictions inherent to the way Western modernity views and practices freedom— the freedom to be dominated and exploited under capitalism.[59] Abolition must be an insurrectionary praxis, the ending and remaking of the world.

But in the context of those inauspicious years, years in which the tensions between the North and South eventually gave way to war, only rebellion could fully maintain the Black savant's philosophical legacy. In the hands of the emerging Black middle strata, nationalism and the pursuit of self-determination did not attempt to contest Western modernity's core conceits. The belief among Blacks that liberation was impossible in America, and that Black people should seek freedom on greener pastures, was, at the time, a radical proposition. Nevertheless, the nationalist/emigrationist faction of Black leaders for the most part maintained the ideological substance of their more liberal contemporaries: the need for education, self-help, and respectability, so that Black people might succeed *within* the capitalist world system and the social relations that comprise its core. The difference was a matter of strategy, and even that strategy oscillated, with thinkers shifting positions from one pole to the other in response to changing circumstances.

~~~

Having sketched, in broad strokes, the material and ideational divide between nonfreedom and nominally free, and the different, though occasionally overlapping, political cultures it produced, we can now move further downstream. These two political cultures, one belonging to the Black slave and the other to the Black bourgeoisie, are the raw materials of Black political development, the "profound grounds," to use Robinson's words, on which it has proceeded.[60] While each iteration of Black struggle owes the specifics of its form to inherited circumstances, the Movement for Black Lives included, "their bases," as Robinson notes, "are in alternative worldviews germinated from radically different Black experiences" and evidenced in the attempt to fashion a collective Black self.[61]

The Changing Same

The logic of uplift and respectability that informed the competing integrationist and nationalist strands of Black thought prior to the Civil War and Reconstruction persisted and mutated throughout the twentieth century, morphing from a structural critique of slavery and white supremacy to one increasingly bound to individual responsibility during and after Jim Crow segregation. A similar ideological mutation informed the idea of the New Negro, which we can think of as "an ensemble of geohistorical relations" that exacted a profound "collective outpouring of political protest, cultural expression, and intellectual debate" across national borders.[62] This collective outpouring reached its creative apex with the cultural interventions of the New Negro (or Harlem) Renaissance in the mid-1920s, before giving way to the intensifying currents of a more leftist political persuasion that began to take hold prior to and during World War I, blossomed during the Depression years, and largely revolved around the Black working class.

With an eye toward the uses and misuses of Black art, the New Negroes within this more radical camp rejected what they thought to be a white-facing, apolitical, and socially detached cultural movement divorced from the lived experience of most Blacks. It was a critique shepherded by a gravitational pull in Black politics and thought toward Marxism and the Communist Party of the USA in the 1930s, which engendered a different and deeper orientation toward Black people and everyday Black life than what was fostered by the Black bourgeoisie. Richard Wright succinctly captured this shift when he claimed that Black writing up to that point amounted to "the educated Negro pleading with white America for justice" and that "rarely was . . . this writing addressed to the Negro himself, his needs, his sufferings, his aspiration."[63]

There was never a singular New Negro. The term was differently understood by Black thinkers and cultural workers over the better part of three decades, laying bare not only "a tension between strictly political concerns" and those that were assumed to be "strictly artistic" but also conflicting visions of Black identity and the desired structure of society.[64] Nevertheless, the New Negro conjuncture still stands as the first and, at the time, most pronounced assertion of a global, Black collective self-image, which included the Negritude movement launched by African and Caribbean writers Aimé and Suzanne Césaire and Léopold Senghor, among others. To put things in familiar terms, it was that era's political and cultural zeitgeist, a "moment in time," to borrow from Davarian Baldwin, "more so than a discrete collection of individuals who thought and acted the same way."[65] Again, generations are not monolithic.

In the spirit of renewal, the New Negro was, in the first instance, a "symbol of plenitude, of regeneration, of a truly reconstructed *presence*" against the persistent idea that Black people were nothing more than a "truly negated" and unworthy "other."[66] This negated other was aggressively depicted and narrated through an array of Black stereotypes, such as the docile image of Sambo, caricatures that not only defined what Blackness was and meant in the context of white visual and popular culture but also continued to influence the terms by which some Black people, particularly those with social privilege and political power, chose to imagine themselves. The purpose of images like Sambo, as Wynter explains, was to (re)produce a general understanding of Black people in the eyes of white America powerful enough to re-create the master-slave relationship that had been (and continues to be) central to the construction of anti-Blackness, white supremacy, and the maintenance of whiteness as such. It was an image that insisted Black people and, more broadly, Black culture must be "devoid of all the characteristics that separate the lower forms of human life from the supposedly higher forms."[67]

Not unlike the public-facing impulses present in the antebellum North, to combat this narrative, the New Negro, as a (contested) political and cultural paradigm, or what Henry Louis Gates refers to as a "coded system of signs," sought to capture and assert an "evolved" Black public-self fundamentally distinct from these racial caricatures and stereotypes.[68] The basic tenets of this public-self were promoted by an emerging class of Black elites, sometimes referred to as the "Reconstruction Generation." Many among this generation were wedded to Victorian ideals of decorum that were dominant in the late nineteenth century, furthering the political-cultural divide between the Black multitude and the bourgeoisie. These ideals served to reinforce the importance of traditional gender roles and the family more broadly, setting the stage for the maintenance of gender-based boundary drawing in the years to come.

The National Association for Colored Women (NACW) provides an instructive case in point. Founded in 1896 as the signal consolidation of the Black women's club movement, and, subsequently, one of the most formidable Black-led organizations in the early years of the new century, the NACW, along with its cofounder and inaugural president Mary Church Terrell, espoused what Erin Chapman has called "Victorian Black feminism."[69] The "Black feminist" part of this equation can be traced to the fact that many "club women"—Terrell and the educator

Anna Julia Cooper, for example—were unambiguous about the unique consequences of anti-Blackness as it pertained to the experiences of Black women. In noting this specificity, they were equally vocal about the role Black women could and should play in Black struggle, despite the sexism of Black men. On the other side of the ledger, the NACW, Chapman writes, could be appropriately called "Victorian" because they often "assumed bourgeois homes to be both women's rightful sphere of influence and the basis for their civic activism outside the home." Consequently, the NACW promoted a politic that made "black people's achievement of such ideal homes a preeminent indication of racial advancement through the demonstration of their 'civilization.'"[70]

Building on the foundations laid by the NACW, and later, the more "masculinist impulses" of the National Association for the Advancement of Colored People (NAACP) and National Urban League (NUL), the primary twist in the Black self-fashioning of this period, at least at first, was that the New Negro aimed to show that Black people were not simply *citizens* of the United States capable of education, culture, refinement, and self-respect.[71] They were also "unapologetically" *Negroes* who understood their worthiness by embracing and taking pride in being both *Black* and *modern*.

In this initial phase, the embrace of Blackness, of "race pride," particularly by the Black middle class, did not, in and of itself, fundamentally change the ideational ground that existed in preceding iterations of Black political thought, a ground weighed down by the influence of liberalism and capitalist social relations. Instead, it tended to reinforce those views, often with seemingly competing strategies that were nevertheless guided by a shared idea that "racial consciousness" was needed to combat anti-Blackness and white supremacy. The New Negro, then, was as much about shifting America's view of Black people as it was about changing Black people's image of and approaches to themselves, which they did by leveraging the political and cultural expanse of the growing Black counterpublic: organizations, newspapers, magazines, music, books, art, public speech, and public performance.

As the (in some ways) overstated differences between and within nationalist and integrationist interpretations make plain, the task of reimagining Blackness exposed fissures, though not necessarily contradictions, in the relationship between Black politics, Black culture, and the Black multitude. For those who, in one way or the other, remained invested in the American project, the goal was to "marshal the masses of the race into the regiments of the New Negroes who, of course, would command them."[72] This position is famously evident in the political thought of Booker T. Washington and, even more explicitly, in a young Du Bois's view of the "talented tenth" as outlined in *The Souls of Black Folk*. But it is also apparent in the latter's vision of political aesthetics, the distinctive "gift" of the Negro "Spirit," and the role art and beauty should play in breaking the fog of anti-Blackness, an argument Du Bois spelled out most clearly in his essay "Criteria of Negro Art."

This reading of the New Negro, endorsed by people like Washington and Du Bois, and echoed by Victorian Black feminists like Mary Church Terrell, Ida B. Wells, and Anna Julia Cooper, reproduced the classist idea of the Black masses as backward and in need of authoritative leadership. At the same time, in the case of Du Bois at least, it simultaneously heralded the "Beauty" of (and "Truth" in) Black expressive culture—the power it held to "vindicate" the race and "redeem" America, which would allow the country to finally fulfill its promise of equality and justice. To put it another way, the New Negro represented an analysis of the "what" and "how" of Black freedom, and this what and how, communicated intramurally and to the broader public sphere, still rested in large part on pushing Black people closer to civilization by adopting "notions of the proper" threaded by bourgeois values that were themselves premised on anti-Blackness.[73]

A desire to place parameters around how Black people comported themselves in the name of a "collective destiny" to be achieved within a revised rather than undone capitalist world system should not surprise us, even as we may recoil from these stances, perched, as we are, in the present. It was a rational, and in many ways inherited, response to a complex array of political and economic forces that followed the failures of Reconstruction—first among them, anti-Black violence, most egregiously in the form of lynching—and the dawn of U.S. empire. The combination of America's growing imperial drive and European colonial exploits in Africa inspired new bonds of international solidarity and helped spur the First Pan-African Conference in 1900, a crucial pivot in the development of Black political thought.

The tack taken by these Black thinkers, in league with the ideological underpinnings of their class, was premised on what they believed would bring about freedom in the context of a global regime of capital accumulation transforming right before their eyes and a newly (re)arranged apparatus of racial rule. These beliefs invariably went hand in hand with normative understandings about the role of leadership in Black struggle and represented positions that the Black underclasses were meant to see, accept, and adhere to. After all, the "backward" should be led, out of necessity and for the betterment of the race.

History teaches us that authority rarely manifests in a neatly woven dialectic of "command and obey." The nascent northern and midwestern ghettos, and the "wayward lives" of turn-of-the-century young Black women, as rendered by Saidiya Hartman, offer one glimpse of how Victorian mores and social control were rejected in favor of autonomous self-possession.[74] By refusing to be governed, these "social visionaries and innovators"—the sex worker, the cross-dresser, the queer vagabond—advanced a Black radicalism that mirrored and embodied the "experiments with freedom" pursued through everyday acts of resistance on the plantation; they reflected the flight of the Maroons.[75] "It is the untiring practice," Hartman writes, "of trying to live when you were not meant to survive" that infuses and unites the techniques of Black rebellion and ushers forward those "in search of a better place than here," someplace else entirely.[76]

In the U.S. South, many among the Black multitude also went their own way, choosing, for example, to use "public community action," which typically took the form of "mass meetings," as the means to create the conditions for Black communal living—actions that, as Painter notes, had little if anything to do with the ideological whims of national leadership.[77] When confronted with the realities of the postbellum South, in other words, the Black masses operated according to a doctrine of separatism and self-determination, of going it alone to the extent that they could, based on locally acute, material concerns and largely without tipping into the conceptual territory of the nation-state. This doctrine helped continue a tradition of mutual aid and other "cooperative enterprises," which coalesced with what Ernest Allen Jr. describes as a "collective Black group culture existing apart from that of the dominant American identity and culture."[78] As with the "fugitive gestures" of the young Black women navigating the northern ghetto Hartman brings to light, it is a tradition that began with the Black slave.[79]

~~~

The more militant vantage on the New Negro paradigm emerged in the 1910s, spearheaded by a post-Reconstruction generation that did not have direct ties to the slave experience and that wanted to advance beyond the parameters put forth by those who had preceded them. This newfound militancy can be sourced, at least in part, to the dynamism and disenchantment that followed the first waves of internal migration of Blacks from the South and the external migration from the Caribbean to the urban centers of the North. It was likewise spurred by the experiences of Black soldiers returning from the battlefields of World War I; the precipitous rise in anti-Black violence, subjugation, and terror that accompanied the coming of Jim Crow, the "red summers," as Ernest Allen Jr. termed it; and the success of the Bolsheviks in the October Revolution of 1917, which provided a model for proletariat revolution. While this militancy held its own internal tensions, principally between bourgeois nationalism and socialism, its proponents were united in their appeal to and support from the Black working class, their Pan-African and internationalist sensibilities, and a belief that now was the time for a Black self-determination organized by Black people independent of white paternalism.[80]

Following in the footsteps of the socialist street orator Hubert Harrison, chief among this group was Marcus Garvey and the martial pageantry of the Universal Negro Improvement Association (UNIA).[81] Garvey famously denounced Du Bois and the NAACP for wanting "us all to become white" while espousing that "to be a Negro is no disgrace, but an honor," and that the members of the UNIA, unlike those in the NAACP, "love our race."[82] However, his actual political agenda, and the justifications behind it, followed the logic of uplift, self-help, and the prevailing capitalist common sense. Additionally, Garvey's Pan-Africanism betrayed a commitment to a state-building project through the "performance of sovereignty" that, similar to the ambitions of previous nationalist thinkers like Delany, not only harbored clear colonial aspirations but reified the nation-state as the ideal political vessel for self-determination— even as the nation-state itself, to borrow once more from Richard Iton, "might be best understood as intrinsically anti-Black."[83] In short, Garvey's radicalism was shadowed and arguably undermined by a fidelity to the modern world system.

The same could be said for the cadre of Black nationalist women, many of whom developed their politics while members of Garvey's UNIA. As Keisha Blain has shown, these nationalist women balanced between conservative and radical points of view to articulate their vision of Black liberation. Though unquestionably more militant than many of their counterparts in the NACW, they nevertheless "embraced heteronormative gender politics and generally advocated civilizationist racial uplift views," despite occasionally flashing proto "feminist beliefs."[84] Like Garvey, Black nationalist women also embraced "Black capitalism" as a principal mechanism for actualizing independence in ways that betrayed their radicality, a position they held alongside and in tension with a critique of the imperial aspirations of the United States and other countries.[85]

Garvey and the Black nationalist women who would carry on and transform his political vision after the decline of the UNIA were joined in dialogue by competing programs to bring about a radical transformation of society. Socialist labor leaders such as A. Philip Randolph and worker-centered "left nationalist" organizations like the Communist African Blood Brotherhood, led by the journalist Cyril Briggs, the Renaissance poet Claude McKay, and W. A. Domingo, a childhood friend of Garvey who, for a time, also served as editor for Garvey's *The Negro World*, all provided alternative imaginings of what would bring about Black freedom. And a rejection of capitalism was at its center.

For galvanizers like Randolph, notions of self-defense and armed resistance against white supremacy, as a "matter of course," marked what was both new and necessary about the Negro in the wake of World War I.[86] Randolph envisioned the New Negro as a "militant, card carrying, gun toting socialist who refused to turn the other cheek, because doing so would only invite more of the same."[87] Much like both the integrationist ethos and the bourgeois nationalism of the UNIA, education was central to Randolph's thinking—just to different ends. "The New Crowd," wrote Randolph in a 1919 issue of *The Messenger*, "must be composed of young men who are educated, radical and fearless."[88] But instead of seeing education as the springboard for respectability and social acceptance, Randolph believed it was the foundation for all efforts toward social transformation. From the perspective of organized labor, the New Negro was also someone who spoke, in the words of W. A. Domingo, "the language of the oppressed" in opposition to the "language of the oppressor."[89] In that sense, the New Negro was not only an adherent to a culture of Black revolt dating back to slave ship mutinies and plantation rebellions—one that argued "no one who will not fight to protect his life is fit to live," as Randolph proclaimed—but also one and the same with the Black masses. Black radicalism should be with and for the dominated and dispossessed.[90]

This more radical, anti-capitalist, and masses-centered take, one that would influence the thinking of Wright, performers like Paul Robeson, writers such as Lorraine Hansberry, and future nationalist formations like the Black Arts Movement would remain a powerful stream in Black political thought. Crucially, Black women who aligned themselves with the Communist Party, paced by radical organizers like Claudia Jones, Audley "Queen Mother" Moore, and Esther Cooper Jackson, to name only a few, were essential to advancing this stream, developing what Erik S. McDuffie terms a "Black left feminism," one that centered the lived experience of Black working-class women, foreshadowing a political analysis of "triple oppression" that would shape the political thought of Black women in the 1960s and 1970s.[91]

Nevertheless, it was Alain Locke and his culturally focused understanding of the New Negro Renaissance that is most associated with the term in the popular imagination, drowning out the militancy that characterized interpretations of who the New Negro was following the

Great War in favor of a view that, if not quite apolitical, centered artistic concerns and innovation. The New Negro, as promoted by Locke and many of his followers, believed it would be "the fine arts and not the political sphere or protest poetry" that would dent the brunt of racial hierarchies and prompt the reevaluation by "white and Black alike of the Negro in terms of his artistic endowments and cultural contributions, past and present."[92] While Locke certainly believed in the cultural value and importance of Black folk and ancestral traditions, he maintained a strong attachment to Victorian ideals and, in general, looked down on the Black working class. He harbored a vision of "old versus new" that placed the Black masses and their "lack of self-understanding," as Locke put it, on a lower rung, while "the thinking few," by virtue of their ability to "[shed] the old chrysalis of the Negro problem," ascended to the arena of "spiritual emancipation."[93]

Despite his influence, Locke's views were not universally embraced. Renaissance writers like Langston Hughes rejected notions of respectability and seized specifically Black signifiers and symbols, asserting, in his essay "The Negro Artist and the Racial Mountain," that "black common people . . . furnish a wealth of colorful, distinctive material . . . because they still hold their own individuality in the face of American standardizations."[94] For Hughes, it was important that Black people "know we are beautiful. And ugly too," which is why his poems were, in his own words, "racial in theme and treatment, derived from the life I know."[95] The sentiment was shared by the "New Negro Women" who rejected many of the pretenses associated with Locke's Victorian vision, along with the persistent projection, even from radicals like Randolph, that the New Negro was, by nature, a man—from fellow Renaissance writers like Zora Neale Hurston and Marita Bonner to singers like Gertrude "Ma" Rainey and Bessie Smith.[96] While these artists embodied and attempted to reflect everyday Black life, the broader Renaissance, as directed by Locke and affirmed by Du Bois's polemic on "Negro Art," was largely consumed by white audiences, patrons, and Black elites, maintaining a degree of distance from the actual "needs . . . suffering . . . and aspirations" of everyday Black people, as Wright and, later, Amiri Baraka and Larry Neal would charge. This distance was punctuated by the decision by some Renaissance writers to adopt expressive forms that mirrored white cultural production, such as the poetry of Countee Cullen, whose work Du Bois and Locke both celebrated. By adopting classic poetic stylings, artists like Cullen simultaneously "sought to erase," returning to Gates, "their received racist image in the Western imagination" and ended up "[erasing] their racial selves" in the process."[97]

These shortcomings notwithstanding, movements like the New Negro Renaissance, in both its political and cultural dimensions, "do not always *settle*," as Margo Natalie Crawford reminds us, at least not completely. Instead, they have the power to set the table for horizons that can only be realized in the future, when the conditions for their emergence are ripe.[98] To take one example, Crawford notes that some Renaissance texts, such as Hughes's "The Negro Artist and the Racial Mountain," "approached the aesthetic, theory, and practice" of the Black Arts Movement (BAM), a fact acknowledged by BAM writer and publisher Dudley Randall, who said that the essay by Hughes, despite important divergences, was "as close to the Black Aesthetic cry of 'I'm Black and beautiful!' as it is possible to come."[99] From this vantage, the efforts to pursue an "integrationist aesthetic," guided, to a degree, by the influence of white patrons but also the aspiration of being considered a human participant in the creation of civilization and the furthering of democratic ideals, do not completely "cancel out" the space Renaissance writers attempted to make for Black self-determination or the valuation of Blackness and Black culture as such.[100]

For Crawford, in understated ways and without yet fully having the tools to articulate a vision of an unapologetic Black aesthetic or maintain an embrace of the idea that Black is "always beautiful," as Dudley put it, Negro Renaissance writers and artists still managed to anticipate a fuller view of Blackness through the prism of everyday Black life and culture. And they did so if only by beginning to suggest, for the first time, that Black "could" be beautiful, and "ugly," that Blackness itself was expansive and therefore difficult to pin down, themes Crawford suggests are even evident in the work of those hesitant to claim a racial mantle, such as luminaries like Cullen and Jean Toomer.[101]

These anticipatory visions, coupled with the political projects of Garvey, Randolph, and Briggs and the sonic signatures of the blues, jazz, and later soul—Bessie Smith, Ma Rainey, Duke Ellington, Sam Cooke, Nina Simone, and others—greatly shaped the more assertive, self-assured tones and aesthetics of the BAM and Black Power era, which arose, in part, out of the perceived political insufficiencies and cultural conservatism of the civil rights order. It was a further step toward unbounding the idea of Blackness, informed by, as Marx put it, the "inherited circumstances" of their historical present and pronounced by way of the axioms offered by those on the periphery of the periphery, a tradition that began with, and therefore gestures back to, the culture and politics of the Black slave.[102]

I Love Being Black

The militant voices of the Black Power and Black Arts Movements, a collection of souls that leading BAM theorist Larry Neal referred to as the "New breed," attempted to cry the song of the Black masses through the tune of an unambiguous Black love. Utilizing the expanded networks of communication and assembly available to the 1960s generation, combined with what James Edward Smethurst describes as a "do-it-yourself ethic that did not wait for the benediction of higher authorities," the BAM embraced the way Black culture, and the Black musical tradition in particular, "[chronicled] . . . the Negro's movement from African slave to American slave, from Freedman to Citizen."[103] In his essay "The Myth of Negro Literature," Amiri Baraka, one of the BAM's brightest lights, drove home this point by leveling a not-so-subtle critique at many of his artistic predecessors, arguing that, in the past:

> the Negroes who found themselves in a position to pursue some art, especially the art of literature, have been members of the Negro middle class, a group that has always gone out of its way to cultivate *any* mediocrity, as long as that mediocrity was guaranteed to prove

to America, and recently to the world at large, that they were not really who they were, *i.e.*, Negroes.

For Baraka, only Black music had thus far been able to withstand the willful abandonment of Blackness and Black people by the Black middle class, allowing Black musicians to "[maintain] their identities as Negroes." They were able to do so because Black music "drew its strengths and beauties out of the depth of the black man's soul, and because to a large extent its traditions could be carried on by the lowest classes of Negroes." Culture for the Black middle-class artist, Baraka charged, was more about the "cultivation" of a white sensibility, which fell to the "'best and most intelligent' of Negroes" to exact. The pursuit of cultivation, then, meant detaching oneself from racial affinities to attain "favor" in the eyes of a predominately white and middle-class public sphere, creating what he believed to be a "separation between Negro life (as an emotional experience)" and Black art.[104]

In contrast to the desire to harness a white sensibility, the BAM believed the aim of Black cultural production should be to "feel one's history." Neal claimed to be after what he termed a "workable concept" that could properly capture the multivalent nature of Black life: the Black experience as lived and understood by everyday Black people and purposefully reflected in Black culture. History and heritage were crucial to and inseparable from this effort, which also informed Neal's understanding of the Black Power and Black Arts Movements more broadly. Black radicalism in the 1960s, he argued, must be seen through the "ideas and persons which preceded it"; they were part of a longer-running conversation, a "synthesis," and a historically situated "emotional response"[105]—in other words, Black political development. For Neal, Black art and culture represented "a living history," encompassing a "great vision, revolutionary and spiritual in nature," but to take part in this tradition and to honor its forerunners, Black people had work to do. We "must liberate ourselves [and] destroy the double-consciousness" Du Bois famously named as Black America's "unreconciled" striving, by doing away with the desire to reconcile with the American project altogether.[106]

To do this, and against the reigning paradigms of a Western culture BAM theorists thought to be "dying" if not already dead, Neal believed Black people needed to "integrate with ourselves" by seeking a "haven in Blackness." Embracing Blackness was seen as an antidote, one that could help resolve the historical "tension" produced by double-consciousness toward, as he put it, "recognizing the beauty and love within Black America itself," that Black is ultimately beautiful.[107] In this regard, the BAM understood Blackness and Black culture to be a "world opening force" and that proudly reclaiming Black heritage was not about, to use Crawford's phrasing, "where one is from but to where one must travel" so that we might "embrace . . . a fuller view of what Blackness is" and all that doing so might bring to bear.[108] By experimenting with "new self-images and ways of walking through the *actual new world* that was anticipated," through poetry, music, dance, visual arts, and theater, as Crawford persuasively suggests, the cultural workers of the BAM "were not waiting for the world to change; they were anticipating change, believing that change could happen."[109] But how did the BAM ecosystem, those "ideological and institutional spaces in which young (and not so young) black artists and intellectuals came together to organize, study, and think about what a new black art (and a new black politics) might be," come to see Blackness and Black culture as a world-opening force?[110] Or to put it another way, what were the conditions under which such a view could emerge?

~~~

The explanation is layered with complexity, but in its simplest form, as Fanon instructs, we might attribute it to "a fundamentally different international situation" than the one encountered by the generation prior.[111] World War II was a catalyzing event, perhaps *the* event, both because of what preceded it—namely, the prevalence and power of the Black left in the 1930s and 1940s—but also because of what followed in its wake. Postwar economic expansion continued a trend of redistributive policies and economic regulations to rein in and ultimately save capitalism from the civil unrest that could arise in response to its penchant for crisis, a process that, in the United States, began in earnest with the New Deal and that later, once the war ended, established welfare state regimes across the West. Globally, the creation of the United Nations and the establishment of the International Monetary Fund heralded a new, integrated, and cooperative world order, though "coercive" is arguably the more accurate term.

At the same time, with the traditional European powers reeling from the battles that took place on their soil, the onset of the Cold War created sharp geopolitical and ideological divides, gifting us the comically absurd notion that America (through the leadership of its president) is the "leader of the free world." The consequence of this divide, and the presence of a meaningful alternative to capitalism in the form of a Socialist state whose influence had to be taken seriously, on every scale, from the local to the global, cannot be overstated. The repression of Black radicals who had previously formed alliances with the "Old left" and the subsequent conflation of Black dissidence of any kind with communism during the height of the "Red Scare" is one such consequence.

Parallel to the seemingly hegemonic (and unequal) conflict between the United States and the Soviet Union, the "transcendent and more enduring dualism," as Robinson framed it, was the world system's other great contradiction: the "struggle to obtain or vanquish racial domination."[112] The spirit of rebellion and the will for liberation were in full bloom, deepening and, in some respects, redrawing lines of Black internationalist solidarity. The Fifth Pan-African Congress, which took place in Manchester, England, in October 1945, a month after the war ended, announced a "new phase of world revolution," led by "colonial and subject peoples of the world."[113] This watershed moment was soon followed, to cite but a few examples, by the Dutch retreat from Indonesia in 1949; the Chinese Revolution that same year; the defeat, in 1954, of the French in Vietnam to close the First Indochina War; the Bandung Conference in 1955; Ghanaian Independence in 1957; the successful end of the Cuban Revolution in 1959; Congolese Independence in 1960; and the start of the Non-Aligned Movement in 1961.

These global developments tracked alongside domestic events—in the courts, in the streets, and eventually in legislation—that would reshape the political landscape and prepare the way for the Black Power and Black Arts moment. Consider the eleven-year period leading up to the founding of Baraka and Neal's Black Arts Repertory Theater and School (BARTS), one of the BAM's "pioneering institutions," in Harlem in 1965.[114] During that pivotal stretch there was, on the one hand, the *Brown v. Board of Education* Supreme Court decision in 1954; the beginning of the Montgomery Bus Boycott in 1955; the founding, in 1957, of Martin Luther King Jr.'s Southern Christian Leadership Conference; the student-led sit-in movement of 1960; the founding of the Student Nonviolent Coordinating Committee (with the guidance of Ella Baker); the Freedom Rides in 1961; the creation of the Revolutionary Action Movement in 1962; the March on Washington in 1963; the passage of the Civil Rights Act in 1964; the founding of Malcolm X's Organization of Afro-American Unity after breaking with the Nation of Islam that same year; the passage of the Voting Rights Act in 1965; and, within a matter of months, the inception of Maulana Karenga's cultural nationalist organization "US."[115]

On the other hand, however, the years that preceded the creation of BARTS were also filled with politically galvanizing tragedies and racial upheavals. The assassinations of Patrice Lumumba in 1961, Medgar Evers in 1963, and, perhaps most consequentially, Malcolm X in 1965; the bombing of the Sixteenth Street Baptist Church in Birmingham, Alabama, in 1963; the urban unrest that took hold across several cities in 1964; the even more explosive uprising in Watts in 1965—all further shifted the spectrum of possibility in Black political thought. Once more, racial violence, premature death, and the insurrectionary flame of Black rebellion pried open the door to a reinvigorated pursuit of Black self-determination, setting the stage for the understanding that Blackness and Black culture could not only be but, in fact, already were a world-opening force, one that was both present and on the precipice of arrival.[116]

~~~

None of this is to say there was ideological uniformity, or a lack of contradictions and related tensions, either within the BAM or across the broader array of Black power organizations, especially as it pertains to how the thinkers and cultural workers of that era understood the term "nationalism" and approached concepts like "self-determination."[117] Nor was any such uniformity possible. The BAM began locally, emerging "across a wide geographic area" before ultimately "coalescing into a national movement with a sense of a broader coherence that, in turn, inspired more local, grassroots activities."[118] In other words, the local character of Black arts initiatives, grounded in specific political and cultural contexts, ensured the presence of ideological diversity and debate underneath a layer of unity that developed over time. Adding to the theoretical crosscurrents was that there was never an organizational or ideological center to the Black Power and Black Arts conjuncture, no dominant force providing the barometer against which all others would stake their political claims, the outsized media coverage of the Black Panther Party notwithstanding.[119]

The absence of a monolithic ideology or set of practices, championed by a hegemonic national organization, produced divisions that, while important to the development of that era's competing forms of nationalism, did not fray what Smethurst describes as "the common thread between nearly all the groups."[120] First and most important among these threads, he writes, was the view that Blacks should be understood as "a people, a nation, entitled to (needing, really) self-determination of its own destiny" and, short of seizing that power, "would remain oppressed and exploited second-class (or non-) citizens."[121] Second was the understanding that Black diasporic culture was distinct, and fundamentally opposed to, the cultures of white Western modernity. This distinctive culture needed to be both nurtured and enlarged as an "absolute political priority . . . linked to the equally emphatic drive for the development and exercise of black self-determination," a way to run free from the enclosures of "mainstream" American life.[122] For the BAM, this meant producing art that blurred the lines between the popular and the avant-garde, a radical cultural expression whose broad range intentionally tried to reach past Black elites and their penchant for respectable, assimilationist craftsmanship that mirrored white forms to connect with the experiences of everyday Black people.[123]

But despite their rejection of white forms, a generative embrace of the Black masses, an expansive view of Blackness, and the belief in the potential of Blackness to alter existing political and cultural frameworks, the BAM and Black Power moment did not completely escape already established ways of thinking, being, and imagining a Black collective self. A masculinist though not inflexible political ideology and a vision of Black liberation that, while not entirely hostile to homosexuality, was still largely heteronormative were both strong winds within BAM, as it was on the left more broadly.[124] This current included, among other things, the "reconstructing and revolutionizing of the black family in which men were men and women were women" and, as Smethurst writes, a "notion of reconstruction . . . predicated on the cultural fall of a prehistoric Africa figured as a loss of masculinity—a familiar trope of African American nationalism reaching back into the nineteenth century."[125] Just as masculinity followed the quest for citizenship by those seeking political belonging and equality, be that in America or elsewhere, the BAM's idea of "natural Black beauty" carried forth modes of policing the Black image and, along with it, the Black body.[126]

Like the limitations of the New Negro, bound by the social forces that produce distinctive, temporally grounded ways of encountering the world and understanding oneself in it, the BAM's policing of Blackness does not undermine what Crawford calls their "collective love affair with Blackness—the *collective* performance of *self*-love," a performance that married "emotions and desire" with "political urgency" to construct a new foundation for imagining the style and substance of liberation.[127] Nor does it erase the very real way BAM artists demonstrated a commitment to everyday Black people and Black social life, as evidenced in local efforts to create "community-oriented institutions," especially in the South.[128] They directly appealed to Black people to see themselves as Black, not so they could prove anything to an anti-Black world but so they could live and breathe otherwise, for the sake of only themselves, a collective self-fashioning that approaches Blackness as a "full space of imagining the unimaginable."[129] And it this space of "imagining the unimaginable" that both returns to the radical politics of the enslaved and anticipates M4BL's abolitionism, its insistence on Black joy, and the politics of the wake.

A Culture of Possibility

The struggle over the meaning and mode of Black politics and thought, over Blackness itself and who has the "authority" to define it, became particularly acute in the post–civil rights era when, as Iton notes, "concerns related to class, gender, sexuality, generation, and blackness in the aggregate emerge[d] and [became] predominant" while, concurrently, conversations around nationalism and integration lost much of the purchase they once had.[130] In other words, the intramural tensions that arose during and following the Black Power era fundamentally shifted the terms of debate, creating a new "horizon of possible futures," particularly as it concerned those living life on the margins of the margins and the types of access they obtained to elite institutions.[131] The ultimate outcome of this shift was not inevitable; it required decades to produce the necessary conditions upon which the marginalized might realize these otherwise possibilities.[132] The horizons that arose out of the Black Power era were also multiple in kind, and that is a critical part of the story.

As Black political elites and a rising Black middle class became acclimated to the terrain produced by the Civil Rights and Voting Rights Acts, the new laws helped facilitate, among other things, the abandonment of the more radical strands of Black political thought by the Black ruling class toward a fulsome adoption of its liberal assimilationist tendencies—a foolhearted belief in the American ethos, a misplaced hope evidenced time and time again in the past. This magnified an atomized view of respectability and uplift, one of individual responsibility that, when coupled with deepening, racially based social and economic stratification, helped generate a slow-building crisis in Black politics that made clear the limits of Black representation and the violent structural imperatives of the neoliberal status quo: same as it ever was. For Dawson, the opening stages of this spiral toward crisis marked the moment the Black counterpublic started unraveling, which, in his telling, is important because up to that point, the Black public sphere had been instrumental in advancing the Black political agenda. Crucially, the Black counterpublic also nurtured spaces through which the various tenets of Black radical thought spread and thrived, which was undermined with the turn toward institutional politics and the inauguration of what Adolph Reed describes as "the Black regime," those elected officials content to leave the institutions of American government intact.[133]

At the same time, those who had been marginalized and policed within the intramural, led most prominently by Black women—and in particular, Black lesbian women—found previously unavailable routes to organize *with and for* themselves: to think together, critique, and create independent networks of action that did not need to adhere to the male-dominated, heteronormative, and civilizationist strictures that had dominated Black movement and political thought.[134] Organizations like the Third World Women's Alliance and the Combahee River Collective, for example, reflected what Kimberly Springer, a self-described "Black feminist memory worker," calls an "unprecedented growth in Black feminist consciousness" that, in turn, enabled "future generations of Black feminists."[135] That the concerns of these marginalized groups— what we would now describe as Black and queer Black women, queer Black men, Black trans and gender nonconforming folks, the Black poor—were unable to completely overtake the contours of Black mobilization at that moment is inconsequential; doing so would have also defied the material and ideational realities they faced. From Iton's perspective, and for my purpose here, what matters most is that the Black counterpublic did not "disintegrate" at all.[136] Instead, it began to reconfigure itself "away from the promotion of the interests," and I would add ideas more broadly, "of primarily straight, middle class (or aspiring middle class) men" in ways that had been unthinkable or otherwise difficult to achieve.[137]

The output of this reconfiguration, alongside the social forces that precipitated the crisis in Black politics and a larger crisis in the legitimacy of government authority hastened by the financial collapse of 2008 and punctuated by the pandemic, all serve as the sociopolitical foundation for the present conjuncture in Black political thought. With the advent of the internet and social media platforms, an already increasing number of the traditionally excluded were able to participate in creating new, horizontal, and deliberative opportunities for understanding, articulating, and performing Blackness, underscored by a celebration of the multifaceted nature of the Black experience and resistant to policing, if only by virtue of the access and control afforded by the ostensibly democratizing nature of engagement. In the twenty-first century, the Black counterpublic thrives rhizomatically online. But social media and the internet also provide the final piece of the picture I have been trying to paint, one concerning the tides of that known river. Facebook, Instagram, Twitter, and other platforms have served as a repository for the circulation and viral visibility of Black pain and death, the repetition of which is, in large part, the material basis that gave rise to the Movement for Black Lives and, later, the uprisings of 2020. In that sense, the ubiquity of Black pain helps me finish where I began, just as it foreshadows the brutality that opens the following chapter.

The uprisings reaffirmed that M4BL is a powerful, political-cultural intervention, a response to the problem spaces of the Black sociopolitical present, enmeshed in a long-standing confrontation with the violent hegemony of Western modernity, and driven by a mission that is simultaneously now, before, and not yet. The failure of Black politics, the inability or unwillingness of Black politicians to address the systemic nature of anti-Blackness, to regard Black pain in any of its many forms as a constituent feature of the capitalist world system, demonstrates, in stark relief, the limits of Black political thought when it addresses itself to Western civilization or when it valorizes aspects of its logic to the detriment of everyday Black life. This failure has not only been true of the mainstream strands of Black politics over the last forty-odd years. As the conjunctural moments I have traced show, to varying degrees, it has also been true of the way Black thinkers, cultural workers, and movements, usually dominated by the political and cultural elite, have crafted a collective self-image: as beautiful, as new, or as citizen. These examples of Black self-fashioning have all gestured toward the Black multitude and their modes of cultural expression, centering them, as it were, as sign and signifier, *anticipating* but never quite *harnessing* their transformative potential to break free from Western paradigms, from the West's "descriptive statement," from white sense.[138]

Abolition, what Marquis Bey describes as a "visionary and political praxis and modality that struggles against the regimes of capitalism, White supremacy, heteronormative patriarchy, and cissexism," gives voice to these limitations; it screams and shouts this impossibility by demanding another world altogether, one unknowable to us now but one we also believe to be possible, or at least toward which some of us are willing to take the "leap."[139] Enacted through the countermodalities of Black culture, Black joy, and other inherited techniques of Black rebellion, those that coursed through the streets in 2020, unapologetically embody this belief, providing evidence of a regard for Black pain and an ethics of care. They are collective expressions of Black presence and prefiguration, a prelude forecasting a future yet to come that, in its multitemporality, its back-and-forth flow, returns us to the vitality and worldmaking necessity of the source: the radicalism of Black folk culture and the plantation politics of the revolutionary Black slave, a political-cultural tradition that, in its essence, "points us toward what freedom might be," a freedom not completely of this world but elsewhere.[140]

TWO

CHAPTER 3

Regarding Black Pain

What do black people say to each other to describe their relationship to their racial group, when that relationship is crucially forged by incidents of physical and psychic violence which boil down to the "fact" of abject blackness?

—ELIZABETH ALEXANDER

The Driver's Seat and the Hold

"Stay with me." These are the first audible words of the Facebook livestream capturing the last moments of Philando Castile's life. Three words entangled with a sharp cry that briefly cuts across the car. Both the words and the cry must compete with the indecipherable growl of a police officer unseen yet evidenced in Castile's breathless tremor and his bloodstained shirt.

Addressing the camera is Diamond Reynolds—the dying man's girlfriend and the mother of the four-year-old girl sitting in the back seat. At this point, we do not see the child's face, but the divide between the front and back is wide enough for Castile's slouched body to break through the imaginary plane that separates our sight from hers. As a result, the girl is forced into early proximity to the gratuitous violence committed against the Black body, a long "acknowledged horror" emanating from the days of the slave ship and the auction block, a time when the law itself made clear that Black people were valuable only to the extent that their labor could be accumulated and exploited.[1] With Castile's killing, in other words, she is made witness to the systemic distribution of Black pain, its sights/sites, sounds, and smells, its relationship to her own body and that of those around her.

Saidiya Hartman might call this moment the "origin of the subject," the first recognition of living in and being vulnerable to an anti-Black world for a four-year-old who, seconds before, might have still been capable of imagining otherwise.[2] A Black girl's childhood robbed of its innocence. "*Mom,*" the four-year-old later pleads, "*please stop saying cusses and screaming cause I don't want you to get shooted.*" The girl is a quick study. She now realizes her mother could be shot for doing nothing more than expressing anger and grief. Not only was this Black child within arm's reach of Castile's murder, a trauma in and of itself; she also seemed to understand the arbitrariness of their circumstance, the assumption of criminality so closely linked to anti-Blackness, and so often carried out in the name of the law.[3]

In this respect, the police radio correspondence that preceded the traffic stop is telling. "*I'm going to stop a car. I'm going to check IDs. I have reason to pull it over,*" the voice on the radio explains. "*The two occupants just look like people that were involved in a robbery. The driver looks more like one of our suspects, just 'cause of the wide-set nose.*" The officer's use of racial codes is hard to mistake; they are also unsurprising. People of African descent, Frederick Douglass explained over 150 years ago, "carry in front the evidence which marks them for persecution."[4] The logic of anti-Black persecution, the chain that links Castile's car to the hold of the slave ship, is simple: "they are negroes and that is enough." His "wide-set nose" is the evidence that marks and justifies the indignity and violence soon to come.[5] It makes Castile's spectacular Black death coherent.

With this as her reality, Reynolds reports live from the scene. "*We got pulled over for a busted taillight in the back. And the police just . . . he's, he's he's covered . . . he just killed my boyfriend.*" At this point Castile is visibly not dead, but Reynolds seems to subconsciously understand how things will end, just as we already know the ending. The camera oscillates between her face, shaken and steady, a pain-ridden (dying) Castile, and the gun pointed inside the car by an increasingly frantic police officer. Castile's audible agony grows louder, but the viewer's attention is drawn to Reynolds; she remains the focal point.

Even as she steers the narrative, her words are bound to the legality of Castile's situation and actions. She tries to pull him from the criminality he has been assigned and into the realm of the "law-abiding" citizen.

"*He's licensed, he's carrying to, he's licensed to carry. He was trying to get out his ID and his wallet out his, ah, pocket, and he let the officer know, that he was, he had a firearm and he was reaching for his wallet. And the officer just shot him in his arm. We're waiting for . . .*" The officer interrupts this report, gun still drawn, and makes an absurd attempt to (re)assert an authority that has long been lost. "*Ma'am just keep your hands where they are.*" But Reynolds has already refused to comply. By pressing play on the camera and by walking the viewer through what happened, she has made clear that what occurred and is occurring represents a violation and that she will not accept it.[6] This drains him of everything but his power to enact violence and provokes the performative submissiveness in the calm of her reply: "*Ok, sir, I will. No worries.*"

Consider for a moment the casualness of the words "no worries," delivered as if someone was telling her they'd be late for dinner. Consider also, and in juxtaposition, what these words trigger. With heavy breath and his gun bearing down, the officer lets loose a garbled scream: "*Fuck!*" This crudely delivered response is not merely an act of desperation and recognition that he has just shot and (as we later learn) killed Castile. Nor is it an acknowledgment that, ultimately, the events were inevitable, that Officer Jeronimo Yanez, who is Latino, had been trained, either formally in the police academy or socially in the world, to proceed as if Castile, like all Black people, posed an imminent threat, and regardless of the perception of danger is otherwise subject to violence, often with impunity—anytime and anywhere.

Instead, the video suggests that it is Reynolds's announcement of premature Black death—"*he just killed my boyfriend*"—her witness and testimony, which makes this moment visceral for Yanez. In doing so, Reynolds presents to us and to the archive a narrative from a Black woman unmuted in the face of not only her present subjugation but also the quotidian violence that marks the Black experience.[7] The "terrible spectacle" from which she speaks—the (viral) Black body in pain—is in this case secondary to the act of speaking itself, to the refusal her testimony represents, and to the cruel reality it outlines.

Reynolds continues her address to the camera, deepening the detail. *"He just shot his arm off. We got pulled over on Larpenter."* Yanez, still frantic, meets her calm with a fruitless effort to justify what we know to be beyond justification.[8] *"I told him not to reach for it! I told him to get his hand out of it."* But Reynolds will not accept this reasoning, and her defiance, exacted through explanation, further undermines his position. *"He had, you told him to get his ID sir, his driver's license."* Of course, there is no possible response for Yanez except to keep his gun trained on Reynolds through the window. And so, he does.

As if in counterpoint, Yanez's breath grows heavier as Castile's grows quiet, a split second long enough to allow the gravity of the situation to weigh on Reynolds. *"Oh my God, please don't tell me he's dead."* Disturbed only by a second *"Oh fuck!"* bellowed by Yanez, Reynolds again addresses the camera, directly and with steel. *"Please don't tell me my boyfriend just went like that."* Once more, Yanez attempts to reassert his authority—*"Just keep your hands where they are please"*—but this demand does not break the stride of the narration. *"Yes, I will, sir. I'll keep my hands where they are,"* Reynolds responds, but then immediately continues where she left off. Now, however, the target is different; she is addressing the heavens for a miracle we know will not come. *"Please don't tell me this Lord, please Jesus don't tell me that he's gone, please don't tell me that he's gone."*

The camera circles back to Castile and remains there, but it's Reynolds we hear and feel. This is a story about both of them, told through her witness. It's a story about how white supremacy ruptures Black bonds and shatters Black lives. It's a story about the way these lives and bonds are always available to be shattered and ruptured. *"Please, officer, don't tell me that you just did this to him,"* she asks as her emotions ramp up. Switching from sorrowful plea to a pointed accusation, the assault on the officer's supposed legitimacy continues. *"You shot four bullets into him, sir. He was just getting his license and registration, sir."* The words "You" and "sir" exemplify her refusal and her witness, as well as their limits. She'll observe Yanez's authority by addressing him as "sir," but the pointed "you" marks Yanez as both perpetrator in actuality and the symbolic carrier of anti-Blackness. It allows Reynolds to partially subvert the power dynamic and at that moment turn "sir" into an ironic gesture of judgment.

With this gesture, the scene begins to shift as additional officers are heard approaching in the background. Their concern is not Castile, who is bleeding to death; it is Reynolds. *"We got a female passenger,"* someone states. Yanez barks orders to the chorus arriving at the car: *"Get the female passenger out!"* The other officers follow suit with seeming eagerness, as if Reynolds produced the previous standoff; as if she were the one pointing a trigger ready gun; as if she were responsible for anything other than her Blackness captured in the hold of the passenger seat. *"Ma'am, exit the car with your hands up! Let me see your hands, exit now. Keep them up. Keep them up."*

The filming continues as she exits the vehicle. We see the line of police cars, lights flashing. We see an officer with his gun pointed. We see precisely what we have come to expect: Black people in pain. What was unexpected, at the time at least, was the live feed—her act of witness and refusal. Moving between this witness and the immediacy of the situation, Reynolds asks about her four-year-old daughter, sitting in the back seat throughout and initiated as "subject" because of her positioning. But the officer orders Reynolds to turn away and walk backward, an instruction meant to reduce the threat she is believed to pose. Reynolds is transformed into agitator, a potentially violent active agent, a criminal who must be controlled. This is the law at work. This is the language of slavery's afterlife. *"Keep walking, keep walking,"* we hear them say. *"Get on your knees. Get on your knees."* She obeys. She also keeps filming.

Suddenly our view shifts upward, just as we hear the little girl scream and the sound of handcuffs. *"Why am I being arrested?"* Reynolds asks. *"You're just being detained as we sort this thing out, ok,"* the subduing officer replies. But there is nothing to be "sorted out." We have watched it in real time. Reynolds acknowledges our gazes as she explains, "*They threw my phone Facebook*," and then transitions into her sadness, the job of witness nearly complete, her refusal to mourn almost at an end. "*Please, Jesus. No. Please no. Please no, don't let him be gone.*"

But he was. His death was evidence of a complete disregard for his humanity, for Diamond Reynolds, her daughter, and everyone else who loved Castile.

Notes on a Deadly Scene

"*Stay with me.*" Three simple but urgent words that carry a charge beyond what many can understand at a distance. Still, from this distance, most of us watched and listened—often with outrage. Perhaps the outrage was predictable given the impossibility of avoiding Castile's bloody scene, to say nothing of the seemingly clear-cut circumstances that propelled its unfolding: a "routine" traffic stop, someone Black behind the wheel, a police officer, and the unfettered license to wield force.

On the other hand, perhaps the outrage was performative, or, better put, "misplaced," in that it located the problem at the scene of the crime rather than what produced it: the law. In either case, today's virally infused field of vision ensured that Castile's death was (and remains) everywhere: plastered across social media, preserved and available on demand. His life, however, is far less vivid. For the most part, we do not encounter Castile as someone having lived at all. His past and present, his aspirations for the future, are all fictive possibilities figured beyond our line of sight.[9] Instead, the portrait we come to know and remember is one of a dying and dead Black (male) body.

This violence underpins the representations of and the discourse around Blackness and the lives of Black people. The parade of murders prior to, during, and immediately after the 2020 uprising—George Floyd, Tony McDade, Breonna Taylor, Ahmaud Arbery, Rayshard Brooks, and a half dozen others—tells us everything we need to know. When it comes to Black America, America tethers her tongue to the grave, which is to say, as Shatema Threadcraft has observed, to the extent that we mount any real political or cultural discussions concerning the

Black body and its standing in this country, "the body that receives the most attention . . . is a deceased one."[10] One might further conclude that, in the eyes of many, stories concerning Black (non-pathologized) *life* have primarily been an afterthought if not unthinkable, especially when juxtaposed with images of bullet-ridden flesh. The world is conditioned to index Blackness and therefore Black people to precarity and premature death. Our pain is naturalized, a matter of course.

American history has given Black folks little reason to expect differently. More than 25 years ago, in the aftermath of the Rodney King beating, the poet and scholar Elizabeth Alexander summed up the circumstance with precision: "black bodies in pain for public consumption have been an American national spectacle for centuries."[11] That spectacle remains with us still. Black subjection can be found in physical violence (i.e., beatings, shootings, lynching); as well as in what Hartman describes as "scenes in which terror can hardly be discerned": on the stage, in the courtroom, behind the blinding letter of the law.[12] It can be found in the statistical imbalance between the life chances (and "successes") of those who have darker skin and those who do not, as well as the prescriptive and demeaning narratives and assumptions that guide policy responses even when enacted by Black politicians and inform the logic of uplift and respectability. Finally, it is found on the psychic level, embodied and reproduced in everyday practices and cultural patterns.

Yet it is the physical dimensions of Black subjection that feverishly work to preserve and obscure the entanglement of knowledge and power that helps make this subjection possible. In other words, the "spectacle" of Black suffering (re)produces and is produced by racialized ways of seeing, knowing, and narrating Blackness. This is not a revelation. "The cultural and political discourse on black pathology," Fred Moten notes, "has been so pervasive that it could be said to constitute the background against which all representations of blacks, blackness, or (the color) black take place."[13] As a result, any affirmative notion of Blackness and Black life "unfolds 'out of the world' by definition," at least in terms of how it is (un)seen and (mis)understood by those unburdened by Black skin.[14]

The implication here is that what actually *does* unfold "in the world"—
what *appears* legible if not expected—is underwritten by the pained
(and pathologized) Black body. After all, as searing as Castile's death
was, the shooting itself recounts a familiar story, one that has been amplified in recent years not merely by the *volume* of similarly wrenching
episodes but by the *visibility* of their repetition.[15] In an essay published
the year before Castile's murder, Calvin Warren points out that, more
than fifty years after the heralded civil rights legislation of the 1960s, "we
are witnessing a shocking accumulation of injured and mutilated black
bodies, particularly young black bodies."[16]

To this I would add, most are witnessing this accumulation against
their will. Thanks in large part to social media, the routine sight of willful
acts of anti-Black violence has become a reality many cannot escape.
"Stop forcing these videos down our throats," pleads one Black organizer in a note posted on Facebook. "Some of us are quite literally still
mourning our brothers and don't need constant reminders of the disdain this world had for them while they were still breathing."[17] These
videos and images—along with the countless deaths that go un(der)
reported—are modern-day slave narratives, different in kind from the
past but no less brutal in their consequence. I call them slave narratives
to make the historical trajectory explicit; from the hold of the slave ship
to the driver's seat of a car proceeds a persistent and assorted process of
subjugation that subsumes Black people in a shroud of vulnerability,
threats that hide and wait. It is a process that ensures, as the poet Claudia
Rankine put it, "the condition of black life is one of mourning."[18]

Beneath this acknowledgment lies a painful reality. Whether autho-
rized by a badge or brought about by vigilantes, anti-Black violence—
the naked assault against being Black—is as sedimented and structuring
as America's national myths and symbols.[19] Such violence is not an
aberration. It is America's condition of possibility and the foundation
upon which the entire project of Western modernity rests. This is
because the underlying logic surrounding post-Enlightenment political
thought was, and in (material) effect continues to be, grounded in a bio-
logical determinism that relegates Black people to non-human status,[20]
a strategy that differentiates and essentializes human beings by narrating

whiteness as the all and everything against the nothingness of Black-ness.[21] It is the defining script of white supremacy, its sacred text, and represents what Charles Mills has called the "unnamed political system that has made [and continues to make] the modern world."[22]

In 1857, Chief Justice Robert Taney (in)famously summed up this sentiment when issuing the majority opinion in the oft-cited *Dred Scott v. Sandford* case. Black people, opined Taney, are "of an inferior order, and altogether unfit to associate with the white race, either in social or political relations; and so far inferior, that they had no rights which the white man was bound to respect."[23] Accounts like the one offered by Taney—salacious through the prism of history—demonstrate a broader framework of physical demarcation and meaning-making. This tribal exchange of symbolic inscription stretches through and across our most salient political characteristics—the way we read race, gender, sexuality, class, citizenship, ethnicity, and religion. Nevertheless, it has been, for perhaps the last seven hundred years, most firmly rooted in the same soil: Blackness.

The accumulation of dead Black bodies, then, does more than haunt the visual field. It also disrupts any pretense that the arc of history bends toward a better, more just world. The increasingly spectral nature of these deaths, a haunt that appears again and again, likewise unsettles the idea that justice and equality are possible while leaving the values, institutions, and techniques that reinforce the capitalist liberal state intact. In other words, the current order of things, the world as we know it, is structurally incapable of genuine care or concern for the actual lived experience of Black people, let alone the matter/ing of Black life.[24]

The long-standing and all-encompassing reality of anti-Blackness—what Christina Sharpe calls "the weather"—requires us to adopt a view geared less toward instances of Black pain as singular events, since doing so only serves to make spectacular that which we know to be routine and by design.[25] Instead, what should become central is the exploration of what that pain generates, what it makes manifest. As Audre Lorde noted during a 1978 interview, "pain is important,"[26] not merely because it is a fact of life, especially if you are a member of a marginalized community, or in light of the layers of power, seen and unseen, that make the pain of marginalization possible if not inevitable. The importance rests in the way pain "moves us to act," what pain "calls on us to do."[27]

The fire that moves this movement and has fueled Black rebellion is, in the first instance, harnessed through the burn of Black pain. Online and in the streets, M4BL's political culture, the movement's demand to defund and abolish the police, is a multimodal response to and an acknowledgment of the wake, the system of signs and symbols—the *language*—that cements "the conventions of antiblackness in the present and into the future," just as it has been in the past.[28] In that sense, the phrase "Black Lives Matter" should not be read as a cry for "recognition," at least insofar as such calls have generally been fastened to rights-based discourse and efforts toward inclusion and protection.[29] Instead, "Black Lives Matter" announces something more foundational, even primal: the collective demand for self-possession, in the United States and throughout the Black Diaspora.[30]

I do not mean the self-possession associated with liberal individualism and self-determination: the "freedom" to determine your future, according to pre-prescribed arithmetic of what that future should look like, how one should behave to achieve it, and who is otherwise provided or denied access. I mean self-possession that lays claim to and over the *body*, to and over space, to and over life, by embracing what Tina Campt calls "a practice of refusal."[31] It is a refusal to accept a world that relegates Black people to subhuman status, as an object or as deviant, negations that differently extend across gender, sex, and class. It is a refusal to believe the world as it is will ever permit Black people to live fully, richly, and without threat. As a result, it is also a willingness to, as Campt writes, "embrace the labor required to directly engage the precarity of Black life . . . to use negation as a generative and creative source of disorderly power to embrace the possibility of living otherwise."[32]

For Black lives to matter, then, the dead must be acknowledged to protect the not-yet, perhaps soon to be dying as/so they can live. To put it another way, "Black Lives Matter" underscores the prevalence of Black pain and Black death to Black life. It "foregrounds the question of unbearable brutality" produced by anti-Blackness and "*compels* us to face the terrifying question despite our desire to look away."[33] But what does it look like for Black people to confront unbearable brutality? More precisely, how does one ethically "[ponder] the historical wounding of black bodies"?[34] What does such pondering suggest, speak to, or create?

Amid the growing body count, and the many images of Black suffering, I found myself watching the video of Castile over and over. It was a masochistic compulsion that, at the time, I found troubling and difficult to understand, especially given that so many around me chose not to watch it at all. Now, following another brutal video of a Black man forcefully brought to death, I recognize what drew me: the visual and auditory details of the murder, including yet *beyond* the image of his dying body, and beyond even Castile himself. One of the most striking and tragic elements of the episode is that Castile was not alone in the car—he was riding with Diamond Reynolds and her four-year-old daughter. They were present at the moment of his state-perpetrated and state-sanctioned murder; and like Castile, their past, present, and future will forever be subsumed underneath the weight of his death.

Their presence, what they were forced to witness, should make clear that what transpired between Castile and the police officer does not represent the whole or even the most crucial aspect of the story. It is part of the territory's map, not the territory itself, as Sylvia Wynter might say. The livestream and the act of refusal its narration illustrates (despite being trapped in the fruitless logic of right and wrong) are just as central, not only to what took place that day but to all that lingers in its aftermath—the video included.

Whether it's Castile's bloodstained shirt, Emmett Till's mutilated face, or George Floyd's contorted neck, the violent, structural, and systemic force of anti-Blackness remains explicit, for me in profoundly personal ways—as a Black man and Black scholar. But more crucially and toward my purpose, what matters in the end is how Black people respond, what we do when we reach the point of saying, like Nichols at the Millions March in 2014, "we're not going to stand for this." The response is crucial to how we read, understand, and theorize Black social movement in the time of #BlackLivesMatter. It should also inform how we position the politics, thought, and culture of the movement along the grain of the struggle for Black liberation and the strategies used to move Black people closer to attaining it.

For centuries, Black activists and thinkers believed that making our pain visible to an anti-Black world would induce empathy, to insist on "a public accounting of white violence," a demand that was itself driven by a deep and abiding concern for Black life.[35] As Courtney Baker explains, pain became "the currency of black liberation from injustice and state sanctioned violence": "if only my pain is recognized, I will be free."[36] For example, writing in the late nineteenth century, Ida B. Wells famously sought to expose the pervasiveness of and impunity for violence waged against Blacks in the South, work that was supported by the NACW before being taken up by the NAACP.[37] To make Black suffering visible, to "turn the light of truth on [it]," she argued, is "the way to right wrongs" and, in the process, insert black voices "into the channels of public discourse."[38] You could say that *The Red Record* and her earlier study *Southern Horrors: Lynch Law in All Its Phases* were both attempts to demonstrate how a politics of visibility could materially produce change. They were attempts to force the world to reckon with Black pain by advancing a critique of the criminalizing legal and extralegal regime developed to maintain Black captivity and subordination following the Civil War. The same is true for the open-casket funeral Mamie Till-Mobley insisted on having for her son Emmett in 1955, as well as the "documents of chaos and control," to borrow Baker's phrasing, that archive the repressive response to the civil rights movement's nonviolent direct actions in the early 1960s.[39]

But what if the point of attending to Black pain and death is not to induce empathy or recognition but *regard*? As a verb, "regard" means to "consider or think of in a specified way." As a noun, to have regard means to give "attention to or concern for something."[40] I am after the *specific* way in which we might give *attention* to and *concern* for Black pain, the ways that the coherence of spectacular Black death opens up new ways of being and knowing, regardless of how horrible and painful it is. In this vein, the telling of Castile's story is not simply one in a long line of others but a political document forged by a Black woman to testify to the *irreconcilable chasm between law and justice* and direct us to "the necessity of engagement" this chasm calls forth.[41] If the law will not and cannot see or acknowledge Black people beyond our wounded Black flesh, what would it mean to fully see ourselves and, in doing so, recognize what must be done?

With these two overlapping definitions of "regard" in tow, the above questions represent a place where we might begin to reflect on the political importance of "sitting (together) in the pain and sorrow of a death,"[42] that is, to see the livestream as a mechanism that makes vivid the underlying violence and vulnerability, the deep-rooted presence of pain that drives Black radicalism and the politics of the wake. It makes abolition both necessary and urgent.

The cases I explore in this chapter—the murder of Philando Castile; the toppling of the Confederate Soldiers Monument in Durham, North Carolina; and BYP100's campaign Our Streets, Our Bodies, Our Voices (OS/OB/OV)—correspond with three ways of thinking about "regard" in the context of Black pain, some of which overlap.[43] The first is to regard Black humanity in and on the pained Black body, which renders the law an historical accomplice in the production of that pain and therefore an impossible recourse for Black liberation. The second is to regard the history and legacy of Black subjection in time and across space, which demands we destroy the structures and disrupt the geographies that reify racial violence so they might be replaced with an as-yet determined future. The third is to regard Black expression and voice, in speech and representation, to break down the "boundaries of Blackness" that fracture Black politics and leave the marginalized among the marginalized left to fend for themselves.

In sum, regard for Black pain is central to the politics of the wake. It is the basis from which healing begins, joy manifests, and care gets inscribed as an ethical (and political) commitment. In other words, if Blackness is the critical and creative potential for rupture, born out of the "tear in the world" that was the Middle Passage, as Fred Moten would have us believe, this potential is generated through and with pain.[44]

Stop Killing Us!

Nearly a year from the day of Philando Castile's killing, Jeronimo Yanez was acquitted. While indisputably responsible for fatally firing seven shots into Castile's car, he was deemed not "guilty" of manslaughter. "The system continues to fail Black people," Philando's mother, Valerie Castile, said at a press conference following the jury's ruling, "and [it] will continue to fail you all."

"You all" implicitly acknowledges the general public's collective, undifferentiated gaze. After all, "we" watched the video, and we were now watching *her*. In pointing to the law's continued failure, Valerie Castile also seemed to suggest the impossibility of justice for anyone, regardless of their race, so long as anti-Blackness underpins our institutions and structures our lives. The "system" she refers to names not only the specific legal proceedings that, through its verdict, announced Castile's murder as permissible under the law. It also names the logic of the law itself, defined by and through its relationship to, juxtaposition with, and dependence on Blackness as a foil. Moments later, she would extend this critique in no uncertain terms: "My son loved this city, and this city killed my son."

For Black mothers living in the United States and across the Diaspora, Valerie Castile's steady rage is familiar. Philando was her "firstborn one son dead." And like so many Black mothers before and since, she has been assigned the "terrible weight" of mourning another Black body brought into its deathly inheritance: an unrelenting world of subjection toward what Hortense Spillers has called the "frontiers of survival."[45] Valerie Castile's choice of dress that day was telling. She honored Philando's life by wearing the fact of his death pinned to her shirt as evidenced by her need to wear his picture in the first place. She is permanently branded by the legal lynching of her child, the lasting imprint of his subjection before the law, just as the law intended it to be.

Perhaps it was a similar structural understanding that gave the immediate reactions to Castile's death their emotional register, elevating not only an already existent atmosphere of collective grief but also the anticipation of where the path through the courts was likely to and ultimately did lead. Valerie Castile articulates a suffering traced in blood, but the pain Philando's death produced was not hers alone:

- "I been crying off and on all morning. 2016. 2016! Same ole crap! #PhilandoCastille #Alton Sterling"
- "Today is canceled. Tomorrow is canceled. The rest of 2016 is canceled. #PhilandoCastille #AltonSterling #StopKillingUs"[46]

These represent a fraction of the responses that flooded social media in the aftermath of Castile's killing. And he wasn't even the first Black person murdered by the police that week; both posts also refer to Alton Sterling, a thirty-seven-year-old Black man who was shot and killed at close range by two police officers in Baton Rouge a day before Castile. Their deaths heightened what, by the summer of 2016, had the feel of an everyday demand, a demand that motivated thousands to take to the streets during the uprisings four years later, a demand that is always on the tip of a Black person's tongue: stop killing us![47]

Less than a month after Castile was killed, M4BL, through its namesake umbrella organization engaged in collective visioning and coordinating strategy, published its most explicit programmatic statement to date.[48] "A Vision for Black Lives: Policy Demands for Black Power, Freedom & Justice" laid out a range of wrongs and outlined solutions to at least begin to remedy them.[49] The headline demands included reparations, economic justice, community control, political power, and divestment from institutions that cause harm in favor of an investment in Black people and communities. These demands and their elaboration are anchored in and by what is arguably the platform's central charge: to "end the war on Black people."[50]

The decision to start the platform this way suggests an intention to make the vulnerability of Black life clear and the cause or perpetrators of that vulnerability plain. The platform framed its demands in the language of combat, playing on the American penchant for adopting war metaphors to describe and defend ineffective, violent, and/or criminalizing policies against Black and other communities of color (i.e., the "war" on drugs and the "war" on terrorism).[51] In doing so, it also located the basis of those demands in an analysis that reads deaths like Castile's as the product of anti-Black structures, carefully crafted and maintained over time, rather than as an "unfortunate" incident perpetrated by a "bad" or "reckless" actor and thus preventable and fixable within existing liberal frameworks.

From this vantage, Castile's livestream and all the other scenes of Black subjection before and since are examples of *war footage*—reels from the forever war waged against Black life. In *Regarding the Pain of Others*, Susan Sontag argues that images of war represent a "species of rhetoric," a language we get so used to hearing that it reduces and flattens the potential of a structural critique of the war itself. This makes it possible to provide "the illusion of consensus" around the damage that war produces and has produced.[52] That damage—and the general sense of outrage it can inspire—initiates a sense of relatability, something shared.[53] This allows images of Black pain to fictively "extend to the dispossessed" what they never truly had in the first place and, as Valerie Castile reminds us, will never truly attain under the current system: full recognition as human beings.[54] While empathy may be possible, *genuine regard* is a taller task requiring a full reckoning with anti-Blackness as the rule, not the exception.

To regard *Black* pain on and through the body means accepting that Black suffering is constitutive to the law and brought to bear in the way it is performed, just as it is constitutive to America's institutions and ideologies, such as the police and policing; the same can be said of the capitalist world system as such. It means caring for and being attentive to not only bullet-ridden flesh but the bodies—the lives—of those around it as further evidence of the totalizing threat posed by anti-Blackness. Black radicalism emerged from Black pain, from dispossession, and M4BL, in its regard for this pain, recognizes that appeals for empathy and recognition within the current order of things will not save us. Nor will the law or the ideas and values of Western modernity, which are historical accomplices in our subjection. Instead, the historical and spatial legacies of anti-Blackness must be undone, which requires a collective desire to abolish all its vestiges and, in its place, reconstitute the community.

Southern Comforts

In the early evening of August 14, 2017, Takiya Thompson, a twenty-two-year-old Black activist and student at North Carolina Central University, climbed a ladder perched against the back of the Confederate Soldiers Monument that stood in front of the Durham County courthouse. The statue was erected in 1924, nearly sixty years after the end of the Civil War. It depicted a uniformed, musket-bearing Confederate soldier proudly resting atop a base marked with the Confederate seal. Like similar memorials constructed in the years following the Confederate Army's defeat, the statue was meant to honor, as its inscription read, the "memory of the boys who wore gray."[55]

The decision to locate the statue in front of the courthouse, a prominent public space and a presumed arena for justice, was neither accidental nor innocent. The memorial's visibility aimed to provide an occasion for passersby to "pause and reflect," as General Albert Cox put it during the dedication ceremony, on the sacrifices made by the many soldiers who fought and died for the South. More than just a reverent homage to the dead, however, this reflection was meant to, in the words of James Mayo, "impose meaning and order" by making sacred and public a political narrative premised on southern identity, values, and heritage.[56] Mayo has called this narrative a "common notion of good" linked to the Civil War, states' rights, and the struggle to preserve the institution of slavery as a heritage beyond reproach. In other words, the statue memorialized the past to reinforce a present and future distinction between Black and white people, not only as descriptive categories but as distinct and incommensurate ontologies.

At the beginning of the twentieth century, just as states across the South were passing laws to ensure the preservation of a racial hierarchy perceived to be under siege during Reconstruction—laws that would come to be known as Jim Crow—there was a parallel uptick in the creation of Confederate iconography in general and monuments in particular, many of which were constructed at courthouses.[57] The swell in memorials during this period was rivaled only by a similar rise during the civil rights movement, another moment in which the imminent "loss of the white man's government" was a catalyst for the reassertion of white dominance.[58] Hitting its peak in 1911, the wave of Confederate statue-building had declined significantly by 1920, evidence of the successful decades-long effort to create opportunities, recalling Cox, to "pause and reflect." By then, North Carolina trailed only Virginia, Texas, and Georgia in the number of memorials paying tribute to the "gallant South"—an imagined community built on the backs of slave labor and war.[59]

Durham, however, would not have its own statue until 1924, well after this decline. The monument Takiya Thompson later scaled had been in the works for nearly two years before it finally came to fruition. The project was backed by a collective of Confederate Army veterans and spearheaded by Julian S. Carr, who served as a private during the Civil War and subsequently established his southern "bona fides" through both discourse and deed. For example, a little over a decade before, Carr had proudly and publicly recounted having "horse-whipped a negro wench, until her skirts hung in shreds, because . . . she had publicly insulted and maligned a Southern lady." Carr's actions, his words, and the statue he promoted were designed to affirm the naturalness, the historical "fact" of racial hierarchies—a hierarchy enforced through physical violence against a Black woman.

The statue's unveiling was celebrated with a front-page story headlined: "Durham Honors Heroic Dead." The brief article described the "hundreds of people," some having traveled "many miles for the occasion," who packed the courthouse and the surrounding lawns, including sixty uniformed veterans of the Confederate Army. They all gathered to watch the rope pull that removed the covering used to conceal the statue and celebrate the latest marker, and further entrenchment, of what Charles Mills calls the "*racing* of space," meaning "the depiction of space as dominated by individuals (whether persons or subpersons) of a certain race."[60]

A very different group crowded the lawns that August night in 2017, chanting with anticipation as Takiya Thompson dared to "insult and malign" Carr's white southern narrative. She tied a noose around the statue's head and tossed the yellow rope into the crowd so they could, as she put it, "decide if they wanted to pull it down." Within moments the statue had crashed to the ground, followed by jubilant celebration and attacks on the toppled memorial. The videos instantly went viral. For Thompson and many of the others gathered at the Durham County courthouse, the meaning of the monument was unambiguous, just as it had been for the people who celebrated it nearly a century before. In her own words, the statue was a "symbol of white nationalism," and such symbols had no place in the country she sought to create, let alone the actually existing America she inhabited.

Though the memorial strove to link the past to the present, it was America in the here and now that pushed Thompson up the ladder. Three days prior, 168 miles north of the scene, throngs of white nationalists and their sympathizers arrived in Charlottesville, Virginia, to protest a plan to remove a different Confederate memorial, this one dedicated to General Robert E. Lee, from the newly renamed "Emancipation Park."[61] The protest crystallized a simmering and overtly racialized battle over space, over narrative, and over what should and should not be celebrated as essential to American culture. The sentiment was perhaps best articulated by then president Donald Trump at his own rally in Phoenix the following week. "They're trying to take away our culture," Trump warned. "They're trying to take away our history."

This "us and them" mentality, long central to creating and maintaining a version of history that erases Black suffering and denies Black humanity, was evident in the sense of grievance that permeated the weekend. Beginning with a throng of torch-wielding men shouting racist slurs and hailing their collective whiteness on the campus of the University of Virginia and culminating in violent clashes with counterprotesters the next day during what had been dubbed the "Unite the Right" rally, the two-day spectacle was a deadly reminder of the deep-rooted racial antagonisms Confederate monuments have come to represent and uphold. The images and actions of resentment struck a nerve across the country, especially among young Black people like Takiya Thompson. For her, "the sentiment expressed in Charlottesville is part and parcel to what built this country" and served as a justification for

not just indignation but also corrective action, expressed in both instances as a matter of principled reason. As she explained:

> What we did, not only was it right, it was just. I did the right thing.
> Everyone who was there, the people did the right thing. And the
> people will continue to keep making the right choices until every
> Confederate statue is gone, until white supremacy is gone. That
> statue is where it belongs, right? It needs to be in the garbage, inciner-
> ated, like every statue—every Confederate statue and every vestige
> of white supremacy has to go.[62]

Speaking in terms of "we" and "the people," Thompson expressed the
collective political will that brought down the memorial. She located
symbols of racial violence—like the statue she helped upend—within
a broader structural critique: the world as we know it was built, and is
sustained, by anti-Blackness. That its removal was not only "right" but
"just" echoes Martin Luther King's "Letter from Birmingham Jail," in
which he famously argued that people have a moral responsibility to
disobey unjust laws, what Lee McBride describes as an "insurrection-
ist ethos."[63]

Yet there is a difference between the nonviolent direct actions of the
Birmingham Campaign that led to King's arrest—which included sit-
ins, kneel-ins, boycotts, and walks—and the toppling of the Confederate Soldiers Monument. The goal was not simply to raise awareness by
"unlawfully" removing the statue, for which Takiya Thompson was later
arrested.[64] The objective—a small semblance of justice—was in the
statue's destruction, promoted as a radical civic act rather than an external appeal, as brave and selfless as those appeals may have been. It was in
the hands of "the people" themselves to ensure the monument was "in
the garbage [and] incinerated," along with every other marker of white
supremacy and anti-Blackness, including the law itself.

The same sentiment—the removal of every marker of white supremacy and anti-Blackness—drove the wave of toppled monuments during
the 2020 uprisings, just as it motivated activist Bree Newsome to scale
the flagpole bearing the Confederate flag above the statehouse in
Charleston, South Carolina, in June 2015, following the murders of nine

Black churchgoers by Dylann Roof at Emanuel African Methodist Epis-
copal Church in Charleston ten days prior.[65] For Takiya Thompson,
"anything that emboldens [white supremacists] and anything that gives
those people pride, needs to be crushed in the same way that they want
to crush Black people and the other groups that they target." Further,
her actions suggest that, along with ridding public space of emblems of
white nationalist pride, equally important and just is ridding our collective visual field of anything that rehearses or serves as a reminder of
Black pain.

Members of BYP100's Durham chapter, several of whom were present during the monument's fall, published a short communiqué several
days afterward, elaborating the action's political significance using a
similar frame. It is worth quoting at length:

> We believe that the 93 years of confederate and white supremacist
> altar worship in Durham must come to a dramatic end. . . . White
> supremacist monuments do not belong in this city. They do not be-
> long in this state. They do not belong in this country. We cannot
> tolerate the New Confederacy. BYP100 Durham believes that the
> people have a moral imperative to break unjust laws. The removal of
> the confederate statue, from our home, reflects a mandate from our
> community to dismantle that which does not represent us. While
> some have criticized the removal of the confederate soldier as un-
> necessary or uncivil, we are clear that the uncivil and often unneces-
> sary are those in power, as they have allowed the statue to stand, as
> they also allow the extrajudicial killing of Black and Brown folks. The
> request that we politely wait for politicians to gather the courage,
> ethic, tact, discipline, rigor, moral compass, and values needed to act,
> is and has always been a demand that denies those marginalized of
> our humanity and self-determination. These same people would also
> ask that we put anti-Black violence aside, that we put the long history
> of ethnic genocide, slavery, colonization, and erasure of history, aside.
> The people of Durham could no longer allow this white supremacist
> monument to tower over us, Monday was the end of that reality. We
> used the current political moment as a catalyst to destroy one of the

historical representations of this country's violent foundation. We as a community demand that enough is enough, and we can wait no longer. As our ancestral mentor Ella Baker said, "We who believe in freedom cannot rest until it comes."[66]

To speak of the "dramatic" in this instance is to embrace the need for confrontational tactics to urgently intervene in and over public space in ways that disrupt, tear down, and seek to replace entrenched narratives like the ones attached to Confederate iconography, regardless of what the law might mandate. As the communiqué notes, these actions are a "moral imperative." They are mandated and pursued not merely by an individual or a particular organization but by a community, for the sake of that community. Two things stand out about this.

First, in making these claims, the authors double down on Takiya Thompson's assertion of *the people* as community constituted and horizontal. The authority to act, to tear down the monument, then, comes from a community-based analysis of and attack against white supremacy, rather than expecting recourse to the liberal democratic state will deliver justice from the top down. It is an assertion of self-possession, or as Thompson put it, an act of "people claiming their agency," before a political system unwilling to do the job or incapable of doing so. The latter point is amplified in the communiqué, when it directly names politicians as complicit for allowing the statue to stand for so long, condemning their tolerance for and celebration of sites of Black pain as an acceptance of "the extrajudicial killing of Black and Brown folks."

In essence, the communiqué questions, if not outright denounces, the legitimacy of "those in power," along with their ability to act on the people's behalf. Instead, it positions its authors and other activists, including Thompson, as representative arbiters of the people's will. To borrow from and repurpose Denise Ferreira da Silva's words, we might say that by simultaneously laying claim to a notion of the people, and by announcing the ability to represent the people's will, "the *object*," the slave, the dispossessed as assigned by Western modernity, and its "arsenal of racial knowledge" transforms and becomes "the *subject*," in ways

similar to the non-dominated action of the enslaved.[67] This (re)center-
ing unmoors the violent logics of anti-Blackness as constituted by the
liberal status quo and represented in the statue as a monument to racial
hierarchies in favor of a world that is yet to come though still not yet
here. Such a procedure makes it possible to *inhabit* a notion of the
people that centers Black and Brown agency and places that agency
within a paradigm of thought beyond the rule of law and thus beyond
the "modern themes" that provide for the law's legitimacy.[68]

Second and closely related, BYP100 Durham destabilizes the "our
history/our culture" paradigm, evoked by Trump and embodied in the
Charlottesville protests, by (re)inscribing a notion of community that
locates Confederate sympathizers as the alienated Other and unwel-
come outsider. Just as the racialized object announces themselves as
"subject," they likewise announce that those who previously claimed the
mantle of subject are, in fact, the "stranger within." We see this not only
in the assertion of acting on the people's mandate but in naming Durham, and thus the lawn surrounding the courthouse, as "our home."
Crucially, in making the territorial claim to space—that Durham is
home—the communiqué also asserts the right to "dismantle what does
not serve us," linking the statue's presence and the multiple forms of
oppression and domination that have historically been used against
Black people in the South and throughout the country. It suggests, in
other words, that the toppling of the Confederate Soldiers Monument
in Durham was never simply about a single statue but instead about the
urgent necessity to address all the ways the "country's violent foundations" continue to incite Black pain—be that on a material, psychic, or
spatial level.

This point of view is part of a broader reckoning with the geographies
of Black suffering—everywhere and in all its forms—undertaken by
Black organizers and cultural workers in the time of #BlackLivesMatter.
During the 2020 uprisings, statues and monuments around the world
similarly fell. It is one way the movement moves to regard Black pain as
a collective, ethical syntax grounded in and produced by care and concern for Black life. I highlight geography not merely to point out the

spatial realities of, or the sense of place that emerges from and against, the "fact of Blackness," where the environment itself is contested ground in the battle for Black belonging, but rather to emphasize the importance of *navigation* to practices of Black resistance and rebellion. That is, I underscore the need to map and remap strategies and tactics of flight from the world as it is toward the world as it should be, just as the fugitive slaves did. As the Durham example demonstrates, the radical cartography born alongside struggles for liberation takes shape in ways that may shift the physical landscape—overturning a statue—and the ideational terrain on the level of discourse—a repositioning of the people and the people's will by (re)constituting *who* the people are to begin with. By not only drawing attention to these foundations through action but justifying that action through a structural critique of anti-Blackness and white supremacy, both Takiya Thompson and BYP100 Durham embody the movement's political culture, tearing down the visual field of Black pain and precarity one monument at a time.

Of course, an assault on the visual field, even if carried out in the name of a more inclusive notion of the people, leaves unaddressed a further dialogue about what the future should look like and what mechanisms might best ensure that those historically positioned on the margins not only have a say but are meaningfully centered. In that sense, to regard Black pain is also to be attentive to voice and representation—not in the shallow, integrationist way people tend to herald the "first" Black this or that but in a manner that strives for the deliberative and democratic ethos of plantation politics. It is to imagine that the world to come will be built from the bottom up, following the lead of those who have too often been overlooked or ignored, because their liberation is synonymous with our own. Building from the bottom up requires devising new and creative ways to speak and relate to one another with and through our differences, to wrestle ourselves away from hierarchical thinking, and to do so even when the conversation is uncomfortable. For Black people in particular, it means finding ways to address and move beyond the schisms within the intramural that have long haunted Black politics and troubled the waters of Black political development.

Staging Captivity

The visual campaign Our Streets, Our Bodies, Our Voices (OS/OB/OV) offers a compelling example of how a margins-to-center approach, guided by a regard for Black pain, not only attends to voice and representation but disrupts the status quo by making meaningful, if temporary, visual interventions in public space. It also demonstrates what the campaign's organizers called the importance of "visibility and projection," in attending to life through pain without needing to reify the pained Black body. But if we peel back the curtain a bit, OS/OB/OV magnifies internal contradictions that bring to the surface a set of challenges inherent in trying to imagine, and put into practice, another world.

Conjured by documentarian and cultural producer Autumn Robinson, and later launched in the summer of 2015 by the New York City chapter of BYP100, OS/OB/OV aimed to initiate a dialogue around policing and safety in Black communities across the city, intentionally seeking out Black people whose voices are typically silenced or ignored by policymakers and the media: intramural kin who are often similarly shunned, sometimes violently, within the community itself. As Ain Raven Ealey, a former BYP100 member and project coordinator for the campaign, explained:

> The idea was to focus on people who do not get recognition . . . when talking about police violence. So women, trans folk, Black folks with various sexual orientations are oftentimes left out the conversation, and there's a hyperfocus on hetero-cis Black men when talking about police and police violence and its impact. So we wanted to get a broader view and provide a space where voices can be heard of Black folks within the community.[69]

Ealey astutely frames the campaign as a rejoinder to narratives about state-sanctioned violence that privilege, as Shatema Threadcraft has noted, "how cis men die, how young men die, how able-bodied blacks die, over all other black dead."[70]

The "how" in Threadcraft's description is essential to the stakes. When Ealey refers to recognition, it is not solely about acknowledging that Black people other than "hetero-cis" men fall victim to police violence, an undernarrated truth at the center of the African American Policy Forum's campaign #SayHerName, inaugurated in 2014, which strove to bring "awareness to the often invisible names and stories of Black women and girls who have been victimized by racist police violence."[71] Recognition also points to *how* that violence bears down on the bodies of Black "women, trans folk, [and] Black folks with various sexual orientations," which is to say, it does so in a manner particular to their intersecting identities. The task, then, is to confront the ways "state power intersects" with the lives of those situated on the furthest tip of the periphery in both publicly visible ways and intimate spaces.[72] The "no-knock warrant" that led to the murder of Breonna Taylor, a major flashpoint for the 2020 uprisings, is, in recent years, one of the most highly visible examples of the latter.

To achieve this "broader view," BYP100 members were asked to take to the streets—of Harlem in Manhattan; Brownsville and East New York in Brooklyn; and around Yankee Stadium in the Bronx—to engage and amplify those who are typically unheard and begin to shift the terms of debate around the police and policing among Black New Yorkers while forging stronger links between BYP100 and the communities the chapter hoped to support and learn from. Robinson describes the imperatives and ethical positioning of the campaign this way:

> OS/OB/OV was a conversation for the community, for those communities and for the Black community more broadly. This wasn't about outside validation, and there is no reason to reinforce Black trauma. I'm tired of asking white people to see us. White people need to see themselves. The project was really like a fuck them what about us project. Let's just talk to each other. We have a hard enough time talking to each other. Let's just deal with this shit and talk to each other.[73]

Robinson makes clear that the project was not intended for white or otherwise non-Black consumption. It wasn't designed to generate "empathy" or galvanize solutions from politicians or policymakers; the goal was not to claim a campaign win. In short, the project was not seeking recognition from the white world. OS/OB/OV was about highlighting the intricacies of Black life as lived in New York's concrete jungle by creating a platform for historically marginalized voices to articulate and take seriously their experiences without reinforcing their trauma. To do so, the street teams carrying out the campaign would need to acknowledge and address challenges Black folks face engaging one another about the well-being and survival of the Black community, including those with points of view contrary to the positions held by people in movement.

The "boundary" in this case concerned the role of the police and notions of safety and criminality, around who is and is not a threat, and, underneath it all, who is and is not worthy of care. For Robinson, it is from this place of dialogue and acknowledgment—from a place that regards Black pain by honoring *all* Black life—holding close the way Black life is shadowed by death and forced to inhabit worlds designed to be uninhabitable, that the community conversation was to proceed. It's by giving ourselves the opportunity to "just deal with this shit" that we begin to not only imagine but conspire with each other to become something other than what we presently are and have been structured to be. But because notions of threat, and the boundaries we construct in response, are inseparable from our embodied experience as racialized, classed, sexualized, and gendered subjects tethered to the yoke of capitalist social relations, arriving there was not a simple task; there were hurdles to overcome, particularly given that Black folks "have a hard enough time talking to ourselves," that is, if we're even talking at all.

The biggest and most daunting hurdle was getting started in the first place. "Street teaming was super awkward, or is, [and] has been," noted Robinson, who used to be the chapter's membership cochair, as we struggled to overcome the chatter in a boisterous Harlem bar. "Oftentimes people have a hard time with starting a conversation with other folks," especially strangers. Though BYP100 NYC had done a lot of street teaming in the past, those attempts tended to take place at events populated by demographics among whom chapter members were already comfortable, like Afropunk, a popular music festival that takes place in

Brooklyn and several other cities in the United States and beyond. Alignment is typically fertile ground when attempting to organize, so Afropunk and similar spaces were ideal sites for identifying and potentially recruiting young Black folks who already possess or lean toward the same values that BYP100 and the broader movement promote. The problem was, such crowds may not always reflect the majority of Black people; in fact, they often don't.

As Robinson confessed, BYP100 was "not necessarily street teaming in areas or among . . . non-college-educated folks," which is to say, the parts of the city where you're most likely to find Black people who occupy a different class position and social status than the bulk of the chapter's membership, which at that time was largely comprised of educated nonnative New Yorkers. So, the question became "how do we actually engage with those folks" and do so in a way that would make people comfortable street teaming.

For Robinson, infusing the process with creativity was one possible solution, since not everyone who wanted to be a part of BYP100 was interested in "straightforward organizing" or eager to be involved in direct actions. As she explained, "The ways in which we'd been organizing prior didn't include any type of artistic vision outside of there being art included. There was nothing that was art driven." In Robinson's estimation, art could be both "a way to organize" and a means to make organizing more accessible to members of the chapter. At the time, she was working on a documentary project that she described as engaging "young Black and Latinx girls on things that they were going through and how they were navigating the world" when the idea for a campaign that could "serve as a conversation starter" and "in itself be a conversation piece" about safety and policing "just came."

The process of initiating this "conversation piece" within Black communities across New York City, the task of taking the complicated entanglements of Black intramural life seriously by centering those positioned furthest away from power, was, in the end, both straightforward and novel. Participants were provided three guiding questions concerning police presence, harassment, and safety where they lived, and then given the option to answer whichever resonated with their experience

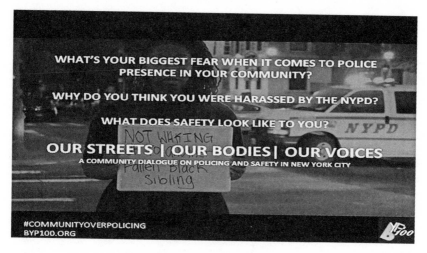

FIGURE 3.1. Campaign questions. Our Streets/Our Bodies/
Our Voices, BYP100 NYC.

(fig. 3.1). The campaign asked: "What's your biggest fear when it comes to police presence in your community? Why do you think you were harassed by the NYPD? What does safety look like to you?" Interviewees then wrote answers to the questions on a dry-erase board. In most cases, participants were then photographed holding their responses.[74]

The decision to use a dry-erase board and take pictures was integral to the creative, documentary-style component of the project. But it was also strategic. "It's easier to talk to people when their guards are a little down," Robinson explained, "and they know that Black folks, white folks, any folks walking down the street with a clipboard is not inviting. Walking down the street with a camera and a whiteboard? Perhaps. People are curious." The novelty of carrying a camera and whiteboard, and the fact that "people are curious," at least more so than they might be if approached in a familiar fashion, such as with a clipboard, were key to getting the conversations started. That people's responses were being documented also offered a sense of security since, as Robinson later elaborated, "everybody wants to know that when they're speaking, they're speaking for a reason and that their words are not just going to fall on deaf ears. And so, if you're capturing it, it kind of gives them a

FIGURE 3.2. Sequoia Honeycutt. Our Streets/Our Bodies/
Our Voices, BYP100 NYC.

little bit of assurance that it's not falling on deaf ears," an assurance that
opened the door to powerful accounts of people's lived experience.

Sequoia Honeycutt's portrait and testimony are in many respects
indicative of what OS/OB/OV sought to achieve (fig. 3.2). To the
question "Why do you think you were harassed?" she replies: "cause
I am TRANSGENDER in a heavily policed area." Sequoia's answer calls
attention to the securitized geographies of marginalized Black folks re-
siding in the city but also to the specific experiences of Black trans men
and women, a point that is deepened by her appearance in the photo
itself, adhering to the goal of visibility and projection. In other words,
it is not enough to simply name the dominating and threatening presence of police in predominately Black and Brown spaces, or the fear felt
by those who call these spaces home. Equally important to consider and
name is the way certain bodies within this spatial arrangement are labeled
and treated as hyperdeviant: the way they are assigned to the negative
register of the already existing negation that the world calls Blackness.
In this regard, there's a way of (mis)reading Sequoia's whiteboard as communicating a more precise message. Her harassment is not only owed to

FIGURE 3.3. Kai. Our Streets/Our Bodies/Our Voices, BYP100 NYC.

the fact that she lives *where* she lives—"*in* a heavily policed area." Instead, because she is a Black transgender woman, her body itself *is* a heavily policed area.[75]

A similar sentiment is expressed in the image of Kai, taken on the same day and in the same neighborhood (fig. 3.3). Asked to respond to the question "What does safety look like to you?" Kai, at the time a prospective member of BYP100, makes clear that the problem is about more than just being a Black body in Harlem. Instead, the answer they provide forces us to see and acknowledge that theirs is a body of a certain kind: "Black, Queer, and ambiguously Gendered." With their response, Kai appears to signal that there should be space enough for that body to exist without always needing to carry the weight of being doubly marked: Black and Queer. For them, then, safety is about the freedom to move; it is about the ability to "navigate the world" exactly as they are. Kai's testimony illustrates a sentiment that cannot be overstated: anti-Blackness restricts movement across categories of difference. It deepens them and makes them worse.

While the images of Sequoia and Kai reflect the campaign's desire to highlight voices typically left out of the narrative about safety and policing, sometimes the conversations were about getting people to see things differently. Take, for instance, an encounter Ain Raven Ealey recounted to me:

> I was in the Bronx where this old dude was . . . answering the question have you been harassed by the police, if so, why do you think that was. And he was talking from the perspective of a young kid. He was like, well, these kids get harassed because their pants are sagging and blah, blah blah. And I was like, well, lynchings happened when people were in three-piece suits and he, he stopped talking and he was like, you're right. And his perspective changed. He was trying to hold onto it, but he couldn't. And those conversations were interesting.

For Ealey, the opportunity to talk to people in the community about their concerns was "powerful," particularly when it prompted them to "rethink a lot of things." In this case, it was an older Black man's fidelity to respectability politics as evidenced in the assumption that the way young people dress is the reason they become targets for the police. By pointing out that the historical legacy of anti-Black terror had nothing to do with how Black people presented themselves, Ealey forced him to question the relationship he'd previously drawn between "sagging" pants and criminality. "It's hard for [older people] to change their mind," she explained, "but to change their minds from a group of young people walking around with a camera and whiteboard in a shirt that says, 'unapologetically Black' and asking questions, that's how communities change. That's why the community engagement piece is necessary."

Getting people to rethink their understanding of criminality, safety, and policing was not exclusively reserved for older Black folks with more retrograde views about the behavior of others. As Autumn Robinson recalled one of her interviews:

> I think one of my most memorable conversations was with this dude. We asked him the question about why were you harassed. Why do you think you were harassed? And he said, because he was standing

outside, and he had no business standing outside. And I was like, what do you mean you had no business standing outside? I shouldn't have been just standing there. And I was like, but you were standing in front of your house, right? In the projects, he was standing in front of the projects. But you know, I was like, well, they can stand outside, right? And you have to actually break it down. Like, why do you feel like you can't just be? Why can't you? It's hot out. It's hot inside. You live in concrete, inside among a whole bunch of bricks. Going outside is a little bit of a relief. Why can't you stand outside? Even if you're just standing there.

The exchange demonstrates the extent to which Black people have absorbed ideas about where we can and cannot be, as well as the nature of criminal transgression justifying police intervention. Or, perhaps more to the point, "we've been taught fear," Robinson surmised, "which makes these kinds of conversations really important . . . it's good to be able to break that down," and not just in the moment. As she sees it, when in dialogue with a community member, "it's also good if the person has somebody else that's around that they know. I can only imagine how those conversations continue after we finish talking." For Robinson, then, the potential for encounters to produce a domino effect that continues the discussion was another upside to engaging people where they live and meeting them where they are.

~~~

As powerful and important as these kinds of conversation could be, and despite Robinson's efforts to make the process more accessible, street teaming still proved to be a task too tall for some BYP100 members, exposing more of the chapter's internal contradictions. On the one hand, it was challenging to get people to buy in and show up for the project, which left Ealey frustrated and disenchanted by what she considered hypocritical behavior. In her own words:

I was super critical because we have these hard critiques about not being connected with the community and there are too many people not from New York in the organization, but these same people would not show up to connect with people in these various neighborhoods.

It isn't hard to see why Ealey was frustrated. To recognize that, as a chapter, we lacked a real connection to Black communities in the city, and to fail to participate in a campaign meant to foster that connection, calls into question our dedication and perhaps our motivations more broadly. As she framed it, "There's starting to be a culture of people joining only when the cameras come, versus people being a part of that very long process to get it into fruition. . . . There were current members who weren't trying to do the work." In other words, for Ealey, there were people in the chapter more interested in final outcomes and the moments the media was present rather than the grind required to make our campaigns and actions a success—a lack of care and attention when there should have been regard.

On the other hand, when people *did* show up, they sometimes resisted talking to "certain" Black folks. "People just weren't comfortable with it," Robinson explained, owing at least in part to the presence of real threats, like street harassment, but also those that were class based and socially ingrained:

> I think street harassment plays a major role. But I guess we still can't be afraid to talk to each other. There were a lot of things, lessons learned, like you had to ensure that certain folks were teamed with other folks in order to combat some of that shit. And sometimes you just had to know when it was time to move away from people. . . . [In] east Harlem, there's a lot of homeless folks, a lot of Black homeless folks, folks dealing with addiction. And so, one time we were street teaming, this, there was like a transaction that happened in front of us. And some folks were uncomfortable. And like, my thing was to keep having a conversation. But it's like, this is some people's reality. And these are the people that are also being policed. Right? These are also people that need to be safe. These are also people that are living on the street.

Intramural fear and discomfort, provoked by predatory behavior and the ravages of social deprivation, undermined people's willingness to engage, which, in turn, compromised the campaign's efforts to reach some of the most vulnerable members of the community: "people that are living on the street." Therein lies another contradiction. It isn't that discomfort when encountering houselessness, a drug transaction, or street harassment is unreasonable and should be frowned upon. And in general, to dismiss concerns people might have when it comes to street teaming, be they real or imagined, is at cross-purposes with a structural analysis that gets at the heart of such concerns and offers tangible solutions to overcome them. Regardless of the challenges, as Robinson put it, "we still can't be afraid to talk to each other," but many folks were and are.

~~~

Staging and archiving what Robinson described as an "honest sharing of stories, experiences, feelings, and concerns among Black New Yorkers" was a multiphase process with an eye-catching conclusion. After months of compiling testimonies and occasionally printing postcards and stickers to distribute around the neighborhoods, the images were projected onto the walls of buildings in participants' communities. As Robinson explained, the projections were "a way to get people who are just walking by to pay attention, or who are driving by to pay attention, or who are riding a cab or whatever, to like stop and pay attention . . . to me it was the best way to like, close out the project" (figs. 3.4 and 3.5).[76]

By projecting the images and testimonies, OS/OB/OV elevated and made available people's experiences on a grand scale. Doing so in turn extended the dialogue from one that unfolded exclusively between BYP100 members and their local interlocutors to one that made possible a broader conversation with the larger community, the domino effect Robinson hoped for. "It was so amazing," Ealey recalled, "just to have people walking by and be like, 'Yo, that's my cousin, what does that say?' And reading the narratives of Black folks in their neighborhood."

FIGURE 3.4. Wall projection 1. Our Streets/Our Bodies/
Our Voices, BYP100-NYC.

This included, perhaps unsurprisingly, a visual confrontation with the police as they surveilled the neighborhood while the images were being projected. "It was dope," Ealey continued with laughter and excitement in her voice:

> Police were mad. They were rolling around trying to figure out what the people in the community that they harass were saying about them and their experience, that shit was so magical. Seeing people come out the projects, like, "yo, what's that?" and "yo, I know him." People driving by and stopping. Yes, I love it. I love that stuff. Because we care this idea that, this classist idea that niggas in the hood don't care. They just like, like we all the same. Like we're fooling ourselves to think that we're different. I'm not saying that all skin folk are kin-folk, but we, we, care, we just don't always have the resources or the outlet to communicate that we care, but we care. And that was proof.

The campaign's attempt to listen, amplify, share, and circulate was an enactment of care and a celebration of life through and with the pain

FIGURE 3.5. Wall projection 2. Our Streets/Our Bodies/
Our Voices, BYP100-NYC.

wrought by the geographies of Blackness in New York City. Despite internal contradictions and the frustration that arose from them, despite our fallibility, OS/OB/OV itself demonstrated regard for Black pain by not only positioning BYP100's work against the ideological forces that further marginalize Black people based on gender, class, and sexuality but by attempting to create a dialogue within the Black intramural that might open up imaginaries that are not bound by or to the authoritative flex of the state or defined by capitalist social relations. In that sense, it's an example of the movement's political and ethical commitments, its wake work, and its choreography of resistance that, in the face of Black pain, is joyful nonetheless.

CHAPTER 4

A Joyful Rebellion

Is an emancipatory figuration of Blackness possible?

—SAIDIYA HARTMAN

Black social life is, fundamentally, the register of black experience that
is not reducible to the terror that calls it into existence but is the rich
reminder, the multifaceted artifact of black communal resistance and
resilience that is expressed in black idioms, cultural forms, traditions,
and ways of being.

—TERRION L. WILLIAMSON

Call and Response

Black joy. The singing, dancing, and chants. The adlibs and improvised
movements. The culture.[1] If Black pain is a spindle around which the
capitalist world system weaves its thread, abolishing that system, through
the adoption of a praxis invested in, as Dylan Rodriguez suggests, "a
radical reconfiguration of justice, subjectivity, and social formation,"
disentangled from the captive logics that ground the "totality of state-
sanctioned and extrastate relations of gendered racial-colonial dominance,"
is the highest form of regard.[2] It's the mechanism by which we build a
Black future.

To make such a claim is one thing; to actualize it is another. And on
that front, Black joy plays an essential role. These community-centered

practices—alongside other forms of "turning-up"—facilitate an embodied sense of being catalysts of transformation, an understanding of ourselves as capable of (un)making worlds. The performance and practice of Black joy, "the variety, and spontaneity of its forms," as Marisa Solomon and I have elsewhere written, offer a "roadmap and prelude authored by the ungovernable." Born out of a tradition that proceeds from the folk culture of the plantation, Black joy prefigures what is yet to come, "just as it announces what has always been here."[3]

I'll never forget the moment I first heard and experienced "Power," a popular movement chant.[4] It was at a weekend retreat in the summer of 2016. We gathered in the kitchen of an Airbnb in Ditmas Park, a south Brooklyn neighborhood that feels more like the suburbs than the city, with its three-story houses and manicured green lawns. I was still relatively new to the chapter at the time, and in many ways disoriented, feeling both that I didn't (yet) belong and an overwhelming sense of belonging, like I was a part of something important, and that importance was connected to our collective Blackness, and the desire to build a movement able to address and overcome the intramural struggles that limited the Black political-cultural formations of the past.

As we prepared to close out the formal portion of the day's agenda, Gabby, a BYP100 member at the time, took the floor and let out a shout that felt like it came from a region of herself seldom accessed—a vulnerability the weekend had opened for many of us. She began the chant, and we repeated in typical call-and-response fashion:

POWER (power)!
I WANT IT (I want it)!
I NEED IT (I need it)!
I GOTSTA HAVE IT (I gotsta have it)!
RIGHT NOW (right now)!
RIGHT NOW (right now)!
RIGHT NOW (right now)!
RIGHT NOW (right now)!

With every word, her body contorted—bending, thrusting forward—while her face betrayed both pleasure and pain. As the momentum built,

we clapped and stomped, each utterance of "Right Now" an accelera-
tion, a heightening. I went along beside myself. When it was over, many
of us embraced. It had been an emotional weekend, and Gabby's rendi-
tion of the Power chant was an emotional apex.

The performance I witnessed and participated in that afternoon—
the hype and holler of the chant—is fundamental to, and an illustration
of, the way Black folks in and around the movement come together. It's
a means to connect and build, both politically and spiritually, in the here
and now, as well as in relationship to the past. For me, it represented a
side of Black sociality I hadn't encountered since I was a teenager
wrapped up in the social and ritual life of the church, where call-and-
response, chanting, and other spiritually uplifting rites were strategies
long used to foster a sense of Black livingness and to further the project
of Black survival.[5] The movement's chants and rituals are cultural enactments of a kind of "Black life politics," as Barnor Hesse has termed it.[6]
These enactments seek community affirmation in the collective rejoice
of everything Black. It's the demand, or rather the expectation, anticipated but not quite fulfilled by the Black Arts and Black Power Movements in the 1960s and 1970s, that Blackness becomes the foundation
upon which our collective future proceeds.

Many no doubt have experienced or at least seen and heard similar
displays of Black performativity firsthand. Celebratory and politically
assertive chants, singing and dancing, along with other movement rituals, have become a constituent feature of contemporary Black protest,
on full display during the uprisings. They are interventions within the
already existing sweep of disruption, revivals that gesture toward otherwise possibilities.[7] Black joy is a way of furthering the movement's claim
to space, of *calling out* white supremacy and *calling in* comrades and
allies, demonstrated in chants like "What's Wrong with You": "*I love Black
people. You don't love Black people? What's wrong with you? What's wrong
with you?*"[8] These rituals bring into view what had once been hidden or
suppressed, announcing and making space for a Black vernacular previously perceived as noise.[9] They mobilize against the anti-Black logic of
the modern world by employing and expanding the fugitive choreogra-
phies of Black folk culture, the radicalism of the Black slave.

When directed toward the public, the movement's ritual life—the call-and-response, the chants—operates precisely along these lines; it intervenes both for and against. It's against the world as it is and for the world that Black and other people of color will manifest. Take the chant "We Ready, We Coming": "*Chant down, Babylon. Black people are the bomb. We ready (ayeee). We coming (ayeee). We ready (ayeee). We coming.*"[10] The intervention here is not (only) hopeful, at least insofar as it does not speak of one day overcoming anti-Blackness within the world as currently constituted.[11] It instead expresses a prideful prescience of a freedom the movement *knows* will come; the wins the movement is steeled for; the liberation young Black folks are *coming* to take. For this, joy is a central ingredient. In the words of one BYP100 member: "let's face it, without joy, we will not win."[12]

But Black joy and celebration are not only enactments of Black presence directed toward the public—dancing, singing, and stomping where we do not belong. Joy is also a mode of communication within the Black community itself. It signals, through our bodies and with our voices, possible futures, the yet to come of Black freedom. If the politics of the wake requires and instills regard for Black pain, it likewise demands and inspires Black joy. This chapter explores where and how joy shows up, and why it has become so central, not only to this movement—its practices and political culture—but to what I have called the time of #BlackLivesMatter. In its essence, Black joy is a refusal to be overwhelmed by pain or consumed by the rage anti-Blackness forces upon us. It is the recognition that, while we can and should be angry about a political and social structure intent to do us harm, it need not define who we are or how we move through the world. Joy is a signal to others and oneself that we are nevertheless here, that we can be here and thrive as we move toward a Black future. In that sense, Black joy expresses and prefigures a future freedom where all Black people can be joyous wherever we are and however we want. Black joy, in other words, is a means to recognize what Christina Sharpe describes as "the largeness that is Black life, Black life insisted from death."[13] That is why, from the vantage of the wake, the rebellion will be—and is—joyful.

The Black Joy Era

In 2014, the same year Mike Brown's murder helped move the movement from a hashtag to an insurgency, the phrase "Black joy" began its ascent in Black popular vernacular. Reflecting on the inner turmoil he experienced while grappling with the rage, horror, and hurt following Brown's death, the poet and scholar Javon Johnson offered the following:

> Rather than thinking squarely about black pain in response to the most recent wave of state-sanctioned anti-black violence and terrorism, I wonder how we might *also* think about *black joy as a theory, a method, and a political device.*[14]

It is precisely within this register of thought—theory, method, and device—that I want to think about the salience of Black joy, a celebration of everything anti-Blackness denies. If the visuality and experience of Black pain are omnipresent, joy is a principal strategy, a "method," deployed in the movement to not only confront pain but move beyond it toward a world where Black subjection does not exist.

Given the tenor of 2014, coupled with the parallel resurfacing of an overtly politicized Black identity—most memorably rendered in the term "unapologetically Black," created by BYP100's former minister of culture Fresco Steez—it is no surprise that ideas about an explicitly "Black" joy would not only emerge but endure. Since then, the term has become widespread across Black political, social, and cultural life. Most commonly, "Black joy" has appeared in the form of hashtags attached to social media posts on platforms like Instagram and Twitter, inspiring a multitude of similarly celebratory sentiments (e.g., #blackgirlmagic, #blackgirlfly, #blackgirlslay, #blackboyjoy, #blackboylit, #melaninonfleek, and so on).

These expressions reflect some of the more recurrent phrasings created and taken up by young Black folks, paced by affirmations like #blackgirlmagic that trumpet Black women and girls. That they do is not without intention or consequence. By enveloping a celebratory approach to Blackness in a generational language, social media has helped

facilitate an interpretation of joy that is not only politically and culturally powerful but can circulate and be understood across geographies,
confirming a collective narrative drawn from collective trauma.[15]

Beyond the hashtag, you can now find Black joy foregrounded in the
headlines of media outlets as diverse as NPR and *Vogue*, just as it once
marked the name and tenor of the popular news and culture podcast
the *Black Joy Mixtape*. The podcast was hosted by Amber J. Phillips, who
colorfully dubbed herself the "High Priestess of Black Joy," and Jazmine
Walker, "Da King of the South" (K.O.S.). In segments of around an
hour, the pair "remix leading headlines with realness, comedy and Black
Feminism, to make the news relatable to our daily lives and worthy of
being pumped through our speakers."[16] Instead of relying on social
media posts alone, theirs is a Black joy driven by and delivered through
laughter and the steadfast point of view of Black women. In doing so,
Phillips and Walker align themselves with the broader movement's aim
to center and uplift the historically marginalized, Black women being
among them.

Further still, the duo positions the *Black Joy Mixtape* within a longer
tradition of using laughter as a tool in Black folk culture generally and
in Black feminist practice in particular.[17] As Lawrence Levine notes in
his seminal work on Black culture and consciousness, "the widespread
existence of laughter throughout Afro-American history is in itself
evidence of the retention and development of forms of communal consciousness and solidarity."[18] Perhaps more than anything else,
laughter—and the hosts themselves—represents the common thread
linking the sixty episodes of their otherwise wide-ranging podcast.

In October 2017, Phillips and Walker hosted a TEDx Talk called
"Blueprint for the Black Joy Era," during which they outlined how and
why they center Black joy in their lives and work.[19] The talk was a live
demonstration of how they get at "hard truths through comedy with
dignity and with flare . . . as Black women in America."[20] With a worldview guided by the experience of being both Black and women, living
in a nation particularly brutal to those who identify as such, the duo
framed Black joy not as a millennial-driven trend but as a redefining and
self-affirming force worthy of exploration and discussion in and beyond

the Black community. This is the "era" of Black Joy, they emphasized, and, like the movement itself, Black women were leading and providing instruction.

While the recent popularity and reach of Black joy have been most visible on the internet, in media headlines, and through social media platforms, it does not belong exclusively to the digital sphere. Over the last several years, Black joy has also permeated more traditional forms of Black expressive culture. For example, in September 2016, two months after Philando Castile's murder, Black joy was the guiding theme of New York City's National Black Theatre's forty-eighth season, titled "In Pursuit of Black Joy." The program included an interactive exhibition, "The Alchemy of Black Joy," that featured photographer Peter Cooper and a performance that nods to popular hashtag affirmations titled "#BlackGirlMagic: The Complexity of Your Smile." The season opened with a panel discussion on the theme cohosted by Afropunk, which was "conceived to celebrate Black excellence and create a safe place for Black folks." Fittingly, it closed with the world premiere of playwright James Ijames's *Kill Move Paradise*, which follows the after-lives of four recently slain Black men and was described in a more recent staging at Chicago's TimeLine Theatre as a "powerful and provocative reflection on recent events, illustrating the possibilities of collective transformation and radical acts of joy."[21] For the theater's CEO, Sade Lythcott, "the inundating images and news of the slaying of young Black people" made a full season exploring Black joy "on our own terms, in our own words" as a necessary "healing space, reminding us all of the awesome power we each have as members of a community."[22]

The previous year, interdisciplinary artist Marc Bamuthi Joseph arranged a suite of performances in New York City's Central Park called "Black Joy in the Hour of Chaos." Publisher and Black cultural critic Ronald Bunn described Joseph's participatory round of "second line" influenced sonic and visual-scapes as "a cycle of musical, dance and spoken word poetry performances that evoke 'black joy'" by recalling and drawing upon the legacies of Black performance, migration, and movement as opportunities to reflect on where we are as a people if not also where we might be going.[23] In that sense, the feeling of community connection Lythcott described when discussing "In Pursuit of Black Joy" is not temporally bound. Joseph's performances show that joy can also function as an opportunity for remembrance, a fulsome embrace of the Black past that, despite pain, produced a culture worth celebrating.

And celebration is central to how Black joy is heralded. Since 2018, Oakland has hosted an annual Black Joy Parade with accompanying merchandise that, among other things, implores people to "be the movement."[24] Like Phillips and Walker, Joseph's performance, as well as the events marking the National Black Theatre's forty-eighth season, by calling the Black Joy Parade a movement, the organizers of the event acknowledge and attempt to signal that Black joy is a cultural and political phenomenon of contemporary significance and collective importance for Black people—a theory, method, and political device, as Johnson put it.

These public-facing and site-specific renderings demonstrate, at least in part, the spatial and material dimensions of the circulation of joy as its importance as an idiom in Black vocabulary and culture has grown. They also make clear the demand to have this intramural experience be accessible in ways that do not feel hidden or wholly commodified. Two additional examples are worth mentioning in this regard, particularly as they highlight the importance of music. Black joy is a principal theme of Party Noire, which is a well-known Chicago-based (and occasionally traveling), queer-centered dance party and community. Started in late 2015, Party Noire describes itself as "an inclusive cultural hub celebrating Black femmes, QWOC, + Black womynhood along the gender spectrum + holds space especially for queer, trans + gender-queer and gender non-conforming Black people." Through an embrace of the movement's goal of radical inclusivity, cofounders Nick Adler and Rae Chardonnay understand Party Noire to be an "intersectional orbit of Black joy" that aims to "love, uplift, and make SPACE for ALL Black joy."[25]

Similarly, BYP100 has created a "national cultural production team," one of the first such efforts undertaken by a Black-led direct-action organization, called the Black Joy Experience (BJE). BJE seeks to "tap into the long history of joy and holistic energy that has been woven in the black radical tradition, especially when our freedom is at stake."[26] The collective does this mainly through the songs and chants that have proven so instrumental to the ritual life of BYP100, as well as Black organizing spaces within the movement more broadly. As they explain:

> BYP100 cultural workers understand that energy can neither be created nor destroyed, only transferred to create movement. We seek to transform the energy in collective spaces and have them be consumed by holistic energy, which is the process of providing an interdisciplinary approach to artistic articulation, erotic truth, music, and anti-oppression work. We merge political education, artistic expression and musical healing towards the goal of curating artistic spaces that create awareness, promote personal healing, surmount institutional barriers and generate Black joy, love, self-care and healing.[27]

Both BYP100's cultural production team and the community built around Party Noire intentionally use joy to transform space in the name of love through performative and celebratory practice.

The sum total of these examples suggests that calling the current political and cultural moment the "Black Joy Era" is a precise claim. Today just about any instance of Black people singing, dancing, doing well, any example of Black people *living* is assigned the label "Black joy."[28] This naming practice indicates that, in a moment when Black pain and premature death appear as constants, there is a strong desire to highlight if not argue for Black life on its own terms and, as Terrion Williamson has put it, "from the vantage point in which it is lived."[29] The "lived" portion of that equation is vital, as it points to the view that, as Black people, we should see ourselves as not only "beautiful" in an aesthetic sense, as was the mantra in the 1960s, but beautiful because we have and continue to survive. Be it performatively or as a description online, Black joy represents a critical juncture in Black political development, a different way of seeing and thinking about ourselves as a collective Black people, Blackness unbounded. And its widespread usage makes apparent one of the movement's greatest strengths: the way it brings together an array of people around a set of beliefs and commitments regardless of their current level of participation on the ground.[30]

Deeper still, frequent evocations of an unbounded Black joy are suggestive of a larger intellectual shift, or "sharpening," in approaches to and understanding of Blackness and Black culture as a counterstatement to the hegemonic forces of the West, its negation and critique. In that sense, Blackness exceeds its role as an identity or relational category. It is, of course, both of these things, but it also can be used as an analytic tool to help forge an alternative future outside of anti-Blackness, white supremacy, and the capitalist world system. Thinking of it in these terms points us in the direction of what Denise Ferreira da Silva has called a "poethics of Blackness," in which the "category of Blackness gets released from the registers of 'object'" to "announce a whole range of possibilities for knowing, doing, and existing."[31]

In other words, Black joy is part of a future tense dialect generated by and through the movement that makes available new terrains of political imagination and political demands unrestrained by, though still indebted to, the legacies of the past. It signals a new frontier upon which social transformation is pursued and evaluated along the ancestral plane of the Black radical tradition, a horizon that centers the historically marginalized in the fight to get free, just as it seeks to celebrate all Black life in-the-meanwhile.

We should approach this with both enthusiasm and caution, making sure to guard against obscuring or commodifying all that makes Black joy, for Black people, not only legible but speakable in the first place. Take the Black Joy Parade in Oakland. It has since become a nonprofit that frequently collaborates with brands and is essentially a brand itself.[32] An identification with Black joy absent context and vision serves the maintenance of the capitalist world system and, as such, facilitates white supremacy and anti-Blackness by draining Black joy of its critical capacity. It is perhaps an allusion to this problem that prompted Phillips and Walker, as they explained why it is important to name "Black joy" as such rather than just "joy" in a general sense, to respond in unison: "White people have no self-control."[33] They continue:

Now that might be alarming for a few of you . . . but if you consider the annihilation of indigenous people, the fact that white folk stole millions of Black people against our will and forced us on the boats to come over here and build this country too . . . girl, the KKK, mass incarceration, phew, and that's just the recent past. When you think about what folks have done to Brooklyn, Oakland, etcetera, what y'all trying to do to the sacred land of standing rock . . . it's crazy.[34]

By outlining a partial but still vivid list of the work of white supremacy against Black and Brown communities, Phillips and Walker seek to ensure that any notion of Black joy does not get separated from its historical and present-day context. The possibility of Black joy is premised on and in opposition to Black pain, the result of white supremacist and anti-Black institutions, attitudes, and the array of social and economic hardships that emerge from them. In other words, they place Black joy and Black life squarely in the context of the wake.

Joy in and as Black Life

Underlying Black joy, then, is a logic of value defined by difference, a contrast sketched in the master narrative of Blackness itself. Joy moves against the terms used to justify racial domination under white supremacy. It celebrates what anti-Blackness denies: Black life and Black worth. Of course, we know this denial does not refute value in the broader sense of the word. If nothing else, from the horrors of the Middle Passage to the glam of celebrity entertainers and athletes, history teaches us that the Black body always has been and continues to be profitable; it has been and continues to be a source of capital accumulation. Instead, anti-Blackness refuses Black humanity, our right to live freely and richly, as equals. For that reason, Black joy is illegible without acknowledging the force of racial violence in all its forms.

To put it another way, the "Black" in Black joy directly corresponds with the social worlds those positioned as Black build with and despite pain and death. While we must be careful not to collapse the Black experience into a monolith, to claim Black joy (and pain) as distinct from general joy and general pain demonstrates what Black people nonetheless share. It's to honor a collective trauma, passed down and repeated, that produces particular ways of being *here* and of expressing ourselves while we are. To say this does not mean joy in and of itself is unique to the current moment. The recognition of and pleasure in singing, dancing, laughing, eating, loving—instances of Black being together, even in the most challenging of circumstances—has consistently been a means for survival and world-making, evidenced in the illicit parties that took place on the peripheries of the plantation, as described by Stephanie Camp.[35]

More than merely serving as a means to soldier on, however, joy makes available speculative imaginings of a world no longer invested in anti-Blackness, and it's an invitation for others to imagine similarly. In many respects, Black joy is a nod to the extraordinary occurrence of Black social life in, through, and despite death where, as Lia Bascomb powerfully put it, the "traditionally thrown away, discarded, or hidden [become] a treasure trove of potential."[36] To borrow a phrase from Clayton Riley's celebratory 1971 review of Melvin Van Peebles's play *Ain't Supposed to Die a Natural Death*, expressions of Black joy act as a "testament, chronicle, and archive" of Blackness in all its possibilities.[37]

One of the ways Black joy marshals its possibilities into a political force is by providing Black people opportunities to see, think, and experience ourselves as more than what the world tells us we are. Joy is a way of exceeding what the world "structures [us] to be," or what Gina Dent refers to as the "potential for our coexistence within another sphere of knowledge."[38] As Johnson notes, these are "profound moments in which black love and laughter 'lifts everyone slightly above the present' and allows [us] to feel, to know in our bones, what black utopia might be like."[39] The sense of "us" implied in "everyone" is crucial, as it indicates that Black joy is simultaneously in the individual body and communal. Because it is recognizable *to* us, we understand it to be *for* us.[40]

Similarly, Cornel West explains that "joy has to do with a connection with others." To have "joy, you need others."[41] These others are not merely those with whom you inhabit space in a given moment. For West, joy "tries to get at those non-market values—love, care, kindness, service, solidarity, the struggle for justice—values that provide the possibility of bringing people together" to create "a community across time" and outside the purview of capitalist social relations.[42] To collapse these thoughts together, we might say that Black joy is the undercurrent of Black social life, and its expression, particularly in the context of M4BL, is an "emancipatory figuration of blackness" aimed at that community across time, a community in which abolition is the only horizon.[43]

Much like the critical space made available by regarding Black pain as structurally embedded in our political system and cause for its demise—an act that requires centering the historically marginalized— joy is both a political resource and a political tactic. It represents one of the ways Black people in this movement moment create a sense of "us," or what social movement scholars call "group consciousness." This identity work necessarily means creating boundaries of distinction that inform who the "us" actually is and who it is not. For M4BL, the boundary is about opening pathways to honor "all Black life" against all systems and practices of domination more than it is erecting enclosures that leave some behind. Black joy practiced in the movement is an expression of community that is sensitive to how some narratives of lived experience gain popular sanction over others and how some ways of living are deemed more worthy. Binding these different but overlapping articulations of Black joy into a unified whole is the underlying acknowledgment of Black pain and the attempt to produce opportunities for refuge and community away from narratives of Black suffering without ignoring them altogether. For this reason, Joy is a practice, not an event.

To deepen this sketch, I consider the *content* of Black joy by further examining some of the ways it manifests itself in and around movement spaces. I take as my first and primary case the creation and evolution of The Black Joy Project, one of the most prominent and widely covered examples of using joy to make a political statement. My second is the Brooklyn-based Black queer and trans-centered party, "A Ratchet Realm," and the way the term "ratchet" augments and elevates joy. Alongside one another, these cases show that Black joy surpasses the event or instance of its occurrence; past the song, chant, or dance; past the food and the laughter, past the talk. It helps foster an exchange between Black people with and for each other—knowingly or otherwise. It is something kept, archived, and circulated. It is intergenerational and seeks to build Black knowledge(s), a form of assembly that never loses the shadow of Black pain but instead harnesses it as a necessary step toward healing. That is what gives it its political weight: the intentional deployment of joy as part of a broader political culture and agenda informed by the wake. The examples explored here take this up, and contain within it, just like pain, *an ethics of care* that outlines the terms of debate, not only within the context of the movement but as a framework for the future. It is part of the road we pave toward liberation.

Variations on a Love Theme

It all happened at once, unexpectedly.
Me typing on the internet.
Feeling like I needed to do this.[44]

This is how Kleaver Cruz describes the calling he received to begin The Black Joy Project (TBJP), a social media–based gallery on Instagram that uses photographs to "exhibit how Black people do and can exist as they are without sensation."[45] Of all the spaces in which Black joy was named and cultivated in the years following the movement's emergence, TBJP was one of the first to directly politicize it by unambiguously asserting that such expressions are, in and of themselves, political acts, that joy is "resistance too."[46] For Cruz, Black joy should be understood as a form of resistance because it demonstrates that those positioned as Black live meaningfully despite the persistent patterns of dehumanization, death, and pain, particularly as they have appeared so spectacularly in recent years. As it was with the enslaved, Black lives are potent reminders that we have survived and are surviving. To borrow from Lucille Clifton, our joy is the evidence that "everyday something has tried to kill me and has failed."[47]

This points to a version of Black representation and Black being that is not predicated on success or power, at least as the capitalist world system has defined them. Against a set of beliefs long cultivated by Black elites and the aspiring Black middle class, it does not rely on notions of uplift, respectability, or advance, concepts that were adopted and evolved with the sometimes explicit aim of subordinating and controlling Black bodies—often through violent means—in the name of "civilization." It is also not about the "Black excellence" attributed to iconic superstars like Beyoncé or the political ascent of politicians such as Barack Obama, however empowering that term has become for Black folks over the last decade. Instead, the Black joy explored by TBJP situates itself in contrast to the way Black people have historically measured one another within the context of the political and cultural status quo— that is, striving to live up to a standard set by white supremacy. TBJP highlights that seeing ourselves *as* ourselves matters for not only how we understand our Blackness and our relationship to others in the Black community but also how we come to understand, analyze, move through, and critique the worlds we inhabit.

Sarah Lewis describes this as the long-standing and critical relationship between vision, culture, and justice, insofar as images, particularly of Black people, can powerfully (re)shape the way we narrate the past, present, and future.[48] With joy we can hold steady in our right to be "without sensation," though not without feeling, as we go about sketching a world otherwise. In this respect, the TBJP's use of images is in a Black photographic tradition that dates back to portraits of Frederick Douglass and includes the work of photojournalists like Kwame Braithwaite, who helped popularize the phrase "Black is Beautiful" in the 1960s. More recently, this tradition can be recognized in the work of heralded artists such as Radcliffe "Ruddy" Roye and up-and-coming photographers like Britt Sense, both of whom have taken up photos of everyday Black people to refigure the dignity of Black life (figs. 4.1 and 4.2).

Deeper still, for Cruz, sharing, thinking, and talking about Black joy is also one possible ground upon which we might come to love and care for each other across our differences and beyond pre-established boundaries (of class, color, gender, sex, geography)—a love and care that comes from being systematically marginalized and subject to the registers of violence and degradation deployed in the service of white rule

FIGURE 4.1. Two Black girls playing in a laundromat.
Brittani Sensabaugh (Britt Sense). Instagram.

around the world. This itself is a political task. As Barnor Hesse and
Juliet Hooker suggest, "political mobilizations of 'blackness' have always had different and dispersed meanings across time and space."[49]
Liberation movements must find ways to effectively maintain political
forms of Blackness that attend to differences along with geographically
specific contexts and the structural conditions that make those contexts
possible.

Seen in this light, Black joy represents a political form of Blackness
that achieves this mandate and does so without needing to foreground
Black death. It is the "capacious conception . . . of black life as an eman-
cipated sociality" that Hesse and Hooker demand; it represents "the
emancipation of black comportment and black identity from the white
regulations and requirements emanating from the dominant regime of

FIGURE 4.2. Black woman with child. Ruddy Roye. Instagram.

race performativity."[50] As a political and "deterritorialized" form of Blackness, Black joy "involves the creative disembedding of particular meanings of black solidarity from local events and settings, where these meanings become transferable to other places, linking previously disparate black communities in affinity and dialogical networks of discourses and activities."[51] In this way, examples like TBJP affirm the idea of viewing Black joy as a feeling and a practice aimed at creating spaces to discuss how *all* Black people can, should, and do live despite the long shadow of slavery, as well as the possible futures we might build through that dialogue.

The everyday images of TBJP underscore the importance of marshaling Joy in its simplest manifestations to build intramural bonds in the United States and around the world. This community is built not only through the images themselves but also through the dialogue around Black joy that the images and Cruz himself invite as they appear in the accompanying comments of his Instagram posts. The opportunity to discuss and define Black joy also works to affirm the power in our survival and perseverance—the power of our own words and image to proclaim *we* are powerful and abundant as Black people connected by and through an overlapping past, even as our proximity to violence and domination may vary.

Taken together, TBJP demonstrates that our attention to and appreciation for the "fact" of Black life is central to how we resist and have resisted. When the formal institutions of power and control continue to prove themselves to be antagonistic to the liberation of the historically marginalized, as they do now, we must critically consider the abolition of those institutions in favor of something better. Tactics that emphasize and make space for who and what we are without sensation are crucial to paving a path toward that world, toward a new politic because sensation is what renders Black life, queer life, on the outskirts of prevailing normative assumptions of what is "good."

In this regard, social media in general and Instagram, in particular, represent a central arena for Black image-making with and through a resurgent Black public sphere, a counterpublic, that is not content to be a subaltern space but instead means to construct a narrative and aesthetic powerful enough to compete with those advanced in mainstream political discourse. It represents, too, the most expansive and accessible frontier upon which young Black political mobilization and identity work takes place, where the politics of the wake—regard for Black pain, a celebration of and care for Black life—circulates.

The story of how TBJP began, which, because of the salience of Black joy in the current moment, has been reproduced in multiple forums, offers a useful lens through which to deepen the way we understand the why and how of Black joy.[52] The quote that opened this section suggests the project's origins were sudden and unexpected. However, the "need"

Cruz names comes from a place of hurt. What rests at the root of his compulsion toward joy is pain.

> A little after Thanksgiving in 2015, I woke up burdened. It felt like a ton of bricks were on top of me that morning and I could not get out of my bed. I laid still, heavy, wondering what was the source of my sadness. I thought about how, earlier that year, my family and I had experienced the sudden and tragic loss of my uncle Ali—may he rest in peace.[53]

Central here is how Cruz narrates the sequence of events. He begins by speculating about his sadness before eventually drawing attention to the death of his uncle. However, he does this only as a continuation of the search for the source, or cause, of his unrest. Uncle Ali is present in this pain but described as one of several possible factors adding to the "ton of bricks" burdening Cruz. Against the conclusion we might jump to draw, personal loss and mourning might not capture the depth of his hurt or explain why he "needed to do this."

Mourning and sorrow often align with what is assumed to be a universal, human experience: the death of a loved one. Few people go through life without being forced to endure the feeling of having someone alive and present one day then gone the next. But in Cruz's rumination, death and loss should not be assumed to exist within the boundaries of universalism. Black pain is not universal. It is specific and non-relational insofar as equality and freedom have never been enough to prevent racial violence let alone afford Black people a level playing field: socially, culturally, or before the law. Black pain *is*, however, a core element of our "democracy," given that liberal democracy—in the United States and elsewhere—is itself predicated on the frequently violent exclusion and subordination of Black people.[54]

To not acknowledge this would mean (re)enacting the erasure of distinction that undergirds most discourses around multiculturalism, inclusion, and rights. These discourses insist on the political and cultural claims of a universal subject with and despite differences that cannot possibly exist without first reconciling oneself to the implications of a social, economic, and juridical order premised on Black containment and death. That this erasure is commonplace is violent on its own but particularly in the way it promotes several dubious presuppositions. The first is the idea that what Cruz was going through that morning is, could, or should be knowable, if not familiar, to all. This vantage foregrounds Uncle Ali and Cruz's solemn acknowledgment of his untimely passing: "may he rest in peace." It concludes, in other words, that all deaths are the same. Second and closely connected: since death is knowable and familiar to all, and since all deaths are the same, Cruz's pain, his rumination and trouble, could plausibly be yours, regardless of who occupies the subject-position of "you" in that phrase: Black, white, or otherwise. This mode of projection allows for empathy by conflating the discursive "we"—what is implied by invocations of humankind and human rights—with the material counterpoint of Black life.

Tying these two assumptions together is the belief that since death is knowable, familiar, and the same for all, there is a grammar available to locate Cruz's burden, that pain and death possess a register that we all share and thus are inherently communicable. But it is precisely the inability to find a grammar, a means of articulation or expression, that forces Cruz to wander further in pain. For this reason, the passing of his uncle, the micro-dimensions of personhood, does not answer for Cruz's unexpected call to the internet. It does not capture what Hortense Spillers refers to as the "primary narrative."[55] He continues:

> I thought about how present I was for and to Black death and pain through my organizing work with various activist collectives in New York City, and the ways I felt bombarded by these things on a daily basis. By the time I woke up that morning, I had already made a commitment to not watch any more videos of Black death and continue refusing to repost them anywhere on the internet.[56]

Here we are brought closer to the real problem: his proximity to a *particular* kind of death, as both a teacher and activist in New York City,[57] as well as through the oversaturation of images of Black degradation shared across social media—those long-familiar sites of Blackness in "varying states of corporeal chaos and decay."[58] But the problem is deeper still. For many Black and Brown kids growing up in the Bronx, where Cruz lived and worked, distance does not mediate Black death. Instead, it is often a regular feature of their everyday lives. As Cruz explained, not everyone is "bombarded by Black death" in the same way; some encounter it more than others.

> Right before even having this experience with The Black Joy Project, I think it was the year Mike Brown was killed, so 2014. I remember going to my school. I was working at a school in the Bronx, and rightfully or understandably, people weren't that pressed, you know what I'm saying? Like what's the difference between Mike Brown and so and so who got shot? The first year I worked [there], the day, like the week before school started, a kid [who attended the school] had been killed, you know, and there wasn't no protests, there was no rallies, and there was no, there wasn't even a candle lit at the school for that kid, you know, so why would they all of a sudden want to be up in arms for Mike Brown, you know what I'm saying? And it made me present to the ways that it's just normalized, Black death, like that, that really Mike Brown in a way was exceptional because of the way all of it went down. But a kid that age that looks like that being killed to a lot of people in the hood is not.[59]

It is this normalized, global, and historically structured dilemma—"the black body in pain, all of the time, a little bit dead, all of the time, and ever almost dying"—that points toward critique and disruption.[60] Cruz's burden is linked to a broader convergence of sentiment, a regard for Black pain and an acknowledgment that Black death and dispossession often shape (but do not always define) the boundaries of Black life. What troubled Cruz, then, precedes and surpasses the familial, most conventional grammars of sorrow, and even the material fact of his restless night, just as it exceeds what can be redressed by the institutional frameworks built to provide care or the discourses of grief meant to offer comfort.[61] We might say that Cruz outlines an experience that plays out on the ontological level, a metaphysics beyond and within the body or, perhaps better put, the "flesh."

As Spillers explains, the distinction between the body and the flesh fruitfully demarcates "captive and liberated subject-positions" forced into existence during slavery and as they continue today in slavery's afterlife.[62] To speak of "the flesh," in other words, is to describe what Calvin Warren calls "the structure of black existence . . . which anti-Blackness incessantly targets."[63] What matters here is not primarily the anatomical attributes of gender—the African male versus the African woman—but the ways the wounding of (Black) flesh was and is a characteristic of the captive shared across gender, age, physical fitness, and so on. Spillers writes:

> The anatomical specifications of rupture, of altered human tissue, take on the objective description of laboratory prose—eyes beaten out, arms, backs, skulls branded, a left jaw, a right ankle, punctured; teeth missing, as the calculated work of iron, whips, chains, knives, the canine patrol, the bullet.[64]

From these various lacerations, markings that represent what Warren describes as "a sign of destruction that is itself a 'witness' of the violation," we are offered, or instead forced to consider, the symbolic "form" in which the laceration is "felt or registered on another plane of existence."[65] Spillers imagines these markings as "a kind of hieroglyphics of the flesh whose severe disjunctures come to be hidden to the cultural seeing by skin color" but nonetheless represent a "cultural text." This text avails itself not only to what Warren calls "a cultural reading and hermeneutical practice" but also, I would add, to political action.[66] Said simply, what shook Cruz was the haunt of anti-Black violence, the laceration that marks and communicates Black suffering in a way that exceeds language.

Aroused from his slumber by this haunt, the weighty sorrow that underwrites "Black being in the wake," and to offer a grammar for that which resides beyond articulation and redress, Cruz turns to images that deliver everyday expressions of joy. Additionally, in what appears as a gesture to and a rejection of the primary narrative, as Spillers would put it—the way Blackness, through the flesh and the laceration, is "passed down from generation to generation"—he calls on his social network to likewise take part in (counter) communicating the mark of violation, how we carry and respond to Blackness in ways that reside beyond language but are nevertheless legible to other Black people.[67] Cruz explains:

> I decided that my Social media timelines needed some smiles amidst the sharing of important information, thoughts, art, photos and videos that can be upsetting and at its worst depressing and traumatizing. I posted a picture of my mom smiling and asked for others to post their #BlackJoy moments. I then decided to take on a 30-day personal challenge (that I kept to myself) to share photos of Black joy.[68]

The word "amidst" helps demonstrate Cruz's logic as one of balance or what he has called "equilibrium." In other words, the project aims to show to others as much as to himself what it looks like when Black people are permitted to just be.[69]

To *just be*, in Cruz's case, finds its first form in the selfie, images, for example, like the one he posted of himself in an empty subway car, adorned with a deep-blue hat that bears a stitched black "X" in the middle, a tribute to Malcolm popularized in the 1990s alongside Spike Lee's now-classic biopic (fig. 4.3).[70] The hat's symbolic value in the photo is augmented and affirmed by the rims of Cruz's glasses—which echo those of the late liberation thinker—as much as it is by the dissonant synchronicity of his green, blue, and beige varsity jacket. Most importantly, the symbolism of the hat is elevated by the excitement shown through the smile that prompted Cruz to post the picture in the first place. Cruz is capturing the joy that comes from being alone in a public space that hardly, if ever, allows for physical solitude.

This way of representing Black people *being* is likewise displayed in the family portrait Cruz took of himself, his twin brother Walter, and his mother, grinning widely, doused in glow-in-the-dark paint after participating in "the color run," smiling with their mouths open as if to shout.[71] It can be the image of one of Cruz's friends "taking the time" to breathe in the fragrance of a fistful of sunflowers, as was the case in one post, marked once more by the silver chrome of the subway car. Or another comrade captured midsentence, almost in motion, in front of the vibrantly painted mural outlining the entrance of the Sixth Street

FIGURE 4.3. Kleaver Cruz on the subway. The Black Joy Project. Instagram.

Community Center on the Lower East Side. It can also be the arms-stretched radiance of a Black elder in the sun-soaked streets of Harlem, uplifting others through her expressions of movement and devotion.

These everyday pictures of the self, chance encounters, of friends and family members, are sourced from what Cruz explained happened to be on his phone at the time. In both their original intent—the happenstance archiving and sharing that camera phones and social media make possible—and their deployment in this context, they serve to reject the more spectacular scenes and stories that permeate the current visual and auricular economy of Black representation. As Cruz put it, for Black people, "the self-portrait, the selfie is political. It means I existed. This is a way of remembering that I was in the world. That other people were in the world."[72]

In the process, this assertion of Black presence through quotidian pictures also does away with what Nicole Fleetwood describes as the "iconicity" of Black image-making and consumption.[73] In place of the spectacular or the iconic, TBJP favors the powerfully mundane moments of Black social life—so powerful that "after a few weeks and a couple of moving responses," Cruz decided to "make [The Black Joy Project] a regular installation and share it more openly."[74] Cruz recognized the need he felt was one that traversed his network, a *need to* that had to include the different gradients of the Black experience. And at the center of that need was Black joy.

The image Cruz chose to formally launch his intervention to the public was the eyes-locked smiling face of a Black child, cheeks resting on the palm of their hands (fig. 4.4).[75] Alongside "this face," as one of the commenters put it, is a call to "bombard the internet with joy" so that we might "trigger love as much as pain." Love, Cruz writes, is "necessary," and imaging joy is meant to conjure love. In other words, evoking joy is a way to break, or at least diverge from, the pain and alienation historically linked to Blackness and the treatment of the Black body. Said another way, joy is a way to *practice* "making loving blackness possible," as bell hooks put it.[76] Returning to the picture, which Cruz tells me was sent to him by his twin brother Walter, the message suggests that it doesn't matter who the child is, where they are from, or where the photo takes place. We needn't, in this case, be concerned with what lies within the blur of the background, or the hand that appears just behind the child's shoulder. We don't even need to know who the photographer is. We needn't attempt to read this image for or as more than what it presents to us in the foreground. It is the *Black smile* that matters. It is the smile that offers a grammar that words could not.

For Cruz, the grammar of joy—the smile—is not just a choreography of love *amid* pain. As he wrote in the comment accompanying this image, joy is a kind of "resistance too." The use of resistance in this context moves parallel to, but is also distinct from, classical modes of

FIGURE 4.4. Black child smiling. Kleaver Cruz, The Black
Joy Project. Instagram.

political action usually marked by more overt steps *against* an oppressive person or system. The source, or existence of oppression, is intentionally left beyond the frame. What remains is the occasion for the
smile to breathe without juxtaposition.[77] This approach works to affirm
in Cruz's project the link between Black resistance and Black social life
dating back to when the first ships carrying human cargo set sail across
the Atlantic, the rebellion steeped in Black folks' ability to "be" in a
world where being is consistently in question and under siege. As Terrion Williamson reminds us, "to speak of black social life is to speak of
[the] radical capacity to live . . . even in the midst of all that brings death

close."[78] The work of The Black Joy Project is imbued with this radical capacity to live "in the midst," as are the space-making practices referenced by the makers of the *Black Joy Mixtape* and exacted by Party Noire, and the Black Joy Experience.

The Beloved Community

If The Black Joy Project's origins suggest both a personal need and a collective haunt, tending to the "collective" is where these images really show their political significance. As Cruz explains, being in community is important, and being in conversation is "powerful." Addressing Blackness through images of joy is a way to "heal without needing to leave the group"; it is a way to hold and embrace one another rather than retreat inward. It also acts as a mechanism to "give a space for people in communities that don't always have a voice."[79] Cruz identifies as queer, which plays a crucial role in his experience of Blackness and marginalization. It also places his desire to give voice to those often silenced or ignored through TBJP in line with the movement's broader posture of centering the historically marginalized: of valuing their experiences and celebrating their lives. This centering operates on two basic levels that track alongside the project's development from its inception in 2015 until the present. Taken in tandem, they demonstrate Cruz's approach to Black joy through TBJP as an attempt at consciousness-raising or group consciousness in the wake: a way of "developing a sense of 'us' that creates shared affect" and "a shared notion of what it means to be in the group."[80] In this case, the shared meaning is premised on the power of, and in, Black joy, that Blackness is worthy of celebration— that *we* are worthy.

The first and most immediate level is Cruz's decision to create and make public TBJP, to begin with, the decision to "bombard the internet with joy" through examples drawn from his own life and experiences. These images are accompanied by simple and often affecting descriptions of the images' content. Who is in the picture, what is taking place, where they are, and so on. Take, for example, the previously mentioned image of the Black elder. In the comment to the post, Cruz writes: "earlier this

FIGURE 4.5. A Black elder. Kleaver Cruz, The Black Joy Project. Instagram.

year after a #BlackSpring action in Harlem, we ended with a drum circle at the State Building Plaza. This beautiful elder was there (fig. 4.5). There was freedom in her dance and liberation in each beat of the drums." In presenting the images with to-the-point yet personal and emotive descriptions like this one, Cruz makes clear his desire to organize more people around the quotidian experiences of Black life, or to put it somewhat differently: the spectacular within the mundane, and the often-unrecognized knowledge of freedom that emanates in and through Black movements, gestures, and being more generally.[81]

The second level is in the project's move away from Cruz's reflections and experience toward a more direct engagement with what Black joy means to others: the moment when, as Cruz describes it, he "started asking the people around [him], instead of just looking at pictures [he] had, or people [he would] hang out with."[82] In this way, Cruz does more than simply encourage images of Black joy; he also promotes a conversation about it. TBJP attempts to build a community that practices and pursues Black joy as a common language, one with potentially different but nonetheless parallel interpretations of its meaning and importance.

As with his personal images, this is evidenced in the direct quotes Cruz posts to accompany the portraits of his subjects. They point toward a shared understanding among the people Cruz captures with his camera around not only what Black joy *is* but what it has been conditioned *by* and positioned *against*. Consider the following examples. "Black joy and black mourning are inherently tied. There is joy in the mourning just as there is mourning in the joy. Black joy is always intermeshed with the knowledge of survival, but that makes it potent." And: "Black Joy is everything else outside of white supremacy. All the possibilities outside of it. All of our potential for happiness outside of white supremacy." Lastly: "Black Joy is the free expression that comes from recognizing the love that our ancestors have allowed us to embody in the face of oppression." Each of these quotes, in their manner, signals the relationship between Black joy, Black pain, and Black death as they are implicated in and produced by white supremacy and anti-Blackness. Further, each signals a crucial relationship with the past. On the one hand, it links joy in the present to a history of suffering. On the other, it connects a legacy of survival born from that history. Finally, each of them suggests futurity and a mode of speculation mapped by and through practices of joy.

On this latter point, as Elizabeth Currans writes, the futures that practices of joy make possible are not primarily meant to signal a utopia "free from [all] pain or struggle."[83] Instead, they are "futures in which the sedimented legacies of oppression and privilege have begun to erode, allowing for new ways of being, individually and collectively," what Paul Gilroy might call a "politics of transfiguration."[84] As a result, they are futures that can be inhabited in and through what is built in the present, premised in part on an acknowledgment of anti-Blackness and other intersecting strategies of persecution and division that permeate the social world. From this frame, Black joy—its place in the current movement and its importance to the politics of the wake—is as much about imagining otherwise as it is about embodying and performing that possibility in the here and now. It is about cultivating a "beloved community," as Martin Luther King Jr. once named it, that can serve as a model for a kind of sociality, for care that can extend beyond Black people—"beyond" even as it is inextricably linked to and born out of Blackness.

This second level has an additional dimension: Cruz's desire to not only ground conversations around Black joy within the United States but pursue it throughout the Black Diaspora. As Hesse and Hooker note:

> Globally, black protest movements originating from local concerns are responding in different ways to the inability of liberal democracy to deliver robust racial justice and inviolable equal rights, drawing attention to the unfinished project of decolonization and the unrelenting dehumanization of black lives resulting from the precarity induced by global white supremacy.[85]

Black pain and death are not, nor have they ever been, a uniquely American or even Western experience. Anti-Blackness is global, and the rejection of it by contemporary Black mobilizations ranges from Brazil to the United Kingdom, to South Africa and beyond. Attending to this worldwide reality has been an aim of not only TBJP but the movement as a whole.

Nevertheless, that anti-Blackness is a shared logic with similar mechanisms of deployment across the globe does not mean that the experience of Blackness for Black people is the same. To this end, TBJP understands Black joy to be an essential contribution to a "revolutionary practice" that can act "in excess of the centrality of the state" and the locally specific violence that this brings about.[86] Like the Black radical tradition that is both its heritage and inheritance, Black joy runs counter to normative notions of Western thought. It is therefore positioned on the front line of the effort to dismantle the capitalist world system by harnessing the power of joy to act as a deterritorialized form of Black mobilization and political action.[87] For Cruz, who is Dominican, Black joy can produce fugitive affinities that bring the Diaspora together across the artifice of borders to heal in the name of all Black life, while still holding the complexities of our differences. These affinities provide opportunities to learn with and from each other horizontally, by letting people "speak for themselves." They are opportunities to deepen our cultural and historical understanding, sharpen our analysis, and develop and strengthen our strategies and tactics, all toward becoming something greater than what we are.

Along with various destinations within the United States and its territories like Puerto Rico, Cruz has taken TBJP to or received images from Brazil, Cuba, Belgium, France, Mexico, England, South Africa, the Netherlands, and Trinidad and Tobago. In each instance, TBJP has sought to cultivate understanding and connection through an acknowledgment of what we share, along with what makes us different. Through the Diasporic pursuit of Black joy, TBJP avers to be a place for "all those things to exist" in their multiplicity. As Cruz has put it, "There is a freedom in expressing and naming Black joy, and I want it for all Black people around the world."[88]

TBJP signals the necessity of Black joy in the wake. This necessity is premised not merely on joy's ability to allow us to balance and counteract Black pain, though this is a crucial part. It is also a tool for building community, for basking in the glow of Blackness in all its possibilities, not only as individuals but as an "imaginary unified" collective.[89] Because much like the affecting resonances produced during the recitation of the Power chant Gabby led during the retreat, when Black people start putting our minds together, that's when the ground begins to shake.

But for such a community to thrive, for it not to topple over onto itself when the shaking begins, the intramural ground beneath our feet must itself be stable. Black joy is an empty gesture unless it encompasses a real embrace of the different ways Joy is expressed and by whom.

The Dance of the Disposable

If on a Saturday night in the summer of 2019 you happened to walk down Wycoff Avenue toward Hancock Street in the Bushwick neighborhood of Brooklyn, you likely passed Luv Story, a "low-key, neighborhood hangout with beer pong tables, bar bites, old-school video games & live music."[90] A typical Brooklyn bar, or so you'd think.

If on a Saturday night in the summer of 2019, in the fall of that year, or in the winter, just before the Covid-19 pandemic took hold, you walked past Luv Story en route to a destination only you could name, and your ears caught wind of big blaring beats, while out of the corner of your eye you saw flashing lights of green and red, you'd be forgiven for assuming that the bar you were passing, that what was transpiring inside, was just another instance of people enjoying another weekend, drinking to wash away the atomized alienation capitalism produces. In fact, let's say you're off to do the same.

What you wouldn't have seen, what you would've necessarily missed and couldn't possibly know, was that later that evening, in the bar you just passed, there'd be a twerk contest: Black trans and queer bottoms bouncing onstage for ten seconds with only one able to take home the cash prize. You would have missed Black trans and queer folks getting low, grinding, flaunting, sweating. You would have missed Black trans and queer folks free.

From June 2019 through March 2020, Luv Story was the home of "A Ratchet Realm": "a party with a Politic that celebrates the liberation of Black Queer and Trans folx," an experience conceived, curated, and hosted by Jewel Cadet, otherwise known as "Jewel the Gem," whom I organized with for a time in BYP100. As she tells it, "A Ratchet Realm" is an "homage to the loud homegirls from the hood with colorful hair, big hoops, tattoos, piercings, and long nails. The ones who were told we were too 'ghetto.'" More than just a typical party, Cadet frames the event as a politically minded, intentional space, one that, in the spirit of radical inclusivity:

> celebrates all body sizes and abilities as people get their lives on the dance floor! In "A Ratchet Realm" you will find tongues out, backs arched, knees to the floor and straight-up BLACK JOY on people's

faces as Trap, R&B, Reggae, and Bounce is played by Black Women and Femme DJs. The Twerk contest and the musical performances by Black Queer and TGNC talent provides an additional unapologetic ratchet flavor to this space; one that is bold, raunchy, and audacious. In these parties, people are free to be their full selves. Societal norms are left at the door and people come alive to the sound of the music and the vibrations of being among the community.[91]

The community vibrations she points to signal the eclipse of socially prescribed restraint, the shunning of shame, and the celebration of self, fashioned collectively on the dance floor. They are examples of what Aliyyah Abdur-Rahman calls the "Black ecstatic," which she conceptualizes as "black queer attachments, affective dispositions, political aspirations, and representational practices that punctuate the awful now with the joys and possibilities of the beyond (of alternate worlds and ways)."[92]

Following a path paved by the Black and Brown pioneers of "queer nightlife," those wayward assemblages "staged in the variety of permanent, temporary, static, and mobile sites that queer people congregate in to get relief from the pressures of everyday life," Black LGBTQ+ organizers and cultural workers in the time of #BlackLivesMatter have created and cultivated liberatory spaces to honor and take pleasure in what society demands be hidden or thrown away.[93] I read "A Ratchet Realm," and the use of the term "ratchet" itself, derived from the word "wretched" and previously deployed to describe "unruly" Black women, as a practice of refusal that channels the sensual experience of Black joy to not only imagine but enact a world otherwise.

The party's jubilant articulation of freedom—the twerks, the splits, the sweat—helps foster a community in which Black LGBTQ+ folks feel seen and safe; it represents "an immediate space of relational joy" wherein "the future is both yet to come and already past" (fig. 4.6).[94] In that sense, "A Ratchet Realm" instills a will to be ungoverned, what Eric Stanley calls an "abolitionist way of life," one that necessarily extends beyond the event itself and points to the radical futurity of being in a world that isn't premised on notions of respectability or capitalist definitions of value, a world without the threat of Black premature death.[95] For Stanley, ungovernability must be understood as "an organized yet

FIGURE 4.6. "A Ratchet Realm." Jamilah Felix. Instagram.

improvisational practice in common that revels in pleasure and expropriation, whose aim is to collectivize exposure towards that exposure's
abolition.[96] "Ratchet," as one illustration of ungovernability, much like
Blackness, marks more than the body. It outlines a way of seeing, being,
and thinking "in common," an embodied analytic for envisioning and
inhabiting an alternative future in the here and now, for willing it into
existence.

However, the question we're forced to confront when thinking about
"A Ratchet Realm" is the same problem that shadows the space-making
praxis of Black joy—the conditions that make and have made such
spaces necessary in the first place. The answer is a deathly recurrence,
the "atmosphere of violence" that "threatens, and at times erupts into
the deadly force that not only kills but makes life unlivable" in ways that
analyses of anti-Blackness alone cannot address.[97]

～～～

"A Black transgender woman was found dead." "A Black transgender
woman was fatally shot." "A Black transgender woman was killed." This

implacable repetition consumes the efforts of the Human Rights Campaign (HRC) to track what they term the "epidemic" of violence against the transgender community. The specificity of their narrative is telling. According to the HRC, there were at least (they stress "at least" because the true number can't be known) fifty-seven transgender or gender nonconforming people fatally shot or killed by other violent means.[98] In 2020, the year of the uprisings, and the historic rally for Black trans lives in front of the Brooklyn Museum, HRC tallied a then record number of fatal incidents against transgender and gender nonconforming (TGNC) folks: a total of forty-four deaths. As in the previous years, the vast majority of those killed were Black transgender women. If anti-Black terror is inscribed in the foundation of the world system, so too is violence against the Black TGNC community, particularly women. And that violence is not only perpetrated by the state. Take the following example from 2019: Muhlaysia Booker was struck from behind. Off-white gloves shielding her assailant's hands paired perfectly with the white of his clothing. The sum of this ensemble made for a sharp contrast with his Black skin as he delivered blows to Muhlaysia's Black face, first straddling her body, then hovering over top, before she stumbled to a stand. That Edward Thomas was wearing gloves at all suggests he planned the encounter, which occurred after a minor car accident in the parking lot of the Royal Crest, a low-income apartment complex in Dallas, Texas. The two hundred dollars later found tucked away in his pocket provided further evidence. The attack was deliberate, commissioned, and paid for. For him, it might have been an honest buck. For her, it was another humiliation in a long line of others, carried out by people within her own community, people among whom she lived.

While the initial blow knocked Muhlaysia down, the subsequent punches, thrown with the force of a prizefighter, likely caused the concussion she suffered. It might also be responsible for her fractured wrist, itself a consequence, no doubt, of her attempts to stave off the beating. Then again, perhaps it was the result of the kicks of enthusiastic disdain provided by the other Black men who circled around the pavement waltz, Black men who might have otherwise intervened. One such man stretched his arms out to back onlookers away. Presumably, this was so the others, hard at work, could carry out their task undisturbed or, more generously, to prevent someone else from mistakenly receiving the beating intended for Muhlaysia alone. After all, the rain of kicks, punches, and homophobic slurs that soaked her body that afternoon offer a clear narrative of justified subjection. She was a Black transgender woman, and they wanted "that faggot out of [their] hood."[99]

The assault continued until several women were able to drag Muhlaysia's unconscious body to safety, recover her shoes from the parking lot, and get her to a hospital. A week or so after the incident, she addressed a small crowd of supporters at a rally, stating as she fought back tears, "This time it was me, the next time it could be someone else. Our time to seek justice is now. If not now, when?" A month later, Muhlaysia Booker was dead, found facedown in the street with a gunshot wound to the skull. According to police, the trigger was pulled by Kendrell Lavar Lyles, another Black man.

Neither the events at the Royal Crest nor the murder that followed should be thought of as spectacular. Though our present may well be a "time of LGBT inclusion," as Stanley notes, "the time of LGBT inclusion is also a time of trans/queer death."[100] In fact, if not for the viral video of the assault (the basis of my narration), there would be significantly fewer utterances of her name, Muhlaysia Booker, another Black trans woman's life recognized now primarily through the prism of death. Her beating and her murder are, however, reflective of the way Black trans women have come to represent a negation of the negation that the world calls Blackness. And this subject-position is imparted on them not simply by an anti-Black, patriarchal, transphobic, and homophobic regime of dominance but from within the Black intramural itself.

The tragedy of these premature deaths, like that of Muhlaysia, along with the ignored or incorrectly reported others unknowable in number, underscore a truth too often ignored. The peril and precarity that haunt all Black life casts a particularly dark cloud over the Black LGBTQ+ community. Subject to the baseline logic of anti-Blackness, these lives are rendered doubly disposable, and not merely by those who see LGBTQ+ bodies as outside the lines of respectability, a worldview governed by a toxic mixture of heteronormativity and transphobia. They are likewise held captive by a capitalist economy that demands work but limits opportunities for Black folks who choose not to deny the fullness of their selfhood, their pleasure and desire, leaving them exposed to a spiral of vulnerability. But from within the brutality of this spiral, and against a world system contingent on Black pain, "rapturous joy," the "aesthetic performance of embrace, the sanctuary of the unuttered and unutterable, and a mode of pleasurable reckoning with everyday ruin" Abdur-Rahman calls the Black ecstatic, becomes a practice of "interdependency otherwise."[101] It becomes a practice of care.

Spaces like "A Ratchet Realm," the sights and sounds of queer nightlife that, though "inseparable from the oftentimes violent political economies within which they emerge," nevertheless celebrate the liberation of Black queer and trans folks, are an essential breeding ground for ungovernability, not simply in or toward a future world to come but for the sake of Black joy in the present tense.[102] They provide and nurture a basis for living and embodying an abolitionist way of life that extends beyond the party, beyond the walls of a typical Brooklyn bar. Asanni York, a Black, gender nonconforming organizer and the founder of "For the Gworls," which is a collective that uses mutual-aid parties to help "Black transgender people pay their rent and get gender-affirming surgeries" by giving money directly to those in need, manifests the ethos and power of these parties precisely in their intended manner:

> I express my full self in my everyday life by not allowing the world to tell me how I need to show up—I tell the world how I need to show up, and it has no choice but to listen. I dress how I want and where I want; I wear my hair how I want; I present how I want. Whether I am at work, on the train, or at an event, I show up as Asanni—unapologetically Black; unapologetically bending the rigid rules patriarchy tries to impose on me and other Black people; unapologetically me.[103]

To this I'd add that Asanni's embodied practice, as an example of what queer nightlife makes possible, bends if not breaks patriarchy's rigid rules altogether and breaking the rules should be our objective.

During the twerk contest, or when folks are grinding, sweating, and "getting their life on the dance floor," when the crowd excitedly looks on while chanting in unison, louder and louder: *"Fuck it up! Fuck it up! Fuck it up! Fuck it up!"*: they're talking about how to live, breathe, move, and, most importantly, love yourself with and through community in a world system that prefers to see you dead than thrive. It's a pedagogical practice and therefore a mode of pedagogical speech about being in the wake, or what Cathy Cohen has called a politics of deviance, one that allows Black trans and queer folks, those on the margins of the margins, to "not only counter or challenge the presiding normative order with regard to sex, and desire, but also create new or counter normative frameworks."[104]

Ratchet, then, is a Black joy–infused counternormative framework positioned to disrupt and undo all that prevents us from finding love and light, pleasure, and desire in ourselves, all that prevents us from seeking and finding all of those things in each other. It is, to borrow from Saidiya Hartman, "an entry on the possible" in opposition to society's enclosures.[105] Similar to the term "wayward," "ratchet" is definitionally akin to and finds common cause with "the family of words: errant, fugitive, recalcitrant, anarchic, willful, reckless, troublesome, riotous, tumultuous rebellious, and wild," words that signal a threat that must be contained.[106] Following suit, to enter "A Ratchet Realm" is to "inhabit the world in ways inimical to those deemed proper and respectable, to be deeply aware of the gulf between where you stayed and how you might live" if free to always do so on your own terms.[107] Ratchet, the loud girls from the hood with colorful hair, big hoops, tattoos, piercings, and long nails. The ones who were told they were too "ghetto," as Cadet reminds us, names the way Black life, and particularly Black LGTBQ+ life, gestures to how we might live, how liberation might look and feel. Because of this ability to point us toward somewhere else, somewhere not yet here, "A Ratchet Realm" participates in, and was itself an illustration of, the operations of care, upholding care's political and ethical commitments, with and through the wake. And how, exactly, might liberation look and feel? Jewel Cadet may have said it best: "tongues out, backs arched, knees to the floor and straight-up BLACK JOY."

CHAPTER 5

The Operation(s) of Care

We are each other's
harvest:
we are each other's
business:
we are each other's
magnitude and bond.

—GWENDOLYN BROOKS

We are making the future as well as bonding to survive the enormous pressures of the present, and that is what it means to be a part of history.

—AUDRE LORDE

Cranes in the Sky

Nov 8, 2016, 11:08pm[1]
D: ugh
S: Y'all this is not fucking good.
E: At all
E: He just won FL
St: The most anxious I've been in years. These numbers are weighing heavy on my heart. I'm confused y'all

J: This is a nightmare

E: Yep. Just violence displayed on a screen.

Nov 8, 2016, 11:39pm[2]

C: I love y'all. We've been through worse and we will get through whatever comes, for real

S: Y'all I think I was willfully blind. But I actually did not think that the country hated people like me enough to elect a literal openly racist nationalist.

S: AND YET HERE WE ARE

Nov 9, 2016, 1:59am

R: I love you all

Nov 9, 2016, 1:59am

Ra: I love you like you was me. And I mean that. Stay safe tonight y'all

Ct: I love yall.

Nov 9, 2016, 2:18am

F: Loves, let's go, how we uniting, organizing for change? We have each other.

~~~

Several days later, in a Brooklyn backyard, a group of us assembled around a worn-white table and a scattering of chairs for a healing circle over the comforting seasonal crunch of red, green, and yellow leaves. Through the speakers, rim taps followed the heavy thumps of a kick drum. The hi-hat shutter broke through our silence as the strings' slow swell matched the cadence of our purpose. The swirl of burning bundles of sage cleansed and grounded the invocation,[3] enhanced shortly after when the first verse of Solange's "Cranes in the Sky" began:

I tried to drink it away
I tried to put one in the air
I tried to dance it away
I tried to change it with my hair.[4]

Donald Trump's surprise victory—everything it represented and magnified about the country's commitment to anti-Blackness, white supremacy, and heteropatriarchy—felt like a punch to the face. That there'd be a particularly emotional response to the election of an "openly racist nationalist" by Black folks encountering the results as "violence displayed on a screen" should not be mistaken as a latent belief in the redemptive power of the state or the presidency, dashed by the soon-to-be occupant of the Oval Office.[5] The Obama years made clear, if there were doubts, that the presidency and the state, regardless of who runs them, are instruments of the same structural logic that has oppressed Black people for centuries.[6] Instead, the anguish reads clearest when thought of in the context of Black pain and death. Just months after the murder of Philando Castile and following the steady accumulation of dead Black bodies since Trayvon Martin's killing, the willful embrace of a man promoting a political agenda driven by white grievance and racial resentment further proved America's continued disregard for Black life and the impossibility of things being otherwise without transformative change.

Given the pernicious and pervasive force of anti-Blackness before and after the election, and no good reason to believe better days might be on the horizon, the healing circle was a moment to remember that, if nothing else, "we have each other." This feeling, the idea that Black people often *have each other*, and that perhaps each other is *all we have*, gives breath to what anchors the politics of the wake in the time of #BlackLivesMatter: an ethics of care. For "Black non/being in the world," to use Christina Sharpe's formulation, care is not a "metaphor" or a moral sentiment but an assemblage of methods that "shape, refuse, inform, [and] speak back to material conditions."[7] These conditions are defined by anti-Blackness, and its entanglement with racial capitalism, but they are also expressed within the enclosures of cis heteropatriarchy and the carceral logic of the liberal state. An ethics of care made manifest through a praxis of interdependence that recognizes the self in relation to the collective, and the collective in relation to the self, works to undermine the legitimacy of the sociopolitical past and present—slavery, coloniality, and their afterlives—along with the ideologies that sustain them.

In this context, care must be understood as a form of study that, if practiced properly, gives way to a concrete analysis of where things stand, the "enormous pressure of the present," to use Audre Lorde's words, in order to grasp how best to proceed.[8] Such an analysis requires us, in the first instance, to be vigilant about how Black pain and the structural violence(s) of the past come to bear on our ability to navigate our day-to-day now, and in the future, even as we refuse to allow it to dominate or define us in any complete sense.[9] Black joy tells us as much. Nevertheless, violence and pain are constitutive to the form and function of the capitalist world system, which makes them impossible to redress or eliminate within its purview, what Calvin Warren describes as our current "cultural space of ethics, relationality, and the sacred."[10] In the face of this cultural space, and its ability to mystify its extractive and exploitative agenda, "Black care," to borrow Warren's framing, represents a "network of strategies aimed at circulating, communicating, and sharing" slavery's lasting imprint—the oscillation between Black life and Black death—"as a vehicle for endurance" while we sharpen our knives and plot our escape.[11]

If we take escape seriously, if we channel the spirit of insurrection offered to us by the revolutionary Black slave, the same spirit that set fire to the Minneapolis Third Police Precinct during the uprisings in 2020, it should be clear that the goal of this ethics of care is not simply to endure the world as it is or to be content with carving out pockets of reprieve, even as such pockets are, at times, a necessity. It is a world undone, a project that seeks nothing less than mustering the collective will to wrestle away from the precepts of Western modernity, such that it becomes possible to see and refuse its penchant for destruction and decay, the consequences of which fall disproportionately on Black, Brown, and Indigenous communities, but also distorts and undermines freedom for all. None of us have every truly been free.

Without question, the way forward will be littered with landmines, some visible, some buried beneath the surface. But, in the final analysis, we are our own biggest threat. To prepare for the possibility of explosion, especially those unintended eruptions that emerge from unresolved harm, it's necessary to understand that the process and practice of undoing the world and our relationship to it are precisely that, a process, to be learned and experimented with through trial and error, where error often provides valuable lessons about how much of the road we have left to travel, particularly when it comes to how we treat each other.

In what follows, I consider the operation(s) of care circulating in the time of #BlackLivesMatter. The operations I sketch include approaches to healing—many reflecting a commitment to African epistemologies—and attempts to create spaces and share resources, images, and sounds to help shoulder pain, adjudicate harm, and promote joy, all in an effort to abolish the institutions, and the parts of ourselves, that function according to the paradigms of the world as it is so that we might more ably move closer toward creating the conditions to bring about a Black future.

We Must Love and Support Each Other

The election results were not originally the occasion for our gathering. At the time, BYP100 NYC typically held chapter meetings every other Sunday. Chapter meetings bring together both active and prospective members to discuss, provide updates about, and, when necessary, vote on the chapter's work and overall direction. Generally, our meetings opened with a check-in question, such as: "What is something that has brought you joy this week?" Then we proceeded with the day's agenda and, more often than not, closed out with the Assata chant, a call-and-response named after its author, the revolutionary freedom fighter Assata Shakur.

It is our duty to fight for our freedom.
It is our duty to win.
We must love each other and support each other.
We have nothing to lose but our chains[12]

Unlike other meetings, however, it was decided that November 13 would be a potluck and kick-back.[13] In proposing the idea, chapter leadership wanted a setting that would allow us to eclipse the formalities of a typical meeting. The goal, as I understood it, was to create space for members to get to know each other better: to eat, drink, and chill as a collective even as we maintained our overall desire to map our way closer to something like liberation. "Knowing," in this case, was not only about building a stronger rapport. It was also about establishing trust: trusting that the people you organize with were ready and willing to "throw down" when needed, that they would be willing to take arrest alongside you or help pack the court on your behalf.[14] It was about knowing they were willing to spend long hours talking through and often disagreeing about strategy, and that these disagreements would be principled instead of personal.[15] It was about trusting that they were willing to hold you accountable and be held accountable themselves. It was about knowing your comrades were ready to show up for you when the weight of the work proved too heavy.

To "know," in this way, is an essential aspect of successful organizing, organizations, and institution building in a general sense, just as solidarity and trust greatly contributed to community cohesion among the slaves, helping give rise to rebellion. But driving the desire to (re)establish trust in this instance were ongoing cycles of interpersonal conflict, political disappointment, and the fallout both produced. Though at the time I'd been a chapter member for only nine months, I'd already witnessed how these cycles of conflict, much of them lingering and unresolved, eroded trust between members and in the chapter itself. The problems ranged from the immediately actionable to those that were more deeply imbedded in and sourced from a social order premised on capitalist social relations. Intimate partner violence, abuse between members, and how those abuses were handled by chapter and national leadership were arguably the most damaging. Not far behind, however, was the (largely accurate) perception that trans-identifying members were not being centered and, to some extent, were being silenced, despite the organizational rhetoric to the contrary. Then there were all the ways toxic, masculinist behaviors were permeating our spaces in contradiction to our values, behaviors that were not only carried out by men, given that the social and cultural logic of masculinity is learned. More broadly, we needed to address the justifiable frustration that male-identifying members were not doing enough to show up for Black women and Black LGTBQ+ folks after their murders. Nor were we doing enough (and I include myself here) to help shoulder the emotional labor of the chapter, particularly in the face of frequent images and reports of Black premature death, labor that generally fell to women and femme-identifying members—the "hidden abode" of Black organizing.[16]

It should come as no surprise that these conflicts mirror or were triggered by the intramural violence and aggression that have long taken place in the Black community along the gradients of class, gender, and sexuality. They were deeply enmeshed in the trauma of secondary marginalization members experienced—often but not exclusively female-identifying and TGNC members—in their everyday lives at the hands of other Black people, to say nothing of the disregard the rest of the world shows them. The anger and hurt members felt, as a result, naturally showed up and reproduced itself during chapter meetings, dialogues, and functions. Harm had a way of diminishing what many viewed as one of the only spaces they could safely (learn how to) be their full Black selves and, on a practical level, made organizing that much more difficult. Returning to Our Streets/Our Bodies/Our Voices adds clarity to this last point. In recounting why the campaign, though successful in her estimation, wasn't as "big" as it could have been, Ain Raven Ealey explained that, at the end of the day, "there were people who, because of personal issues or debacles didn't show up and their roles were super important . . . and I was like, damn, this isn't like what the [Assata] chant says, this isn't protecting, supporting, and loving each other at all. I'm like, at least show up for the work."[17] For Ealey, not showing up because of issues with others was to renege on the duty Assata taught us to honor, our duty to fight for our freedom.

The political frustration was equally vexing, if not less personally charged. Some members felt the chapter's structure and leadership reproduced hierarchies that our political lens was meant to disrupt. For them, core leadership, as it was known, lacked transparency when it came to making decisions on behalf of the chapter in ways that made accountability for those decisions and their subsequent impact on our work difficult to exact. In other words, the deliberative and horizontal plantation politics that were the foundation of leadership models promoted by organizers like Ella Baker and pursued in the organizational structure of youth-led organizations like the Student Nonviolent Coordinating Committee (SNCC) appeared as symbolic rather than evidenced in our everyday practices.

Similar concerns about accountability and transparency were leveled at the national organization, especially when it came to decisions about its overall direction and the degree to which the values we claimed aligned with the actions we took and were taking. On the one hand, these critiques revolved around the organization not being sufficiently "radical," in part because it was too enmeshed in the world of nonprofits and their associated structures to support and promote an abolitionist and anti-capitalist agenda guided by Black queer feminist praxis. The relationship between BYP100 and the M4BL organizational ecosystem was also a point of contention, insofar as the latter was seen as taking public positions that did not fully reflect the views of all BYP100 members. At the time, at least, there were no real attempts to garner buy-in or consider objections.

A few of these instances played out publicly through social media, fanning the flames of the issue, the embers of which remain to this day. Since January 2021, for example, several BYP100 chapters have severed their relationship with the organization, citing, among other things, the organization's engagement with electoral politics, lack of transparency around budgeting, interpersonal harm, and an unwillingness to make space for, or adequately engage, substantive critique. These issues are by no means exclusive to BYP100. In late November 2020, following the summer of uprisings and, subsequently, a dramatic uptick in donations to movement organizations, ten local chapters of the Black Lives Matter Global Network (BLMGN), known as the BLM 10 (now the BLM 10 Plus), publicly broke with the organization over a similar lack of transparency and accountability, especially when it came to money.[18] As they wrote in a subsequent statement released in June 2021:

> The issues we raise are bigger than simple complaints about individual leaders, but about the ways liberalism and capitalism have

manifested in BLMGN and the current iteration of the Black liberation movement as a whole, co-opting and deradicalizing this critical
historic moment of revolutionary possibility.[19]

In both instances, the demand for transparency and accountability reflects what had been a growing tension that can be traced back to at least
2016, and in the case of BYP100 NYC, the decision to have a kick-back
instead of the usual chapter meeting.

So, beyond a general belief in establishing deeper ties to bolster our
organizing work, there was an equally urgent need to create the kind of
environment that would make it possible to constructively address and
move beyond some of the chapter's internal contradictions.[20] But as the
kick-back approached and the election results became apparent, there
was a general understanding among some of us that the tenor we initially
imagined needed to be different, that we would have to ground and re-
orient ourselves to a new, unexpected political dynamic beyond our
control. We carried this need collectively, knowing its traces would be
borne on our faces, hinted in our laughter, and suggested in our tone.
The afternoon of the meeting, before the mac-and-cheese and soy-
soaked brussels sprouts; the veggie lasagna and rotisserie chicken; the
chips, dips, and doughnuts; the rum, vodka, champagne, and assorted
mixers; we gathered in the backyard to summon the strength to heal
and find joy in and against a world that continuously demonstrates its
need to, and pleasure in, causing us—and all Black people—harm.

At the outset, the healing circle's facilitators—Jewel Cadet, the cura-
tor of "A Ratchet Realm," and Charlie, a NYC chapter member at the
time—asked us to name and "lift up" someone whom we'd turned to—
in actuality or remembrance—during the difficult week after Election
Day. From the table, Jewel picked up a large pitcher of water filled to the
brim. The water had two functions: to honor the source of support we
identified and to invite them, in spirit, to participate in our healing. This
aspect of the circle evoked the ancient libation pouring ritual, which
is global in its origins and performance, including West African cultures
and religions that then found a place in the cultural practices of the
plantation. The latter was BYP100's point of reference. One by one, we

held the pitcher close to our bodies, conjured our names (silently or aloud), and poured a splash of water to the ground as the rest recited in unison, "Ashe," before passing the pitcher clockwise to the next person.[21] The still of the moment, the simultaneity of sadness and strength, it was a somber ritual of pain, recognition, and care. But the ceremony did not end on that note.

After the pitcher made the rounds, another facilitator—Je Naé Taylor, at the time a member of the DC chapter as well as what was then known as BYP100's Healing and Safety Council—commanded the circle's attention.[22] Her mission was to complete the healing process on an uplifting note. To do this, she began by recounting an anecdote of loss not attached to the present moment. Instead, it was from the past, a Black child in one of her classes who was killed in 2012. Fighting back tears, Je Naé proceeded to teach us all a chant she'd written and introduced to her students to help her and them get through the pain of her student's premature death, one that, as she explained, still provides her and others uplift: "I Love Being Black."[23] It started slowly as a call-and-response but gradually picked up energy and volume until everyone was singing as if the song was their own, because for many of us that day it was:

> I love being black
> I said I love being black
> I said I love being black
> I said I love . . .
>
> I love the color of my skin
> Cuz it's the skin that I'm in
> I love the texture of my hair
> And I will rock it everywhere
>
> I love being black
> I said I love being black
> I said I love being black
> I said I love . . .

The chant-turned-song seems, in retrospect, a fitting way to conclude the ritual. It permitted us to set aside, even if temporarily, what the election meant—the hurt that it caused—and what a President Trump would likely bring about by creating room for both self and collective care and affirmation: "I love being Black." Like the healing ceremony and the kick-back itself, the chant was a refusal—to be weighed down by pain and struggle, to be overcome by contradictions, even though it was necessary to acknowledge them first. It was an active choice to care— for ourselves and each other. With and through that care, we were able to find some semblance of joy and to celebrate Black being in the wake.

~~~

The ceremony marked a turning point in my understanding of the culture of the movement and its relationship to the past. I began thinking more deeply about the place of healing, altars, rituals, ancestor veneration, and, more broadly, African cosmology and how this aligned with the dual emphasis on self-care and mental health I'd been observing for some time. They all represent an expression and practice of care. Just as importantly, however, they are tools sourced from African traditions and Black folk culture to acknowledge and move through pain and trauma in a way that not only refuses (white) Western practices and knowledge but does away with them altogether in search of something else. Through their performance, we assert a sense of belonging, a shared membership in and spiritual and political devotion to the continuum that is the Black Diaspora, and the force of the Diaspora's critique. In that sense, communing with ancestors, returning to and adopting African and Black folk practices, is a process and practice of undoing toward a remade spiritual world in the here and now and a path toward the yet to come.

Honoring Blackness

A world undone is an aspiration requiring individual vigilance and collective understanding, especially given how deeply rooted, long-lasting, and all-encompassing violence against Black people and Black communities has been. Feelings of pain and trauma extend far beyond one's singular experience, even as their markings appear most pronounced on the individual Black body and how we subsequently interact with others. These affective states are also collective and generational. They represent the lasting consequences of slavery and colonialism as a shared memory enacted and responded to in the present.[24] The viral visibility of Black death marks the series of violations that have created what Elizabeth Alexander calls the Trayvon generation.[25] The ensuing experience of trauma has become a community narrative warranting a community response. Since Trayvon Martin's murder in 2012 and the subsequent emergence of #BlackLivesMatter in 2013, this narrative has helped fortify a sense of being "a people" among younger Black folks, though equipped with new ways of approaching and embodying the full spectrum of Blackness.

Yet, as the internal conflicts that roiled BYP100 NYC before (and after) our healing ceremony suggest, pain and trauma are not tied to a sense of "bottom-line blackness" alone. We cannot reduce them entirely to how anti-Blackness has impacted Black people's lives as if we are all the same. Instead, we must not shy away from the way pain and trauma are also deeply connected to the violence that has stemmed from—and continues to plague—gender, sexuality, and class-based differences, beyond but especially within the Black intramural. To truly begin healing from these harms and avoid repeating them, as Audre Lorde instructs, "we must allow each other our differences at the same time as we recognize our sameness."[26] To repair and increase our ability to practice care as both a political and ethical commitment to a world undone, we must develop the capacity to attend to differences, along whatever lines they may be drawn, with careful attention and a commitment to being held accountable.

It is here, in this ethic, that the influence of Black feminism shines particularly bright and demonstrates that the arc of Black political development—in the late twentieth century at least—has in large part advanced through the interventions of Black study and feminist praxis, because, again, care must be seen and pursued as a form of study. After all, it was a specified and experientially based analytic within Black radical thought—promoted by Black women and anchored in care for the Black lives lived on the margins of the margins—that most forcefully sought to address the entanglements of identity within the Black community. It was Black radical feminism that demonstrated how those identities, and the conflicts they produce, were intrinsically linked to power. It was Black radical feminism that put forth the argument that if we understand oppression to be interconnected across various nodes of difference, so too is our collective liberation.

Lorde's meditation on difference and remembrance during her 1982 speech, "Learning from the 60s," delivered at Harvard's "Malcolm X Weekend," provides a useful frame and foundation. Lorde reminds us that "in the 1960s, the awakened anger of the Black community was often expressed, not vertically against the corruption of power and true sources of control over our lives, but *horizontally* toward those closest to us who mirrored our own impotence."[27] In her view, the 1960s marked a particularly telling though by no means unique moment. The power of Black mobilization, fueled by shifts in Black people's self-understanding, was ultimately undermined by the "scars of oppression that lead us to war against *ourselves in each other* rather than against our enemies."[28] Lorde's point here is not to say that these scars led Black people to withhold their fire against anti-Blackness, white supremacy, and other related structures of domination—at least not in totality. Instead, she wants to make clear that pain also tended to sharpen existing differences within the Black community itself. These differences were both ideological and, even more harmfully, rooted in how we inhabit Black flesh—the essence of who we are as Black people in the singular.

Part of what explains these self-defeating practices, Lorde argues, is that "historically, difference [has] been used so cruelly against us that as a people we [are] reluctant to tolerate any diversion from what was externally defined as Blackness."[29] And this is what makes Black self-fashioning a valuable lens with which to observe Black political development. From slavery onward, in the division between the free and enslaved, the respectable middle class and the backward Black masses, and the image of the masculinist militant during the Black Power and Black Arts Movements, Black people have "policed" each other and, in doing so, (re)produced narrow and or anti-Black notions of Blackness and its possibilities. In Lorde's reading, this blinded many from fighting "against those oppressive values which we have been forced to take into ourselves," like narrating Blackness as a "problem" or that Black expression was not befitting the proper performance of personhood.[30] Transformation and the pursuit of liberation are equal parts external and internal; they are addressed to an anti-Black world and the anti-Blackness many of us harbor within ourselves.

Lorde's critical reflections on difference, directed in this case toward Black movement in the 1960s, outline the parameters that guide current attempts to repair oppression's past and present scars and extract ourselves from their root causes. Acknowledging our differences and the aspects of those differences that make us uncomfortable is just as crucial to healing and undoing the world as recognizing the collective and structural nature of Black pain. They are, in other words, the key to making scars not only manageable but politically actionable. Regardless of how radical we imagine ourselves or our politic to be, Lorde urges we practice watchfulness such that we continually ask, self-reflectively: "In what way do I contribute to the subjugation of any part of those who I define as my people?"[31]

These mediations, concerning difference and how to work through them, demonstrate the importance of an honest engagement with the past, to honor and care for what it might teach us about becoming something other than what we were and are. In that sense, the past is both a source of pride and a cautionary tale that should inform our present growth and build a better and different future:

> Through examining the combination of [Black] triumphs and errors, we can examine the dangers of an incomplete vision. Not to condemn that vision but to alter it, construct templates for possible futures, and focus our rage for change upon our enemies rather than upon each other . . . Black people have been here before us and survived. We can read their lives like signposts on the road and find . . . that each one of us is here because somebody before us did something to make it possible. To learn from their mistakes is not to lessen our debt to them, nor to the hard work of becoming ourselves, and

effective. . . . We are powerful because we have survived, and that is what it is all about—survival and growth.[32]

For Lorde, as it was for Frantz Fanon, the past has taught us to understand previous visions of Black liberation as necessarily incomplete. They have been experiments pursued with, and therefore limited to and by, "the weapons they possessed at the time."[33] Their vision did not have the benefit of what we now know.

What this has meant for M4BL, and what it has meant for Black political development, is clear. Though our positions may be different, this positionality—our difference—is not an excuse to blindly eat our own. Black pain and trauma are insufficient reasons to repeat within the intramural so stridently what has been done to us for centuries. As Lorde poignantly argued in an interview, "I don't have to be you in order to work with you. I don't have to be you to honor your Blackness."[34] Honoring Blackness does not require a strict view of what Blackness is or how Black people should be—quite the opposite, in fact. However, it does demand we recognize what anti-Blackness has meant for, and the harm it has caused to, all Black life, regardless of what other identity gets affixed to it. A radically inclusive ethics of care toward a world undone similarly requires a process of undoing the parts of ourselves that remain bound to the principles of the already existing world: anti-Blackness, racial capitalism, cis heteropatriarchy, and the punitive carceral state. It requires us to understand that, as Gwendolyn Brooks writes, "we are each other's magnitude and bond."[35] If we fail to do so, revolution won't just fail, it will never start.

The Tear in the World

Given the enormity of the challenges we face, the belief that confronting difference and working through generational trauma are essential components of Black struggle has made healing a cornerstone of the movement's political culture. While I encountered this firsthand as a member of BYP100—through ceremonies meant to address harmful events and more quotidian practices of altar-making, sage-burning, and other grounding exercises—the ethos was never confined to any one organization or to organizations at all. The Black Lives Matter Global Network (BLMGN), to take one example, used to have an entire page on its website devoted to healing and "healing justice." While that page has since been replaced with an assortment of related tool kits, the original language provides valuable insight into what makes healing synonymous with radical praxis in the time of #BlackLivesMatter. It read:

> In many ways, at its essence BLM is a response to the persistent and historical trauma Black people have endured at the hands of the State. This trauma and pain, unresolved and unhealed lives on in our bodies, in our relationships and in what we create together. Since the inception of BLM, organizers and healers have taken this understanding of historical and generational trauma and made it the foundation of our healing circles, of creative and liberatory space held amidst actions, of our attempts to resolve conflict and division in ways that don't replicate harm or rely on carceral ways of being with one another.[36]

From the outset, the statement calls attention to a central conceit pertaining to the politics of the wake, that M4BL is a direct response to Black pain as historically perpetuated by the state, the capitalist world system's premier institution, and the extrastate actors it almost always shields. The residual damage this causes not only "lives on in our bodies" but also infects how we relate to and build with one another. What's being described, then, is slavery, colonialism, and their afterlives, the initial "tear in the world," to use Dionne Brand's phrasing, and how that tear has subsequently breached our ability to just be.[37] Calling attention to the breach, to sit with the modes of relating to each other it engenders, offers clarity around the extent to which our social relations are conditioned by the brute force of anti-Blackness and its attendant technologies of domination, a force that demands a response.

In that sense, healing justice also gives an account of the wake in a more agentic register, not just what has been done to us but, with and through that knowledge, what we must then commit ourselves to do—wake work. As Prentis Hemphill, who was formally BLMGN's Director of Healing Justice and likely the author of the now deleted page, describes, "How we protect and care for each other along the way, how we come through connected and stronger on the other end, are possibly the most critical and meaningful questions we face."[38] The way to counter the persistence of "racial hurt," a cycle passed down and reproduced for generations, is to respond to that hurt with care.[39] In the present conjuncture, an ethics of care requires both an "understanding of historical and generational trauma" and the will to create liberatory spaces from which we might begin to seek and adopt practices that run contrary to carceral and otherwise punitive ways of being together; it's how we build collective strength.

Regarding Black pain is the terrain through which such imaginaries begin and become possible, and that possibility is aligned with a tradition. The page continued as such:

> Cara Page and Kindred Southern Healing Collective, through their work and commitment to our communities, offered and recovered from ancestral knowledge a framework for healing justice that guides and supports BLM's vision. We see healing justice as necessary in a society that criminalizes Blackness, and structurally ensures trauma for Black people while creating no space, time resource for healing. In this context how we treat ourselves, how we treat each other, and how we move through conflict become deeply political explorations in liberation.[40]

As was the case with the healing circle I took part in, "ancestral knowledge," what Black people have done for centuries to create a culture of reinvention beyond the tenets of anti-Blackness, is at the forefront of movement praxis. It "guides and supports" a notion of justice through healing that does not name a juridical or legal term but instead outlines a path toward repair, a road to be with and for each other on the outer bounds of captivity. This kind of care is not secondary to notions of the "political" but is itself a deeply political act, necessary for and inseparable from explorations in liberation. Much like Black joy, liberation is a practice, not just a destination; it is something we work toward and develop strategies around, rather than something already known or knowable. The page concluded in the following way:

> Healing justice requires that we listen beyond the understandings we've been given of spirit and ancestors, and asks us to both recover and create self-determined and effective rituals, processes for the kind of healing we need. Healing justice, then, makes room for the role of healer, for the practice of community care, in our work to get free.[41]

Here we are told once more, if any doubt remained, that the movement's points of reference, revision, and innovation are not shaped by structures and institutions that have pathologized Black or other marginalized communities. They are grounded in the recovery of practices that have "always sustained us and informed our struggles for liberation," a tradition that inaugurates with the enslaved.[42] By highlighting the importance of healers, calling on the ancestors, rituals, and other healing processes to guide and sustain our organizing, to build trust and solidarity in service to the battles that lie ahead, they make an argument for and express a commitment to care in ways that prior instances of Black social movement did not or that otherwise were considered of secondary importance to "political" work.

Ultimately, the shift toward healing justice in the movement is premised on the conviction that Black people can no longer afford to let pain go unchecked. Nor can we permit emotional labor, and those who take that labor on, to rest at the margins of political struggle, just as we can no longer allow the historically marginalized to remain on the periphery of our visions for the future or allow them to be scapegoats for why those futures are challenging to attain. In M4BL, then, healing makes care operative, often by drawing on tools our ancestors have used for their own survival and sustenance—such as sage, altars, chants, songs, rituals, and ceremonies.[43] It attempts to draw on knowledge and value systems that are not solely or even primarily reliant on Western ideas and beliefs. In that sense, healing is a refusal of the modern world as we know it and represents an opportunity not only to imagine but to practice alternative futures, Black futures that are drawn from a past (pain) we have learned to claim, in order to overcome. As Prentis

Hemphill poignantly put it: "healing justice is [an] active intervention in which we transform the lived experience of Blackness in our world."[44]

~~~

In BYP100, the movement's focus on healing justice and its critique of carceral power led to innovations like the Healing and Safety Council (HSC), the organizing core of which has, in recent years, been renamed the Healing and Safety Community Care Circle. Drawing on Christina Sharpe's work, whom they directly cite, the change was made to reflect a "sincere and thorough . . . attempt to move away from carceral, state, and police logics," logics that are often attached to words like "council" or efforts to offer "advice," a further step afield from the path the capitalist world system presents us.[45] "Care" names the way the HSC aims to relate and the types of relationships it seeks to build. "Circle," which "references the memory of the circles of elders that have existed in our communities for centuries," is likewise about being in relation; it points to our connection, not simply with each other or our communities but ecologically.[46]

The HSC was originally created in 2014 to adjudicate harm within the organization by using mediation processes grounded in an ethos of community accountability and transformation, to hold space for reimagining justice "from an abolitionist perspective and through diverse practices of Black radical care."[47] When I was involved, each of BYP100's chapters had at least one and ideally two HSC representatives dedicated to supporting this task, and the organization maintained a paid staff member charged with coordinating and advancing this aspect of our work. While the HSC's mandate hinged on intervening when conflict or harm occurred in ways that did not reproduce the carceral state's desire to exact and profit from Black disposability, a tactic that itself reflects the hold of Black (social) death.[48] The intention was also to *prevent* such harms and conflicts from happening in the first place, to be, as they put it, "a proactive and preventive means for Black queer activists to practice healing in community, collective, and self" in order to help, in the last instance, "seed Black liberation organizational work that is radically caring, deeply accountable, and wondrously inclusive."[49]

At our national convenings, for example, the HSC curated dedicated healing rooms where members could access a variety of ways to touch base with and center the self so as to proceed with the sometimes difficult work of being in community. As described by former HSC core members, these included "one-on-one sessions with Reiki practitioners, somatic practitioners, herbalists, tarot-card readers, guided meditations, yoga classes, tables for quiet crafting, and areas simply to rest."[50] The motivation behind maintaining a healing space was to provide a sanctuary where people who needed to ground themselves, in one way or another, could do so. By offering such an environment, the HSC hoped to help quell any tensions that might arise and cultivate a container for any past trauma people might have brought with them.

One of the most meaningful and potentially enduring ways the HSC has tried to be proactive and preventive is by creating a guidebook called *Stay Woke, Stay Whole: A Black Activist Healing Manual*. First published in 2017 then subsequently updated and expanded in 2019, the manual aimed to be a resource people could hold and take with them, allowing activists in the movement to effectively pursue "transformative justice by working through our own hurt and harm so that we are not harming ourselves or others."[51] Both editions include "a compilation of resources, stories, interviews with elders, ancestral healing practices, and other remedies for healing" to concretize the healing process as an integral part of our collective praxis, armed with a structural understanding of Black trauma and pain and the knowledge that we've inherited a long tradition of Black survival, resistance, and rebellion predicated on community well-being.[52]

Activist- and practitioner-generated tools like *Stay Woke, Stay Whole* are important not only because they offer an invaluable, educative resource for people actively engaged in on-the-ground organizing work but because they allow in this case healing practices, and the motivations behind them, to circulate beyond the organizations themselves in ways that do not rely on those who already possess such knowledge. It was the first edition of *Stay Wake, Stay Whole*, which includes a section devoted to understanding and unpacking examples of how Black people use and have used "spirituality and culture as a mode of resistance," that provided further context for me to think about the different elements at play in the healing circle I participated in after the 2016 election.[53] In a similar way, BYP100's *The Black Joy Experience Resource Guide* makes possible the circulation of chants and other freedom songs prominent in the movement among those not already in the fold.

These and other efforts to outline and implement a healing justice framework beyond and against the punitive and individuating protocols of the capitalist world system demonstrate how and why healing toward transformation, as an abolitionist praxis, has become a central operation of care in the time of #BlackLivesMatter. They also show that, when it comes to imagining otherwise, a sociality premised on non-domination and horizontal community exchange in league with the plantation politics and folk culture of the enslaved, the movement is doing more than just toiling in theoretical ideas of what *could* or *should* be. Instead, the aim is to, in Je Naé Taylor's words, "model what a commitment to loving Black lives means."[54] This commitment is a collective and intramural charge, grounded in a belief that the "weight of care does not belong to one person" and more broadly that care for all Black people, no matter their station, is perhaps the most powerful (and accessible) weapon we have to wield against an anti-Black world—a testament to our strength.[55]

Harnessing this power such that it can seed and sustain the revolution we need involves being accountable to each other and ourselves. It consists of acknowledging and learning from differences. It means being vulnerable and open to personal growth. It requires tending to the traumas of the past. The HSC was not impervious to these requirements in reflecting on its own work and trajectory. In a brief letter that opens the second edition of *Stay Woke, Stay Whole*, Christopher Roberts, a scholar of Black memory and one of the HSC's founding members, writes the following:

> We would be remiss if we did not say that there have been many times where we failed, where we caused harm when we were asked to help, where we were unable to hold people accountable, where we were unable to be our best selves, where we left people disappointed

and hurt. There were many times where we were, as Mariame Kaba and Shira Hassan say, "fumbling towards repair."[56]

Roberts's admission is further proof of just how messy this work is, has been, and will be, even when our efforts are aimed in the right direction—against punishment and carcerality. I've witnessed firsthand instances in which the HSC, as an experiment in Black radical care, fell short. But by owning up to past failures, by clearly articulating responsibility for harm and disappointment, Roberts points to how we can fumble toward repair instead of falling back into harmful repetition. This means holding ourselves and each other accountable but also analyzing and taking steps to address the things that went wrong—care as a form of study.

Taken as a whole, healing in M4BL is deeply connected to Black living precisely because it directly engages Black pain and Black death, which represent the baseline conditions for Black life. We do this with intention and with an understanding of the stakes. As Je Naé Taylor explains, "This is not for the faint. It means meeting people in the darkest and most uncomfortable situations, practicing patience and compassion in trying times. . . . We are trying, we are daring to imagine the world we want in our lifetime."[57] A healing justice framework seeks a world that "promote[s] healthy Black people who love themselves," a world that is not yet here but in the making.[58] It seeks a society that cares. The same pursuit animates many of the social media–based initiatives of the Black counterpublic, particularly the culturally focused work of the Very Black Project, which brings together images and texts that cut across traditional definitions of the political to encourage an expanded dialogue around Blackness and the radical potential of Black social life.

#Very Affirming

In the opening pages of *Scandalize My Name*, Terrion Williamson presents the "kitchen table" as one of several sites where "black folks gather together in the name of perhaps nothing more than themselves."[59]

Similarly, Zenzele Isoke—who identifies as a "Black feminist theorist, urban ethnographer, and political storyteller"—calls the kitchen table "the place where we speak freely and practice caring for one another."[60] Isoke's narrative testimony is clear about the space's parameters and principles: "Whoever sat down at the kitchen table was family, that is, if'n they was anything but white," family because sometimes we're all we have.[61]

For both writers, everyday Black geographies like the kitchen—or the barbershop, the beauty salon, the block, the house party, the front porch, the barbeque—are reservoirs of Black world-making and essential to the sustenance of Black being in the wake.[62] They afford indispensable opportunities for intimacy, exchange, and fugitive practices of/as Black living that have long proved difficult for Black people to exact elsewhere. There are, after all, very few "elsewheres" Black folks are permitted to congregate without being seen as a threat to be controlled, cleaned up, or done away with, which renders Blackness as a kind of elsewhere in and of itself, a revolutionary spring.[63]

To that end, Isoke names the kitchen as a place "where we hatched the strategies for our next uprising" and where "stories are told" about Black social life, the traditions we've kept and passed down. She reminds us that quotidian spaces like the kitchen are "often the place where our initial imaginings of social life are birthed" and then nurtured.[64] Williamson makes a more far-reaching point, arguing that the kitchen and other such sites are "where black social life fulfills its greatest potential."[65] While the substance of this potential is never articulated outright in Williamson's text, reading her work alongside Isoke's underscores the argument that arenas for Black contemplation, remembrance, healing, creative conjuring, celebration, and joy exact a counterpoint to the past, present, and future logics of racial violence and decay. By bringing Black folks together for "perhaps nothing more than themselves," these locales affirm Black aliveness by creating opportunities to be Black "without sensation," as Kleaver Cruz would put it. They likewise act as a refuge, or at least provide its possibility, from the pain wrought by the capitalist world system's long-standing antagonism to (and reliance on) Blackness and the degraded Black body, a sanctuary from which to plot our next rebellion.

Isoke's and Williamson's observations about sites of Black sociality, and the potential for "unself-conscious affirmation" they possess, offer an opening to think further about spaces of care and their attendant geographies in the time of #BlackLivesMatter. This is particularly true of the "kitchen talks" that helped initiate the Very Black Project (Very Black) and the ways we might understand Very Black as another example of, and space for, care's operation. That these talks took place in the kitchen is not incidental but instead speaks to the everyday, (inter)personal, and often organic nature of how the movement's political culture has spread in and across the cultural realm to become the spirit of our moment.

Very Black has been described by its cofounders, Andre Singleton and Justin Fulton, as a social media–based "digital space unapologetically celebrating blackness in its entirety."[66] The idea of Blackness in its entirety closely echoes the mantra of all Black life and the desire for an unbounded Blackness distinctive to the present conjuncture in Black political development. Like The Black Joy Project, Very Black uses their platform to, in their words, "encourage relatable dialogues around the vast experiences of all people who identify as black across the global diaspora," primarily through the circulation of found images, videos, and texts drawn from a variety of digital sources, all of which reflect a wide-ranging engagement with Black life, politics, and culture.

The circumstances that led to the creation of Very Black and the methods used to encourage relatable dialogues—what Cruz calls the power of "being in conversation"—are instructive. They help us see the way modes of remembrance are deployed to help navigate social contradictions or, as they put it, productively "chann[el] frustrations and negative experiences" into an "inclusive narrative" of Black empowerment and celebration captured in the phrase "Very Black." Exacting this balance is paramount to the politics of the wake, wherein Black pain and Black joy are political accomplices that mobilize action and further a political and ethical commitment to care toward a world undone. At heart, care makes possible an affirmation of Blackness that builds community with and through a reimagined vision of "us"—who "we" are and can be, despite the structural antagonisms that define the world system. It destroys and makes new.

In an interview for Darian Symoné Harvin's podcast, *Am I Allowed to Like Anything?*, Singleton provides a rundown of how Very Black began, centering first and foremost the relationship between himself and fellow cofounder Justin Fulton:

> Justin and I lived together for years . . . so, it's a family dynamic. And people have to understand what living in New York City is like. I don't think a lot of people understand what it's like to live in the city as a young person who does not have the means to live comfortably but builds community and makes it work. And that's when culture always is created. And you know, um, so Justin and I will have these kitchen talks, like just, he will leave his bedroom, I would leave my bedroom, we'd be in the kitchen; either someone got off work earlier, or someone got in late, someone's tipsy, someone's happy, someone's dealing with like, I don't know, drama. But we end up having these conversations, and I guess the core of it [would] always be linked to being Black in some way.[67]

In Singleton's estimation, precarity—specifically, how difficult it can be for young Black people to get by economically in increasingly gentrified urban centers like New York—forces a reliance on one another to make ends meet and is a reminder that collective struggle is how "culture always is created." Culture, in this case, outlines an environment of reciprocity, exchange, attachment, and aid that directly contradicts the atomist drive of capitalist social relations. In short, he's describing a *culture of care*, one created not simply with Justin but through the larger community the two of them share. The kitchen talks Singleton describes, then, are premised on both a personal relationship and a collective one, responsive to material needs, and that is of a tradition traced back to the plantation.

Singleton also emphasizes the racial dynamics that drove the spontaneous instances of coming together in the kitchen, noting they were "always . . . linked to being Black in some way." Despite this linkage, the two never tried to cast their Blackness as a negative or as an excuse, as Singleton explains later in the interview; they never said, for example, "it's cause I'm Black."[68] Instead, their reflections on Blackness produced the opposite sentiment, one of recognition: "It would literally be like, 'Yo, that's very Black' . . . you know what I mean? Like, 'you are crazy, you are so Black.'"[69] This led Singleton and Fulton to conclude their conversations with the phrase "hashtag Very Black," a play on one of social media's most powerful tagging practices.[70] So even as their kitchen talks centered around their own personal exploits, they were built upon a celebratory connection to and articulation of Blackness and Black people, one that is now recognizable, widespread, and affirming rather than policed or punitive.

In honor of these "very Black" conversations, for Singleton's birthday, Fulton had the phrase printed on a T-shirt that marked the moment the duo began to open up their conversation to others as the Very Black Project (fig. 5.1). They did this by selling T-shirts and other merchandise like the one Fulton gave Singleton. They also started an Instagram account, and later a Tumblr page and Twitter handle, extending the scope of the kitchen table and thus inviting more people to take a seat.

That they refer to their work as a "project" has both a practical and more conceptual explanation. Concerning the practical rationale, someone had already adopted the handle Very Black, much to their surprise, but in keeping with the moment.[71] Their first option taken, as a tandem, they found a way to connect their personal interests and experiences with the broader Black community. Singleton explains their thought process:

> So I love projects, and like, Justin also is project based. We are project oriented; we went to the New School. So thinking in a project format was like, "why not the Very Black project?" And also . . . the spin on, in terms of the projects, you know, we live in Bed-Stuy and we live across the street from the [projects] and having grown up in public housing at times, all these different things. It's just like, it's just a nod to the Black experience.[72]

With this nod to their own creative orientation and to their lived experience in proximity to public housing, a common site of Black city life,

FIGURE 5.1. Andre Singleton. The Very Black Project. Instagram.

the newly minted Very Black Project became a space to consider the visuality of Blackness and create a community around what it means to be very Black beyond, in his words, "just our apartment and our small circle of friends."[73] The result "was really explosive," as Singleton put it, evidenced in the more than 154,000 social media followers they have amassed and the 53,214 posts that have attached #veryblack to their social media pages.[74] Employing the hashtag has allowed Very Black's creators, along with anyone who chooses to look, to see the different ways Blackness is understood and expressed on a global level, variations that Singleton considers "beautiful and powerful."[75]

The breadth of the explosion stemming from Very Black cannot be divorced from or understood without the wave of Black insurgency that began to find its footing in the summer of 2014 after the murder of Mike Brown and the Ferguson uprisings. It cannot be separated from the pain and trauma that amplified for a new generation the need to be Black unapologetically, to champion Black joy, and to spread that message to other Black people as not only an act of refusal but one of care in and through the wake. The Very Black Project is, for Singleton, "a call to action. And the action is to love ourselves and each other in the postmodern world deeply, openly, and unapologetically." With a deep and open love for themselves and others, Very Black communicates M4BL's ethics of care, making their work fundamental to and representative of what this movement is—so much so that Very Black's posts often directly mirror movement themes and ideas, which furthers the lack of separation between the political and cultural in Black radical praxis.

As gestured to in outlining the project's origins, crucial to how Very Black echoes the movement's political culture, and its debt to Black feminism, is the way Singleton and Fulton's lived experience, as Black, gay, millennial men, is made visible through many of the project's images and videos. These lived experiences, marking the individual in relation to the collective, the part in relation to the whole, are the basis upon which the intimacy of the kitchen table extends and defines the strategies used to enlarge it. In its most basic measure, Very Black is a platform for telling stories about Black culture and Black life throughout the Diaspora, past, and present. It emphasizes joy while not shying away from posts that speak to the violence, pain, and terror lingering in the background. In that sense, Very Black promotes a kind of healing, the opportunity to learn from both pain and joy, sometimes explicitly. That people identify with them—that words like "explosion" seem on point— shows how sites that enable us to see Black people do "Black" things, to see us think and move "Blackly," have become such a life-offering asset for Black movement in the time of #BlackLivesMatter. It facilitates and deepens counternarratives that allow for an ever-expanding vision and discussion around what Blackness is and might help usher in, one

VERY AWARE PRO BLACK TREATED LIKE A 'BLACK PERSON' TOOLS TO MANEUVER THROUGH OPPRESSION LOOKING AT OUR HISTORY NOT TAKING AWAY FROM OUR HISTORY TAKING THE BATON FROM OUR ANCESTORS PICKING UP WHERE THEY LEFT OFF THIS IS HOW BLACK PEOPLE ARE EVERYTHING STAYS WITHIN THE COMMUNITY THROUGH FRUSTRATIONS AND CONFLICT WE IRON OUT THINGS OUR LIFE AND SECURITY #VERYCOMPLICATED #VERYCONTEMPORARY #VERYBLACK

FIGURE 5.2. Sounds of Blackness. The Very Black Project. Instagram.

anticipated but not quite grasped in the Black political-cultural formations that came before. Let's take a closer look.

Black Citations

There are hundreds of thousands of impressions stretched across the digital repositories of the Very Black Project. These pictures, memes, screenshots, text-based messages, and videos reflect what we might call a Black citational and "counterarchival practice," delivering an archive built with, through, and most importantly by Black people (fig. 5.2). This practice of radical (re)memory work refuses what Hartman and McKittrick both describe as the "tomb" that is the archive of the Black Diaspora, to catalog and demonstrate Singleton and Fulton's devotion to what they call "the exceptional texture of Black life."[76]

The presence of such an archive, a collection of Black citations, reminds us that Black people are not nor have we ever been bound by the absences and silences clouding our stories, the ledger of violence that fills the archives of slavery, colonialism, and their afterlives, even as that violence walks with us still. Black people are a reservoir. We are an expanse. In that sense, their work illustrates the way Black (re)memory can help us move through pain and struggle so we can, returning to their words, "unapologetically celebrate blackness in its entirety" as a prefigurative politics. By demonstrating Black life's exceptional texture, then, Very Black models a way to make visible and (learn to) embody the radical potential of Blackness as the basis upon which we undo and re-make the world. The dynamism of the citational texture they index is not limited to the breadth of the source material they draw on to visual-ize and instigate conversations around Black life and culture, content that embraces rather than polices the variances within and the global breadth of the intramural. It's also in the way they use and interrogate Blackness to engage our collective past(s), present(s), and future(s).

This interrogation is perhaps most pronounced in posts that grapple with the subject of Blackness directly, such as the one in figure 5.2, posted in March 2015, which, in a free-flowing form reminiscent of jazz improvisation, outlines what they dub "the sounds of blackness," taking note of its complications and performing its fluidity. Then there's the post from November 2017, where the duo asks their followers to "insert what [Blackness] means to/for you," prompting people to reply in kind and, as they do, participate in the type of communal reflection social media uniquely provides (fig. 5.3).[77]

The Black political and cultural past, and its relationship to how we think, feel, and act in the present, is a prominent feature of Very Black, closely linked to the message-oriented nature of the discussions they try to provoke. The time given to "looking at our history not taking away from our history," as the post from March 2015 declares, is a telling case in point. On the one hand, it shows they understand Blackness as some-thing that is shared and passed on across time and space and, on the other, something that has been made and remade through struggle. In their acknowledgment of this expanse, this making and remaking, Very Black offers an opportunity for other Black people to consider, com-ment on, and find meaning in Black life, mainly through a celebration of all the things that Black people are and have been despite the pain and generational trauma caused by being subject to the violence, fear, and forms of objectification the capitalist world system requires to re-produce itself.

Behind Very Black's commitment to care, in other words, is the sometimes explicit recognition of, as Christina Sharpe writes, "how slavery's continued unfolding is constitutive of the contemporary conditions of spatial, legal, psychic, and material dimensions of Black

FIGURE 5.3. "Blackness is." The Very Black Project. Instagram.

non/being as well as Black aesthetic and other modes of deformation and interruption."[78] Very Black interrupts the world-destroying logics of anti-Blackness by harnessing the sounds of Blackness as tools to maneuver through oppression and a mechanism of repair, the groundwork for a world undone.

The first image of the project, posted to their Instagram in December 2014, offers insight into the political-cultural matrix Singleton and Fulton would go on to assemble. Fittingly, given the month, it is a digital reproduction of the cover of *Jet* magazine's post-Christmas issue forty

FIGURE 5.4. Esther Rolle on the cover of *Jet*. The Very Black Project. Instagram.

years earlier in 1974. The cover features a photo of actress Esther Rolle dressed as Santa Claus. Her hands are up and spread as if to gesture, open-mouthed and approaching a smile just on the edge of talking or singing (fig. 5.4).

Most would recognize Esther Rolle's face, even if they could not quite place where they knew it from. The dancer turned actress, whose career spanned decades, was most famous for her starring (and pioneering) role in the sitcom *Good Times*, which aired between 1974 and 1979.[79] Set in a Chicago housing project in a poor, predominately Black neighborhood on the city's north side, *Good Times* told the story of Florida Evans (Rolle), James Evans (John Amos), and their three children. The family struggled to escape the kind of inner-city precarity that prompted the turn to Black Power in the mid-1960s and that Singleton noted as part of Very Black's beginnings. A spin-off of a spin-off—Rolle's and Amos's characters first appeared on the show *Maude* (Rolle played Maude's housekeeper), which featured *All in the Family*'s part-time player Bea Arthur—the show was the first Black sitcom to center a Black family in this way. In doing so, it tried to tell serious stories about Black life that reflected, rather than caricatured, the material realities of the Black experience, not unlike the storytelling impulses of Very Black.[80]

Many will also recognize the magazine itself. Begun in 1951 by Black publisher John H. Johnson, *Jet* magazine was a staple of Black households in the second half of the twentieth century. I can recall stacks of them piled up in the garage of my parents' house as a child growing up in suburban New Jersey, with others scattered around the house. As Elizabeth Alexander notes in her short essay on the magazine, more than anything else, *Jet* was dedicated to a particular form of "racial-uplift," in that the magazine invested its pages in the "curious tales of black life" and recognized "the primacy of blackness" in the United States.[81] By invoking *Jet* magazine in their opening image, Very Black stakes a claim to a similar tradition of celebrating and acknowledging the primacy of Blackness. They also point to the critical role of media platforms in ensuring others among the intramural understand that primacy as well, especially in an era where such platforms don't require the same riches possessed by media powerhouses like the Johnson family. In short: they point to the critical role the Black counterpublic plays in providing counternarratives to the dominant discourses of anti-Blackness and white supremacy.

Similarly, by choosing a picture of Rolle as Santa, the project announces and invites an engagement with a familiar face and moment in Black popular culture as reminders not only of Black cultural production and its victories but the intertwinement of that production with the structural inequalities, violence, and (yet) resilience of all Black life. The life worlds that become visible in Black popular culture are important because they help fill gaps that traditional political formations, carried forth mostly by Black elites, have failed to adequately address.[82] As Richard Iton reminds us, in the decades following the civil rights era (this issue of *Jet* magazine falls right at the beginning of this moment), Black popular culture became more politically significant both as a site for "intramural black discourse" and increasingly as a space for previously marginalized groups (in America but also within the Black community itself) "to mobilize and develop their own communicative networks."[83]

As it plays out in the movement's attempt to reconfigure Black dialogical space, this sentiment is evident in the caption that accompanies the image: "We've met Santa and she's a #veryblack woman," which is echoed on a poster Singleton is standing next to in figure 5.1—"I met God she's Black." Two things are made clear with this caption. First, by reimagining Santa (or God) as a Black woman, Very Black moves to destabilize and redefine iconic (and white) male figures as both Black *and* female. It is a figurative approach to centering the historically marginalized generally and Black women in particular, elevating them to their rightful place as cultural pillars of equal importance to men. Second, by saying she is a "very" Black woman, they call on us to consider one way of thinking about what the "very" in Black should and could mean. We can find that definition and meaning in the buoyant visage of Esther Rolle's dark Black skin as she graces the cover of "black America's national organ."[84]

Black popular culture—Black magazines, television shows, music, sports, fashion, and so on—represents one strategy of signification used on Very Black to tell stories about the past, present, and future of Black social life. But they likewise look to the broader expanse of Black intellectual and cultural output. Works by and/or images of James Baldwin, Audre Lorde, Frantz Fanon, C.L.R. James, W.E.B. Du Bois, Toni Morrison, bell hooks, and others appear in conversation with references to, for example, the music of Miles Davis; the paintings of Kerry James Washington; Carrie Mae Weems's "The Kitchen Table" series; Julie Dash's *Daughters of the Dust*; Marlon Riggs's documentary *Tongues Untied*; and Octavia from Jennie Livingston's documentary *Paris Is Burning*, among others.[85] That these latter two examples not only appear but do so multiple times makes clear Very Black's dedication to Black queer life and the importance of giving voice to the experiences of those who suffer secondary marginalization within the Black community. If Very Black is a "call to action," as Singleton claims, that call is predicated on operationalizing care for all Black people, not just those deemed respectable.

The rejection of respectability is not only registered by highlighting path-breaking work that examines LGBTQ life. It comes through in posts that articulate the generational dimensions of the movement's commitment to radical inclusivity. One example of this is a screenshot they uploaded in September 2015 of a Facebook post by activist and theologian Rahiel Tesfamariam introducing an article she penned for the *Washington Post*, in which she argues against the "constraining rules of our elders."[86] "For this generation," she writes, "there's no need to hide behind a veil of purity or wear a suit to have an authoritative seat at the table." That Tesfamariam invokes "rebellious" and "ratchet" in the same sequence crystallizes the genealogical link between slave insurrection to parties like "A Ratchet Realm," and its promotion of an abolitionist way of life we live right now.

Alongside the post itself, however, is a contradiction in the form of a comment from one of Very Black's followers: "I just don't know how I feel about 'ratchet' having a seat at the table." The comment is a direct reference to, and, in a sense, a refutation of, Tesfamariam's assertion that this is a movement that encourages all to come as you are, and that everything is acceptable. It's critical to see this ambivalence as equally instructive as the sentiment expressed in the main post. By suggesting a sense of discomfort with "ratchet," the commenter demonstrates that not everyone who follows Very Black necessarily agrees with the broader movement's position on inclusivity, that unlike the feeling of openness and ungovernability that inspires "A Ratchet Realm," for some Black folks, all Black people still might *not* deserve a seat at the table. Importantly, this contradiction also shows that dissenting voices are comfortable enough to raise difficult questions or positions, long present in Black intramural discourse, on Very Black's platform.

The response to the comment illustrates why creating a space for exchange and disagreement is important, and that Very Black has at least partially been successful at producing such a space.[87] The first follower to reply explains:

> If we are not fighting for them or having them fight [for] us as well, then what does it mean? Ratchet is just our generation's ghetto. They are us and [excluding] them undermines the entire movement.

To this, the initial commenter responds simply: "point taken." A second Very Black follower then hammers home the message with even greater gusto. She writes, "say.it.," affirming the questions raised by the first person to challenge the lack of ease with allowing those identified or who identify themselves as ratchet have a voice, and then continues, "The PRECISE reason we as a community consistently stand stagnant #exclusion of our OWN." In both cases, the heart of the critique is how difference divides and stalls efforts to move the Black community forward.

We can't know whether this exchange shifted that person's opinions about "ratchet" Black folks. But we *can* say that the opportunity to learn and "unlearn" the ways internalized anti-Blackness have harmed Black communities and stifled Black movements is precisely the kind of *action* Very Black seeks to inspire through dialogue. It's one of the ways they work to strengthen solidarity within the intramural and spread a commitment to radical inclusivity, a desire to love and embrace Blackness unbounded, a point articulated in a meme posted in September 2021 (fig. 5.5). The post features a young Black man holding a tweet that says "Pro Black also means letting Black people exist in ways that differ from your view of Blackness," with an accompanying comment from Very Black: "And what a gift to belong to such a dynamic and diverse group of Peoples!"

Along the Ancestral Plain

Unlearning requires a willingness to accept that your ideas and practices may be harmful to others, access to resources that can help guide your journey, and people open and able to support it. BYP100's healing manual is a rich example of such a resource. So too is the deployment of

FIGURE 5.5. Meme of a young Black man holding a tweet.
The Very Black Project. Instagram.

healers and other care practitioners within the broader movement eco-system. Notably, in each instance, the ancestors are cited as an essential spring of inspiration. Very Black has a similar educative dimension and directly references the ancestors as part of its mission. Returning to the "sounds of blackness" post that began our dive into Very Black's coun-terarchiving practice, the caption to it includes the line: "taking the baton from the ancestors[,] picking up where they left off."[88] Combin-ing these two themes, a large number of the entries on Very Black are dedicated to teaching or reminding their followers about West African gods, culture, and languages, such as in a post from July 2015, which

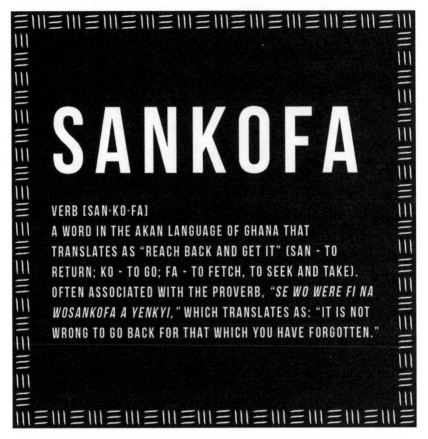

FIGURE 5.6. The definition of "Sankofa." The Very Black Project. Instagram.

highlights the Akan word "Sankofa" and the proverb it is said to be associated with (fig. 5.6).

The accompanying comment offers insight into why they chose to highlight this. It also signals the ethos of Very Black in a broader sense. "One's past," they write, "is an important aspect of one's future. So in order to make the best of one's future, one must visit one's past." This post was part of an initiative they carried out in 2015 called #veryblack-wordoftheday, which included words as diverse as "access," "love," and "negritude" but that nonetheless point to the essence of what Very Black is: an ongoing conversation.

The focus on words, even after they stopped being labeled "word of the day," remains a mechanism for Very Black to engage their followers around topics and themes they deem essential to and for Black people. In many cases, these themes echo the priorities of the movement and demonstrate the extent to which action in traditional organizing spaces like BYP100 is intertwined with social media, culture, and the Black counterpublic. One of the most poignant examples of this linkage appears in a screenshot of the word "heal," posted in November 2016, not long after the election of Donald Trump and the healing circle I participated in. Accompanying the post is a reminder that healing is something we cannot do alone and that our knowledge—regarding how to heal or in a more general sense—is not just out there in the world but "within our bones, skin, blood [and] spirit." Naturally, in declaring us "#veryinterdependent," as the caption does, they give an additional "shoutout to the ancestors," whose bones, skin, blood, and spirit are channeled throughout the movement and anchor Very Black's mission to use their platform to engage Black folks around Black life—to imagine and attempt to create a world where being "Very Black" is celebrated rather than hunted, a world that must first be undone.

They are likewise clear about their commitment to care and the role it plays in building and maintaining community, despite the many tensions and contradictions that can arise from it. In November 2018, Very Black posted another screenshot, this time defining the word "care," which was combined with this caption: "Imagine if we all cared/about for each other." Similarly, in July 2022, they posted an image and explanation of the word "Ujima," the third of Ron Karenga's seven principles of Kwanzaa, which means "collective work and responsibility" (fig. 5.7). The beginning of the caption paired with the post, in typical Very Black fashion, perfectly distills what inspired Singleton and Fulton to extend the kitchen table beyond themselves and their friends through a commitment to Black citational and counter archival practices: "I care . . . right now I'm about to give another fuck! It's the being my brothers and sisters and loved ones keeper for me. Periodt."

In the final analysis, we cannot repair the rupture caused when those ships carrying human cargo set sail across the Atlantic. We cannot

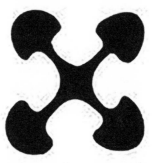

FIGURE 5.7. The definition of "Ujima." The Very Black Project. Instagram.

redress the pain that has followed in its wake, pain the capitalist world system feeds off for its survival. We cannot simply erase the archives of the Black Diaspora that tell this story. What we can do is follow the lead of initiatives like the Very Black Project, resources like BYP100's healing manual, and noncarceral innovations like the Healing and Safety Community Care Circle. We can attend to the full expanse of Black life, celebrate it unapologetically, honor all that has survived and more despite the ceaseless siege of anti-Blackness. In short: we can choose to "give another fuck." And if we do, if we commit ourselves to undoing and remaking the world, to abolition and an abolitionist way of life, maybe, just maybe, we'll produce the conditions under which that world emerges, a Black future premised on the idea that, as Katherine McKittrick teaches us, "liberation is an already existing and unfinished and unmet possibility, laced with creative labour, that emerges from the ongoing collaborative expression of black humanity and black livingness."[89]

Politics in (and of) the Wake

A civilization that proves incapable of solving the problems it creates is a decadent civilization. A civilization that chooses to close its eyes to its most crucial problems is a stricken civilization. A civilization that uses its principles for trickery and deceit is a dying civilization.

—AIMÉ CÉSAIRE

Now, comrades, now is the time to decide to change sides. We must shake off the great mantle of night which has enveloped us, and reach for the light. The new day which is dawning must find us determined, enlightened and resolute.

—FRANTZ FANON

Living as I have argued we do in the wake of slavery, in spaces where we were never meant to survive, or have been punished for surviving and for daring to claim or make spaces of something like freedom, we yet reimagine and transform spaces for and practices of an ethics of care (as in repair, maintenance, attention), an ethics of seeing, and of being in the wake as consciousness; as a way of remembering and observance that started with the door of no return, continued in the hold of the ship and on the shore.

—CHRISTINA SHARPE

Césaire's searing critique in the opening lines of *Discourse on Colonialism* was written over seventy years ago, but the spirit of its condemnation remains true to this day, with perhaps one small amendment. Our "decadent" and "stricken" civilization is not dying; it's already dead.[1] There's nothing left to redeem or revive, nothing for us to mourn. Without hesitation and absent remorse, "we must abandon our dreams and say farewell to our old beliefs and former friendships."[2] The burial is long overdue. Let's hurry to our shovels.

To believe otherwise, to remain impervious to social decline—the farce of so-called democracy, the deprivation fostered by widening inequalities, the creep of fascism, the coming climate catastrophe already here—is the height of self-deception and a betrayal of the first order. Look around. Violence traces the capitalist world system in ways both visible and sometimes hard to see; it always has. Social contradictions abound and spread, producing a fog that obscures our collective agency and interdependence when not properly addressed; they always will—if we let it. The choice is ours to make.

As Fanon instructs, "now is the time to decide to change sides."[3] Now is the time to break free from the darkness that underpins the present state of things, the darkness wrought by capitalism's forward march, "and reach for the light."[4] But what defines the light we all should reach for? The answer, for Fanon, was unequivocal. Rather than concede to extractive and altogether obsolete ways of doing, thinking, and knowing by looking to the West as a model, rather than following in its bloody footsteps, we must set our sights elsewhere and, in so doing, endeavor to create a new world, a social order history has not yet seen. This directive was not meant as hyperbole. During a period of intensified anticolonial struggle, when the possibility of something else seemed, for a time, at least, achievable, Fanon believed a new day was dawning, that a new history of man was in the making, if only we steeled ourselves for the challenge.

In retrospect, we know that independence in Africa was "a short century," and the radical promise of the 1960s was extinguished.[5] We mustn't lament the failures of the past, be that on the continent, in this country, or throughout the Black Diaspora; the urgency of our morbid symptoms disavows it. Instead, we must ask, can a new day dawn in our present, and if so, how?

～～

It remains to be seen whether the current crisis in world capitalism gives way to a global movement with the power to dismantle and radically reimage our society, such that a skeptical observer could confidently declare a new day has, in fact, dawned. Time of course will tell, but we need not await its message. There are possible futures building right before our eyes—Black futures—and the uprisings in 2020, marked most dramatically by, to borrow journalist Tobi Haslett's phrasing, "the infiltrated precinct feasted on by flames" and "the sound of shattering windshields mixed with the rebels' howls and cheers" were a righteous case in point.[6]

This book has been about that beacon of possibility, a politics in and of the wake: how a new generation of young Black organizers and cultural workers, those whose political awakening arrived in the time of #BlackLivesMatter, rejuvenated Black radicalism to help "reimagine and transform," as Christina Sharpe so eloquently writes, "spaces for and practices of an ethics of care (as in repair, maintenance, attention), an ethics of seeing, and of being in the wake as consciousness."[7] This consciousness and ethics of care, fastened to a regard for Black pain and an insistence on Black joy, are the pillars of what I consider to be the political culture of the Movement for Black Lives, defined in these pages as both a network of organizations and activists and a borderless political and cultural zeitgeist that circulates widely online, this generation's public square.[8]

To briefly retrace our steps, Black pain has always shadowed Black life, but social media has rendered that subjection hypervisible. The viral repetition of Black death further exposed the inadequacy of the Black political status quo and the impunity offered by a white supremacist state, spearheading a white supremacist world. This brutal realization not only helped mobilize a more militant political appeal but encouraged a more expansive understanding of what Blackness itself is—to be unapologetically Black, while attempting to disabuse many of the constraints assigned by previous political-cultural formations, particularly as it pertains to gender, sexuality, and class-based differences. The power of this expanse is suffused with Black joy's ability to assert Black presence and prefigure a future free of anti-Black terror, threaded through a radically inclusive ethics of care in the spirit of Sharpe's description of being in the wake as repair, maintenance, and attention.[9]

Upholding a radically inclusive ethics of care is not without contradictions to overcome. In the main, it requires we organize with and for the historically marginalized, those within the Black intramural positioned furthest from power, by championing their concerns and holding ourselves accountable when we inevitably fall short of shaking free of hierarchies we've been socialized into accepting. It also means circulating resources and creating new institutional forms to both heal and adjudicate harm, forms that forgo the punitive logic of the carceral state. In other words, care is not a figure of speech but a form of study; it represents a countercivilizational force, pushing us away from capitalist social relations, away from white sense, away from cis hetero patriarchy, and toward the complete abolition of the world system, including the ideological trails within us that have always disrupted our collective drive for liberation.

The movement's abolitionist vision, nurtured as it has been by Black feminist praxis, a vision that is simultaneously now, before, and not yet, did not emerge from nowhere. As I've sketched, the making of M4BL is a story within a story, part of a conversation Black folks have been having for centuries, one that, returning to Sharpe, "started with the door of no return, continued in the hold of the ship and on the shore."[10] Black political development describes the responsive and circular process through which this dialogue—addressed outward to the world and inward toward the Black community—has taken place. It's meant to capture the shifts in Black consciousness and collective self-fashioning, the debates and competing theories about what Blackness is and what liberation might mean as they've unfolded over time, in accordance with the historical limits and possibilities of the conjunctures in which they came to view. Said somewhat differently, Black political development helps us understand "why now?" and "to what end?"

Situating M4BL within a longer trajectory of Black radical world-making, a path that begins with the originating cleave between the Black slave and the nominally free and stretches to today's upheavals, avails us to two interconnected points of departure that color the pages of this book. The first is the proposition that, in its circularity, its back-and-forth flow, Black politics, culture, and thought builds and repurposes rather than simply breaks away, making clear what Margo Natalie Crawford calls "the power of anticipation" in the Black radical tradition. This promotes a correspondence between the Black present and the Black past in accord with period-specific racial regimes and the political-cultural responses they generate, such that each generation pursues a political praxis and aesthetic that "anticipates" but can't fully actualize the approaches their successors are able to take.[11]

The second is the suggestion that the current movement's advancement of an abolitionism that aims to undo and remake the capitalist world system is best understood as a philosophical return to the source: the radicalism of Black folk culture and the plantation politics of the revolutionary Black slave, the Black multitude, those who set their sights elsewhere, inaugurating a tradition of flight, insurrection, and revolt, in anticipation of Fanon's call; those who cultivated cultural practices of collective reinvention, and a horizontal approach to community deliberation, a "politics without rule," to uphold Black life against the imperatives of profit, property, and accumulation, the deadly dictums of anti-Blackness.[12] The cultural practices and horizontalism nurtured in community were not ancillary to struggle. To the contrary, they fostered trust and solidarity, facilitating the capacity for rebellion; in many respects, they were its precondition.

Following Sylvia Wynter, I'm suggesting that this is the basis and the blueprint for social revolution in the time of #BlackLivesMatter, the abolitionist praxis of a world undone, a politics in and of the wake, a way to not mistake the map for the territory. The ethics of such a praxis is clear and appropriately antagonistic to what we've been taught and come to know. To return to a Hartman quote from the opening pages of this book, "the demands of the slave on the present have everything to do with making good the promise of abolition, and this entails much more than the end of property in slaves. It requires the reconstruction of society, which is the only way to honor our debt to the dead."[13] To that, I say "ashe," let's grant ourselves the power to make this reconstruction a reality, for only we can do that.

Now is the time. The new day Fanon spoke of, a Black future, is a matter of will, not of chance. Our mandate is unambiguous. As Mary Hooks, a southern Black organizer, implores, we must "avenge the suffering of our ancestors, earn the respect of future generations, and be willing to be transformed in the service of the work."[14] May we be judged accordingly.

Just as during the uprisings in 2020, I hear there'll be singing and dancing when at last we lay Western civilization to rest. They tell me there'll be Black joy. Join us. The shovels are waiting.

ACKNOWLEDGMENTS

Book writing is a journey: intellectually, emotionally, and all that might fall in between. It's hard to imagine an author of any kind who is not in some way "changed" by the process, though the nature of that change may not always be obvious or easy to articulate. In my case, the precise character of the transformation is clear and concrete (at least in my head), and not just because the life of this book began while I was still a graduate student. I'd go as far as to say that embarking on this journey initiated a rupture in the most positive sense of the word. The ripple effects of that rupture, the sometimes painful exercise of shedding one layer of skin to give rise to what was perhaps always beneath the surface, are ongoing, and for which I have an endless amount of gratitude. It has made me a better version of myself, a debt for which there is no possible repayment.

There are countless people to thank in this regard, but I'd be remiss if I didn't begin with my family, especially my mother, Angeline Carroll, and my late father, Acie Harris Jr. Because of them, their care and support over the years, I've had the opportunity to pursue life according to my own premises, a long and winding road, to be sure, but one that has brought me to where I am today, doing things I genuinely love and that I hope will make an impact, no matter how small. My dad passed very early on in graduate school, but I later learned, by discovering some of his books and through talking with my aunt some years after, that he was deeply interested in Black political thought. I regret that we never had the chance to talk about it, and that he won't be able to read this book (or any of my writing, for that matter), but I'd like to think he'd be excited to engage, perhaps even proud. I dedicate this book to him and his memory.

If I have my family to thank for providing a foundation to chart my own wayward course, it was my comrades in BYP100 who shifted that trajectory toward personal and political transformation, particularly with respect to my relationship to Blackness. "Coming to Blackness," which is how I like to describe the process of radicalization that took place while a member of BYP100, represented a reorientation not only to the world and how the world works on a structural level. It also meant a deeper interrogation of gender, class, and sexuality, and how Blackness inflects upon these categories in ways that need to be tended to on a micro level as much as it needs to be at the center of our analyses and critiques. For me this entailed beginning to grapple with my own toxic masculinity and related traits, to be open to criticism on that score, and to be accountable for the ways I was showing up in space, be that in the context of organizing or in everyday life. In effect, coming to Blackness meant learning how to unlearn, slowly and with plenty of slip-ups along the way. I will always be thankful for the folks in BYP100 who were willing to "call me in," and for the way being in community with other young Black radicals opened a path I might have otherwise missed.

Around the time I started getting seriously involved with BYP100, I also began a predoctoral fellowship at the Museum of the City of New York (MCNY). During that fellowship I gave my first public lecture about the Movement for Black Lives, co-curated an exhibition case on the movement, and organized a public event that featured movement organizers, among other formative experiences, all of which were fundamental building blocks in the steady advance of my thinking. A heartfelt thank you is owed to everyone I worked with at MCNY, especially in the education department, where the fellowship was housed. That relationship has since produced more opportunities for collaboration after the fellowship ended, which is a testament to the bonds we built as much as it is to the continued salience of the work itself.

Another formative intellectual site in the early life of this book was the Graduate Institute for Design, Ethnography, and Social Thought (GIDEST) where I was among a cohort of doctoral and faculty fellows. Along with being a generative and transdisciplinary space, GIDEST was one of the first (and one of the only) chances I had to workshop a chapter. The book version of the chapter in question—"A Joyful Rebellion"—does not dramatically depart from the draft I presented at GIDEST.

I'm grateful to all the careful and generous comments I received during my session and for the collegiality we cultivated over the course of the fellowship, shepherded by Victoria Hattam, who served as interim director that year.

As I prepared to complete and defend the dissertation, I was hired by Alondra Nelson, who at the time was the president of the Social Science Research Council, to lead the digitization of the Carnegie-Myrdal Study of the Negro in America memoranda archive housed at the Schomburg Center for Research in Black Culture. The resulting digital platform, *An American Dilemma for the 21st Century*, turned out to be more of an undertaking than either of us imagined, but the work offered me a much-needed excuse to step outside of my own head, not to mention resources, at a pivotal moment. Teaming up with Alondra and her chief of staff, Vina Tran, also paved the way for meeting and collaborating with Myriah Towner, who remains a dear friend.

Since so much of the book started as my dissertation, I can't go any further without thanking my committee: Deva Woodly, David Plotke, Jeremy Varon, Jessica Pisano, and Claire Potter. I met Jeremy as a master's student at the New School for Social Research (NSSR) prior to starting the PhD and he remained an invaluable interlocutor throughout the process. David was my assigned faculty mentor when I started in the politics department at NSSR and thankfully took the reins in steering committee coordination. Aside from that, he was a wise and steady hand, especially when it came to navigating the job market and, in many respects, life as an academic. Jessica and Claire provided excellent commentary when it came time to defend, and it was Claire, with whom I worked as an editor at *Public Seminar*, who suggested I reach out to and put me in touch with her agent, Roz Foster (more on Roz in a moment). While everyone on the committee made important contributions to this project and to me personally, Deva spent the most time down in the trenches and was a model mentor while doing so. Deva and I have yet to get around to laughing over a drink about how much stress I probably caused—operating according to my own premises—but things seem to have worked out in the end and she was a big reason why. Thanks for giving me the space to be (and find) myself.

The two years that I spent as a postdoctoral fellow in the African American Studies department at Northwestern is when the book, in its current form, really took shape. Gratitude to Celeste Watkins-Hayes, Martha Biondi, and Mary Pattillo for checking in on me at different points over the course of my time there; to Alex Weheliye for agreeing to meet for coffee very early on; to the department's graduate students for being so welcoming and warm; to Marquis Bey for being a friend and co-conspirator; and to Barnor Hesse for being my primary and most influential interlocutor of that period. An early version of chapter 2 and a few paragraphs from chapter 1 appeared in an article published in a special issue of *South Atlantic Quarterly*, edited by Barnor and Debra Thompson.

While at Northwestern I also began working with Roz, who helped me revise a chapter to circulate and craft a book proposal and guided me through the process of choosing a publisher, for which I will be forever grateful. Thank you as well to my amazing editors Bridget Flannery-McCoy and Alena Chekanov for helping me sharpen my writing and thinking; to the rest of the team at Princeton University Press for supporting this project in all the ways that you have and continue to do; to Jenn Backer for stellar copy-edits; and to the reviewers of the manuscript for reading carefully and responding thoughtfully—the book is better because of all of you.

Lastly, I want to thank my chosen family who, in different ways and at different stages, have contributed to this journey, many of whom continue to do so, even though I haven't always made that easy. Thank you to my NSSR comrades in the politics department and beyond for helping make graduate school bearable; to Anna Reumert, for the years of adventure and companionship that took us around the world and back, and the community we cultivated along the way; to Pernille Reumert and Anders Østergaard, for facilitating some of those adventures and for welcoming me into the fold, a gratitude I extend to the entire family; to Daniel Kressel, Daniel Strand, Rikke Kühn Riegels, and especially Liz Oliver, who have been there from virtually the beginning and persist in making space for me after all these years; to my brilliant sister/ friend and collaborator Marisa Solomon and her equally brilliant partner, Nadja Eisenberg-Guyot, for loving, caring, and showing up for me in all the ways that you do; to Viola Bao, for our long, sometimes meandering conversations, for being a willing reader, for insisting on Marx, and most importantly for being you; to Wendell Marsh and Diego Arispe-Bazan—the writing accountability crew—for helping make Chicago a home to which I still return and for the brotherhood we've built, one I expect to carry on for the rest of our lives (as long as we have no more than two drinks at Marty's); and to Jordie Davies, for your joyful spirit, your care and compassion, your encouragement, your willingness to listen, and your presence during some truly troubled waters, when nearly everything else seemed in disarray, including this book.

NOTES

Chapter 1. We're Not Going to Stand for This

1. According to the event's official Facebook page at the time, the number of marchers reached 60,000. This differs from the account offered by the *New York Times*, which puts the number at closer to 25,000. Brown, Garner, and Gurley were the only names cited explicitly on the event's Facebook page, which is why I name them here. The page also employs the phrase "people of color" (POC). I have added "Black" to assert the distinction between Black and Brown people, a distinction POC erases when it is used to describe Black people. The event description from the perspective of its organizers was but no longer can be found here: "Millions March NYC," https://www.facebook.com/events/washington-square-park/millions-march-nyc/959630214065046/. For the description offered by the *New York Times*, see Benjamin Mueller and Ashley Southall, "25,000 March in New York to Protest Police Violence," *New York Times*, December 14, 2014, sec. New York, https://www.nytimes.com/2014/12/14/nyregion/in-new-york-thousands-march-in-continuing-protests-over-garner-case.html.

2. Keeanga-Yamahtta Taylor, *From #BlackLivesMatter to Black Liberation* (Chicago: Haymarket Books, 2016), 153.

3. This quote was drawn from the now defunct website for the march, www.millionsmarchnyc.org. It is important to note that the two lead organizers of the march, Nichols and Umarra Lynass Elliot, were both young Black women. The emphasis on "new generations" is my own.

4. The phrase "day of anger" was featured prominently on most of the march's flyers.

5. For more, see Barbara Ransby, *Making All Black Lives Matter: Reimagining Freedom in the Twenty-First Century* (Oakland: University of California Press, 2018), 152. See also Deva R. Woodly, *Reckoning: Black Lives Matter and the Democratic Necessity of Social Movements* (New York: Oxford University Press, 2021), 55.

6. A reference is made to this in both Ransby, *Making All Black Lives Matter*, and Taylor, *From #BlackLivesMatter to Black Liberation*.

7. I refer here principally to the generation(s) born during and after the 1980s.

8. Michel-Rolph Trouillot, *Silencing the Past: Power and the Production of History*, 2nd rev. ed. (Boston: Beacon Press, 2015), 1.

9. Christina Sharpe, *In the Wake: On Blackness and Being* (Durham: Duke University Press, 2016).

10. Anthony Reed, "The Black Situation: Notes on Black Critical Theory Now," *American Literary History* 34, no. 1 (2022): 283, 285, https://doi.org/10.1093/alh/ajac001.

11. Frantz Fanon, *The Wretched of the Earth*, trans. Richard Philcox (New York: Grove Press, 2005), 2.

12. Karl Marx, *The Political Writings*, ed. David Fernbach (London: Verso, 2019), 481.

13. Saidiya Hartman, *Lose Your Mother: A Journey along the Atlantic Slave Route* (New York: Farrar, Straus and Giroux, 2007), 45.

14. Wendy Brown, *In the Ruins of Neoliberalism: The Rise of Antidemocratic Politics in the West* (New York: Columbia University Press, 2019), 9.

15. Neil Faulkner, *A Radical History of the World* (London: Pluto Press, 2018), 471.

16. Dustin Jones, "What Is the 'Great Replacement' and How Is It Tied to the Buffalo Shooting Suspect?" NPR, May 16, 2022, sec. Race, https://www.npr.org/2022/05/16/1099034094/what-is-the-great-replacement-theory.

17. Faulkner, *A Radical History of the World*, 471.

18. "(1977) The Combahee River Collective Statement," November 16, 2012, https://www.blackpast.org/african-american-history/combahee-river-collective-statement-1977/.

19. Sut Jhally, "Stuart Hall: The Last Interview," *Cultural Studies* 30, no. 2 (2016): 332–45, https://doi.org/10.1080/09502386.2015.1089918.

20. This was yet another excruciating instance of viral Black death preceded months earlier by the killings of Breonna Taylor and Ahmaud Arbery, unquestionably the most morbid of the previously mentioned symptoms.

21. Roudabeh Kishi, "A Year of Racial Justice Protests: Key Trends in Demonstrations Supporting the BLM Movement," *ACLED* (blog), May 25, 2021, https://acleddata.com/2021/05/25/a-year-of-racial-justice-protests-key-trends-in-demonstrations-supporting-the-blm-movement/.

22. Geo Maher, *A World without Police: How Strong Communities Make Cops Obsolete* (London: Verso, 2021), 1.

23. John Berger, "The Nature of Mass Demonstrations," *International Socialism*, 1st ser., 34 (Autumn 1968): 11–12, https://www.marxists.org/history/etol/newspape/isj/1968/no034/berger.htm.

24. "Black Lives Matter beyond America's Big Cities," *Washington Post*, July 8, 2020, https://www.washingtonpost.com/politics/2020/07/08/black-lives-matter-beyond-americas-big-cities/.

25. Stefano Harney and Fred Moten, *The Undercommons: Fugitive Planning & Black Study* (New York: Autonomedia, 2013), 140.

26. Ibid., 140–41.

27. Gaye Theresa Johnson and Alex Lubin, eds., *Futures of Black Radicalism* (London: Verso, 2017), 9.

28. Sylvia Wynter, "On How We Mistook the Map for the Territory, and Reimprisoned Ourselves in Our Unbearable Wrongness of Being, of Desêtre: Black Studies toward the Human Project," in *A Companion to African-American Studies* (New York: John Wiley & Sons, 2006), 107–18, https://doi.org/10.1002/9780470996645.ch9.

29. Richard Iton, *In Search of the Black Fantastic: Politics and Popular Culture in the Post–Civil Rights Era* (Oxford: Oxford University Press, 2008).

30. Victoria Carty, *Social Movements and New Technology* (New York: Routledge, 2019), https://doi.org/10.4324/9780429493119.

31. Audre Lorde, *Sister Outsider: Essays and Speeches,* reprint (Berkeley, CA: Crossing Press, 2007), 136.

32. Christopher Paul Harris and Marisa Solomon, "Black Grammar: Repertoires of Abolition's Future, Present, and Past," *Social Science Quarterly* 102, no. 7 (2021): 3115, https://doi.org/10.1111/ssqu.13070.

33. Richard Fry, "Millennials Overtake Baby Boomers as America's Largest Generation," *Pew Research Center* (blog), April 28, 2020, https://www.pewresearch.org/fact-tank/2020/04/28/millennials-overtake-baby-boomers-as-americas-largest-generation/.

34. David Scott, "The Temporality of Generations: Dialogue, Tradition, Criticism," *New Literary History* 45, no. 2 (2014): 161, https://doi.org/10.1353/nlh.2014.0017.

35. Ibid.; June Edmunds and Bryan S. Turner, *Generational Consciousness, Narrative, and Politics* (Lanham, MD: Rowman & Littlefield, 2002), 7.

36. Fanon, *The Wretched of the Earth,* 145.

37. Scott, "The Temporality of Generations," 159.

38. Hartman, *Lose Your Mother,* 100.

39. In addition to being Black, being between the ages of eighteen and thirty-five, and attending an orientation, to "officially" join the chapter you had to pay dues ($10 per month) and attend at least two additional meetings and a chapter-sponsored event or action.

40. Fanon, *The Wretched of the Earth,* 145.

41. "#FergusonFridays: Not All of the Black Freedom Fighters Are Men: An Interview with Black Women on the Front Line in Ferguson," *Feminist Wire,* October 3, 2014, https://thefeministwire.com/2014/10/fergusonfridays-black-freedom-fighters-men-interview-black-women-front-line-ferguson/. Also quoted in Taylor, *From #BlackLivesMatter to Black Liberation,* 161.

42. Ransby, *Making All Black Lives Matter,* 100–101.

43. Manuel Castells, *Networks of Outrage and Hope: Social Movements in the Internet Age* (Malden, MA: Polity Press, 2012), 9.

44. Michael C. Dawson, *Black Visions: The Roots of Contemporary African-American Political Ideologies* (Chicago: University of Chicago Press, 2003).

45. Ibid., 23–24.

46. Alicia Garza, "A Herstory of the #BlackLivesMatter Movement," *Feminist Wire,* October 7, 2014, https://thefeministwire.com/2014/10/blacklivesmatter-2/.

47. Danny Katch, "#BlackLivesMatter Looks to the Future," *SocialistWorker.org,* February 4, 2015, http://socialistworker.org/2015/02/04/blacklivesmatter-looks-ahead.

48. Abdul Alkalimat and Saladin Muhammad, "Three Waves of Struggle: Notes toward a Theory of Black Liberation and Social Revolution" (Self-published, 2016), https://alkalimat.org/writings.html.

49. Ibid.

50. Donna Murch, *Assata Taught Me: State Violence, Racial Capitalism, and the Movement for Black Lives* (Chicago: Haymarket Books, 2022), chap. 9.

51. Ibid.

52. Marcia Chatelain, "#BlackLivesMatter: An Online Roundtable with Alicia Garza, Dante Barry, and Darsheel Kaur," *Dissent* (blog), January 19, 2015, https://www.dissentmagazine.org/blog/blacklivesmatter-an-online-roundtable-with-alicia-garza-dante-barry-and-darsheel-kaur.

53. Information on Million Hoodies and their mission was found on their website, which is no longer under their control.

54. Fredrick C. Harris, "The Next Civil Rights Movement?" *Dissent*, Summer 2015, https://www.dissentmagazine.org/article/black-lives-matter-new-civil-rights-movement-fredrick-harris. See also Taylor, *From #BlackLivesMatter to Black Liberation*, 182.

55. Ransby, *Making All Black Lives Matter*, 34–37.

56. Ibid.

57. Chatelain, "#BlackLivesMatter: An Online Roundtable."

58. Sarah Jaffe, "Young Activists Occupy Florida Capitol, Demand Justice for Trayvon," *In These Times*, July 25, 2013, http://inthesetimes.com/article/15356/young_activists_occupy_florida_capitol_demand_justice_for_trayvon.

59. Garza, "A Herstory."

60. Ibid.

61. Ibid.

62. Katch, "#BlackLivesMatter Looks to the Future." The ellipses in the quote are in the original.

63. Garza, "A Herstory."

64. For an inside account of the Black Life Matters Ride, see Akiba Solomon, "Get on the Bus: Inside the Black Life Matters 'Freedom Ride' to Ferguson," *Colorlines*, September 5, 2014, https://www.colorlines.com/articles/get-bus-inside-black-life-matters-freedom-ride-ferguson.

65. As of this writing, neither organization plays a significant role in the movement ecosystem. While Millennial Activists United (MAU) appears to have disbanded completely, individuals associated with it are still engaged, especially on the local level. Hands Up United was active locally as of 2022.

66. "#FergusonFridays."

67. Ibid.

68. Ransby, *Making All Black Lives Matter*, 40.

69. https://www.byp100.org.

70. Charlene Carruthers, *Unapologetic: A Black, Queer, and Feminist Mandate for Radical Movements* (Boston: Beacon Press, 2018), 10.

71. Kai M. Green et al., "#BlackHealingMatters in the Time of #BlackLivesMatter," *Biography* 41, no. 4 (2018): 909–41.

72. Garza, "A Herstory."

73. Alkalimat and Muhammad, "Three Waves of Struggle."

74. Ibid.

75. The Black Visions Collective describes itself as a "Black-led, Queer and Trans centering organization whose mission is to organize powerful, connected Black communities and dismantle systems of violence."

76. Manisha Sinha, *The Slave's Cause: A History of Abolition*, reprint (New Haven: Yale University Press, 2017).

77. "(1977) The Combahee River Collective Statement."

78. Margo Natalie Crawford, *Black Post-Blackness: The Black Arts Movement and Twenty-First-Century Aesthetics* (Urbana: University of Illinois Press, 2017).

79. Sharpe, *In the Wake*.

80. Jeremy Gilbert, "This Conjuncture: For Stuart Hall," *New Formations*, no. 96–97 (March 2019): 6, https://doi.org/10.3898/NEWF:96/97.EDITORIAL.2019.

81. Jhally, "Stuart Hall," 335.

82. Vincent Harding, *There Is a River: The Black Struggle for Freedom in America* (San Diego: Mariner Books, 1993).

83. Dylan Rodriguez, "Abolition as Praxis of Human Being: A Foreword," *Harvard Law Review* 132, no. 6 (2019): 1575–1612.

84. Crawford, *Black Post-Blackness*, 19, 40.

85. Antonio Planas, "Black Man Grabbing Tea from Car Shot by New Jersey Police and Paralyzed, Lawsuit Says," NBC News, March 18, 2022, https://www.nbcnews.com/news/us-news/unarmed-black-man-grabbing-tea-car-shot-new-jersey-police-paralyzed-la-rcna20640.

86. Kishi, "A Year of Racial Justice Protests."

87. Ibid.

88. Ibid.

89. Neil Smith, "Global Social Cleansing: Postliberal Revanchism and the Export of Zero Tolerance," *Social Justice* 28, no. 3 (2001): 72.

90. Brown, *In the Ruins of Neoliberalism*.

91. Rodriguez, "Abolition as Praxis of Human Being," 1589.

92. Taylor, *From #BlackLivesMatter to Black Liberation*, chap. 4.

93. For discussion on the "yet to come," see Rinaldo Walcott, *The Long Emancipation: Moving toward Black Freedom* (Durham: Duke University Press, 2021); Hortense J. Spillers, "The Idea of Black Culture," *CR: The New Centennial Review* 6, no. 3 (2006): 7–28.

94. Fabiola Cineas, "Oluwatoyin Salau Found Dead in Tallahassee, Florida, after Sharing Story of Sexual Assault on Twitter," *Vox*, June 16, 2020, https://www.vox.com/2020/6/16/21292237/oluwatoyin-salau-death.

95. JusticeForToyin [@dr_hemphill], "Toyin Was NOT Homeless. She Just Wasn't Safe at Home! THERE IS A DIFFERENCE! & Regardless, She Stayed at MY HOME before Her Disappearance," tweet, June 15, 2020, https://twitter.com/dr_hemphill/status/1272529258754314240.

96. Amber Jamieson, "The Man Accused of Killing Toyin Salau Allegedly Admitted It to Police and His Mother," *BuzzFeed News*, June 21, 2020, https://www.buzzfeednews.com/article/amberjamieson/toyin-salau-aaron-glee-confession.

97. siempre fresco. 🕯 [@saintsolidgold], "Movement Has a Rape Problem. A Patriarchal Violence Problem. But Particularly a Sexual Violence Problem," tweet, May 31, 2022, https://twitter.com/saintsolidgold/status/1531672092902666243.

98. Robert Gooding-Williams, *In the Shadow of Du Bois: Afro-Modern Political Thought in America*, reprint (Cambridge, MA: Harvard University Press, 2011).

99. Sylvia Wynter, "Sambos and Minstrels," *Social Text*, no. 1 (1979): 156, https://doi.org/10.2307/466410.

100. Christopher Freeburg, *Counterlife: Slavery after Resistance and Social Death* (Durham: Duke University Press, 2021).

101. Hartman, *Lose Your Mother*, 169–70.

102. Wynter, "Sambos and Minstrels," 156.

103. Hartman, *Lose Your Mother*, 170.

104. Cedric J. Robinson, *Black Marxism: The Making of the Black Radical Tradition*, 2nd ed. (Chapel Hill: University of North Carolina Press, 2000).

105. Imperfectly translated as "the good life" or a "good way of living," *buen vivir* is premised on the idea that one can only live well in community, including the natural world.

106. Ashon T. Crawley, *Blackpentecostal Breath: The Aesthetics of Possibility* (New York: American Literatures Initiative, 2016).

107. Sharpe, *In the Wake*, 17.

108. "The Mandate: A Call and Response from Black Lives Matter Atlanta," *Southerners on New Ground* (blog), July 14, 2016, https://southernersonnewground.org/themandate/, from a note in the coda.

109. Hartman, *Lose Your Mother*, 100.

Chapter 2. New Forms/Known Rivers

The title of this chapter is a reversal of, and a nod to, the title of the opening chapter of Richard Iton's canonical book, *In Search of the Black Fantastic*.

1. Harney and Moten, *The Undercommons*, 49.

2. Steven Hahn, *A Nation under Our Feet: Black Political Struggles in the Rural South from Slavery to the Great Migration* (Cambridge, MA: Belknap Press, 2005), 4.

3. Gooding-Williams, *In the Shadow of Du Bois*, 3.

4. Iton, *In Search of the Black Fantastic*, 4, 20.

5. Ibid., 26–27.

6. Cathy J. Cohen, *The Boundaries of Blackness: AIDS and the Breakdown of Black Politics* (Chicago: University of Chicago Press, 1999), 70.

7. Derrick R. Spires, *The Practice of Citizenship: Black Politics and Print Culture in the Early United States* (Philadelphia: University of Pennsylvania Press, 2019).

8. Robinson, *Black Marxism*.

9. Gooding-Williams, *In the Shadow of Du Bois*, 191; Hahn, *A Nation under Our Feet*, 17.

10. Sterling Stuckey, *Slave Culture: Nationalist Theory and the Foundations of Black America*, 2nd ed. (Oxford: Oxford University Press, 2013).

11. Patrick Rael, *Black Identity and Black Protest in the Antebellum North* (Chapel Hill: University of North Carolina Press, 2002), 45.

12. Cedric J. Robinson, *Black Movements in America* (New York: Routledge, 1997), 40.

13. Katherine McKittrick, *Dear Science and Other Stories* (Durham: Duke University Press, 2021), 153n5.

14. Ibid.

15. Stuart Hall, "Black Diaspora Artists in Britain: Three 'Moments' in Post-War History," *History Workshop Journal*, no. 61 (2006): 3.

16. Ibid., 4.

17. Stuckey, *Slave Culture*, 1.

18. C.L.R. James, *The Black Jacobins: Toussaint L'Ouverture and the San Domingo Revolution*, 2nd ed. (New York: Vintage, 1989), 8.

19. Stuckey, *Slave Culture*, 1.

20. Jennifer L. Morgan, *Reckoning with Slavery: Gender, Kinship, and Capitalism in the Early Black Atlantic* (Durham: Duke University Press, 2021), 208, 217.

21. James, *The Black Jacobins*, 9.

22. For more on this, see Eric Williams, *Capitalism & Slavery*, 3rd ed. (Chapel Hill: University of North Carolina Press, 2021); James, *The Black Jacobins*.

23. Eugene D. Genovese, *Roll, Jordan, Roll: The World the Slaves Made* (New York: Vintage, 1976), book 4.

24. W.E.B. Du Bois, *The Souls of Black Folk*, unabridged ed. (New York: Dover, 2016), 37.

25. Stephanie M. H. Camp, *Closer to Freedom: Enslaved Women and Everyday Resistance in the Plantation South* (Chapel Hill: University of North Carolina Press, 2004).

26. Robinson, *Black Movements in America*, 30–31.

27. For more on looting, see Vicky Osterweil, *In Defense of Looting: A Riotous History of Uncivil Action* (New York: Bold Type Books, 2020).

28. Genovese, *Roll, Jordan, Roll*.

29. See James, *The Black Jacobins*.

30. Robinson, *Black Movements in America*, 39.

31. Ibid., 40.

32. For more on this discussion, see Freeburg, *Counterlife*; Vincent Brown, "Social Death and Political Life in the Study of Slavery," *American Historical Review* 114, no. 5 (2009): 1231–49, https://doi.org/10.1086/ahr.114.5.1231; Saidiya Hartman, *Scenes of Subjection: Terror, Slavery, and Self-Making in Nineteenth-Century America* (New York: Oxford University Press, 1997).

33. Herbert Aptheker, *American Negro Slave Revolts*, 5th ed. (New York: International Publishers, 1983).

34. Genovese, *Roll, Jordan, Roll*.

35. Ibid.

36. Gooding-Williams, *In the Shadow of Du Bois*; Hahn, *A Nation under Our Feet*, 3, 16–17.

37. Gooding-Williams, *In the Shadow of Du Bois*; Hahn, *A Nation under Our Feet*, 3, 16–17.

38. Quoted in Robinson, *Black Movements in America*, 92.

39. Stephanie M. H. Camp, "The Pleasures of Resistance: Enslaved Women and Body Politics in the Plantation South, 1830–1861," *Journal of Southern History* 68, no. 3 (2002): 537, 540, https://doi.org/10.2307/3070158.

40. Ibid., 540.

41. Stuckey, *Slave Culture*, xi.

42. McKittrick, *Dear Science and Other Stories*, 153n5.

43. Ibid.

44. Ibid.

45. Ibid., 159.

46. Harris and Solomon, "Black Grammar."

47. Robinson, *Black Movements in America*, 51.

48. Rael, *Black Identity and Black Protest in the Antebellum North*, 2.

49. Robinson, *Black Movements in America*, 51.

50. Quoted in ibid., 47.

51. "Maria Stewart," *Fractals: A Black Feminist Organizing and Movement Building Timeline*, https://fractals.blackfeministfuture.org/fractal/maria-stewart/.

52. Robinson, *Black Movements in America*, 52.

53. Ibid.

54. Ibid.

55. Quoted in ibid.

56. For more on revolutionary violence, see Fanon, *The Wretched of the Earth*.

57. Robinson, *Black Movements in America*, 53.

58. "David Walker, 1785–1830. Walker's Appeal, in Four Articles; Together with a Preamble, to the Coloured Citizens of the World, but in Particular, and Very Expressly, to Those of the United States of America, Written in Boston, State of Massachusetts, September 28, 1829," 79, https://docsouth.unc.edu/nc/walker/walker.html.

59. Joy James, "Afrarealism and the Black Matrix: Maroon Philosophy at Democracy's Border," *Black Scholar* 43, no. 4 (2013): 124, https://doi.org/10.5816/blackscholar.43.4.0124.

60. Robinson, *Black Movements in America*, 93.

61. Ibid.

62. Davarian L. Baldwin and Minkah Makalani, eds., *Escape from New York: The New Negro Renaissance beyond Harlem* (Minneapolis: University of Minnesota Press, 2013), 5, 404.

63. Richard Wright, "Blueprint for Negro Writing (1937)," in *African American Literary Theory: A Reader*, ed. Winston Napier (New York: New York University Press, 2000), 45–53.

64. Henry Louis Gates Jr., "The Trope of a New Negro and the Reconstruction of the Image of the Black," *Representations* 24 (1988): 130, https://doi.org/10.2307/2928478.

65. Baldwin and Makalani, *Escape from New York*, 20.

66. Gates, "The Trope of a New Negro," 130.

67. Ibid.; Wynter, "Sambos and Minstrels."

68. Gates, "The Trope of a New Negro," 133.

69. Erin D. Chapman, *Prove It on Me: New Negroes, Sex, and Popular Culture in the 1920s* (New York: Oxford University Press, 2012).

70. Ibid.

71. Ibid.

72. Gates, "The Trope of a New Negro," 136.

73. Fred Moten, *In the Break: The Aesthetics of the Black Radical Tradition* (Minneapolis: University of Minnesota Press, 2003).

74. Saidiya V. Hartman, *Wayward Lives, Beautiful Experiments: Intimate Histories of Riotous Black Girls, Troublesome Women, and Queer Radicals* (New York: W. W. Norton, 2020).

75. Ibid., xv.

76. Ibid., 227, 228.

77. Robinson, *Black Movements in America*, 53.

78. Ernest Allen Jr., "The New Negro: Explorations in Identity and Social Consciousness, 1910–1922," in *1915, the Cultural Moment: The New Politics, the New Woman, the New Psychology, the New Art & the New Theatre in America*, ed. Adele Heller and Lois Palken Rudnick (New Brunswick, NJ: Rutgers University Press, 1991), 49.

79. Hartman, *Wayward Lives, Beautiful Experiments*, 227.

80. Allen, "The New Negro," 53–54.

81. Paul C. Taylor, *Black Is Beautiful: A Philosophy of Black Aesthetics* (Hoboken, NJ: Wiley-Blackwell, 2016).

82. Manning Marable and Leith Mullings, eds., *Let Nobody Turn Us Around: An African American Anthology*, 2nd ed. (Lanham, MD: Rowman & Littlefield, 2009); Larry Neal, "The Black Arts Movement (1968)," in *A Sourcebook on African-American Performance* (New York: Routledge, 1999).

83. Iton, *In Search of the Black Fantastic*.

84. Keisha N. Blain, *Set the World on Fire: Black Nationalist Women and the Global Struggle for Freedom* (Philadelphia: University of Pennsylvania Press, 2018), 7.

85. Ibid.

86. Gates, "The Trope of a New Negro," 147.

87. Ibid.

88. Quoted in Allen, "The New Negro," 50.

89. Quoted in Gates, "The Trope of a New Negro," 147.

90. Quoted in ibid.

91. Erik S. McDuffie, *Sojourning for Freedom: Black Women, American Communism, and the Making of Black Left Feminism* (Durham: Duke University Press, 2011), 3–4, 217.

92. Gates, "The Trope of a New Negro," 147; Alain Locke, "The New Negro," in *The New Negro: Voices of the Harlem Renaissance*, ed. Alain Locke, reprint (New York: Touchstone, 1999).

93. Locke, "The New Negro," 4.

94. "The Negro Artist and the Racial Mountain by Langston Hughes," Poetry Foundation, https://www.poetryfoundation.org/articles/69395/the-negro-artist-and-the-racial-mountain.

95. Ibid.

96. Chapman, *Prove It on Me*; Allen, "The New Negro," 50.

97. Gates, "The Trope of a New Negro," 148.

98. Crawford, *Black Post-Blackness*, 19.

99. Quoted in ibid.

100. Ibid.

101. Ibid., 19–20, 23–27.

102. Marx, *The Political Writings*, 480.

103. James Edward Smethurst, *The Black Arts Movement: Literary Nationalism in the 1960s and 1970s*, new ed. (Chapel Hill: University of North Carolina Press, 2005).

104. Quoted in LeRoi Jones, *Home: Social Essays* (New York: Akashic Books, 2009).

105. Larry Neal, "And Shine Swam On," in *Black Fire: An Anthology of Afro-American Writing*, ed. Amiri Baraka and Larry Neal (Baltimore: Black Classic Press, 2007), 637–56.

106. Ibid.

107. Ibid.

108. Crawford, *Black Post-Blackness*, 24, 32.

109. Ibid.

110. Smethurst, *The Black Arts Movement*, 368.

111. Fanon, *The Wretched of the Earth*, 146.

112. Robinson, *Black Movements in America*, 134.

113. Adom Getachew, *Worldmaking after Empire: The Rise and Fall of Self-Determination* (Princeton: Princeton University Press, 2020), 73.

114. Smethurst, *The Black Arts Movement*, 367.

115. Ibid., appendix.

116. Ibid., 369.

117. Ibid., 16–17.

118. Ibid., 9.

119. Ibid., 15.

120. Ibid.

121. Ibid.

122. Ibid., 16.

123. Ibid., 371.

124. Ibid., 87.

125. Ibid.

126. Crawford, *Black Post-Blackness*, 197.

127. Ibid., 220.

128. Smethurst, *The Black Arts Movement*, 14.

129. Crawford, *Black Post-Blackness*, 201.

130. Iton, *In Search of the Black Fantastic*, 23.

131. Ibid.; Taylor, *Black Is Beautiful*.

132. Crawley, *Blackpentecostal Breath*.

133. Dawson, *Black Visions*, 36.

134. Iton, *In Search of the Black Fantastic*, 20; Taylor, *Black Is Beautiful*.

135. Kimberly Springer, *Living for the Revolution: Black Feminist Organizations, 1968–1980* (Durham: Duke University Press, 2005).1, 173.

136. Iton, *In Search of the Black Fantastic*, 20.

137. Ibid.

138. Harris and Solomon, "Black Grammar"; Wynter, "On How We Mistook the Map for the Territory."

139. Marquis Bey, *Anarcho-Blackness: Notes toward a Black Anarchism* (Chico, CA: AK Press, 2020), 93.

140. Walcott, *The Long Emancipation*, 5.

Chapter 3. Regarding Black Pain

1. Christina Sharpe, *Monstrous Intimacies: Making Post-Slavery Subjects* (Durham: Duke University Press, 2010), 3.

2. Hartman, *Scenes of Subjection*, 3.

3. As Stephen Marshall has argued, "the criminalization of blackness," as evidenced in recent years by the rash of premature Black death instigated by the police, should be understood as a central "political institution of the post enslavement liberal order." It is indicative of "a distinctive structure of political antagonism." This is most ardently expressed in the "political logic of repetition" at the heart of what Barnor Hesse has termed "racial policing." By this Hesse means

"the routine racial profiling and racial problematization of the black presence, in whatever form, that is aligned with obliging or coercing black social and political assimilation and conformity." Stephen H. Marshall, "The Political Life of Fungibility," *Theory & Event* 15, no. 3 (2012); Barnor Hesse, "White Sovereignty (. . .), Black Life Politics: 'The N****r They Couldn't Kill,'" *South Atlantic Quarterly* 116, no. 3 (2017): 582, https://doi.org/10.1215/00382876-3961494.

4. Frederick Douglass, Peter J. Gomes, and Gregory Stephens, *Narrative of the Life of Frederick Douglass* (New York: Signet, 2005).

5. Ibid.

6. I am referencing a violation that, in effect, illuminates the "general dishonor" bestowed to Black people. As Frank Wilderson, drawing on the work of Orlando Patterson, explains, general dishonor means that Black people are "dishonored in [their] very being. . . . You're dishonored prior to your performance of dishonored actions." General dishonor, along with gratuitous violence and natal alienation, represent the three dimensions of social death that define the slave–non-slave and thus Black-human relation. For a detailed elaboration, see Frank B. Wilderson III, *Red, White & Black: Cinema and the Structure of U.S. Antagonisms* (Durham: Duke University Press, 2010).

7. I invoke the archive here to suggest that Reynolds's recording belongs among other instances of documenting Black pain, including the absence of such documentation.

8. It is beyond justification or logic unless understood as a constituent feature of a world system dependent on Black death.

9. I say this notwithstanding the care work he undertook in the nutrition department of the Saint Paul Public School System, along with generalities about his character and his purported penchant for following "the rules." But these elements of his life do not escape the fact of his death. They are often intertwined. See, for example, Melissa Chan, "Philando Castile Was a Role Model to Hundreds of Kids," *Time*, July 7, 2016, https://time.com/4397086/minnesota-shooting-philando-castile-role-model-school/.

10. Threadcraft aims to critique the necropolitical dimensions of contemporary Black politics and discourse, mainly for their failure to account for the Black female and LGBTQ bodies within their discursive frame, as well as their inability to locate violence beyond the actions of the state. See Shatema Threadcraft, "North American Necropolitics and Gender: On #BlackLivesMatter and Black Femicide," *South Atlantic Quarterly* 116, no. 3 (2017): 553, https://doi.org/10.1215/00382876-3961483.

11. Elizabeth Alexander, "'Can You Be Black and Look at This?': Reading the Rodney King Video(s)," *Public Culture* 7, no. 1 (1994): 78, https://doi.org/10.1215/08992363-7-1-77.

12. Hartman, *Scenes of Subjection*, 4.

13. Moten, *In the Break*, 177.

14. Sexton's use of "out of the world" is drawn from the title of the fifth chapter of Achille Mbembe's 2001 book *On the Postcolony*, published by University of California Press. Jared Sexton, "'The Curtain of the Sky': An Introduction," *Critical Sociology* 36, no. 1 (2010): 22n4, https://doi.org/10.1177/0896920509347136.

15. Here I mean "episode" as distinct from "event" insofar as the word "episode" suggests a continuity—a structure—whereas "event" implies something exceptional—structured, perhaps, but nevertheless outside the norm.

16. Calvin Warren, "Black Nihilism and the Politics of Hope," *CR: The New Centennial Review* 15, no. 1 (2015): 217, https://doi.org/10.14321/crnewcentrevi.15.1.0215.

17. To Shatema Threadcraft's earlier point, the gender specificity in her comment is noteworthy.

18. Claudia Rankine, "'The Condition of Black Life Is One of Mourning,'" *New York Times*, June 22, 2015, sec. Magazine, https://www.nytimes.com/2015/06/22/magazine/the-condition -of-black-life-is-one-of-mourning.html.

19. The myth is perhaps best articulated in the form of what Gunnar Myrdal once called the "American Creed," which has long served to obscure this country's basis in and reliance on racial hierarchy, violence, and expropriation.

20. As Sylvia Wynter has explained, the success of this logic, this regime of knowledge, was achieved through a process of narrativization that served to naturalize the inferior status of Black people, meaning that within the context of scientific reason and self-reliance, which serves as the ethical demand of this epoch, Black (the non-human) and Brown (the subhuman) people are "rightfully" excluded. For more, see Sylvia Wynter, "Unsettling the Coloniality of Being/ Power/Truth/Freedom: Towards the Human, After Man, Its Overrepresentation—An Argument," *CR: The New Centennial Review* 3, no. 3 (2003): 257–337.

21. See Denise Ferreira da Silva, "Toward a Black Feminist Poethics: The Quest(ion) of Blackness toward the End of the World," *Black Scholar* 44, no. 2 (2014): 81–97.

22. Charles W. Mills, *The Racial Contract* (Ithaca: Cornell University Press, 2022), 1.

23. *Dred Scott v. John F. A. Sandford*, 60 U.S. 393.

24. To give another, less visible example, the number of Black women who suffer premature death because of complications related to giving birth is four times as high as that of white women. Similarly, "black mothers also suffer severe complications twice as often, including disproportionate rates of hypertension and blood disorders." Derecka Purnell, "If Even Beyoncé Had a Rough Pregnancy, What Hope Do Other Black Women Have?" *Guardian*, April 23, 2019, sec. Opinion, https://www.theguardian.com/commentisfree/2019/apr/23/beyonce -pregnancy-black-women.

25. It likewise obscures the reality that "there is such a thing as bottom line blackness with regard to violence." Alexander, "'Can You be Black and Look at This,'" 81.

26. Joan Wylie Hall, ed., *Conversations with Audre Lorde* (Jackson: University Press of Mississippi, 2004), 26–44.

27. Ibid.; Sharpe, *In the Wake*, 20.

28. Sharpe, *In the Wake*, 20–21.

29. Some scholars have notably argued the opposite. For them, Black Lives Matter reflects, as Barnor Hesse put it, "an appeal to the liberal democratic institutions to implement protections and justice" ("White Sovereignty," 599) even as it seeks to apply pressure on those same institutions for their failure to live up to their promises. While I understand why such a reading is plausible, I suggest and demonstrate in this chapter that the meaning of Black Lives Matter exceeds the semantic appeal to liberal democratic institutions.

30. Central here is the argument that the material and discursive violence represented and carried out in spectacles of Black suffering has always been fundamental to the creation of a Black "people," despite significant divergences among us. It forges what Alexander refers to as "group knowledges and strategies," the markings of a shared history or "linked fate" that can be

(and has been) manipulated, diverted, and suppressed but never truly erased or forgotten These knowledges and strategies are suggestive of a version of "habit memory," which David Scott has defined as "the social disciplines and rituals and techniques by which the body . . . learns to be, and acquires the memory of being . . . a body of a certain kind." In other words, pain acts as a form of "tribal" production—how a sense of being Black is fostered and renewed. Alexander, "'Can You Be Black and Look at This?'" 78; David Scott, "Introduction: On the Archaeologies of Black Memory," *Small Axe* 12, no. 2 (2008): xvi. For more on linked fate, see Michael C. Dawson, *Behind the Mule: Race and Class in African-American Politics* (Princeton: Princeton University Press, 1995).

31. Tina Marie Campt, "Black Visuality and the Practice of Refusal," *Women & Performance: A Journal of Feminist Theory* 29, no. 1 (2019): 79–87, https://doi.org/10.1080/0740770X.2019 .1573625.

32. Tina Campt, lecture delivered at the symposium "Refusal and Radical Hope," hosted by the Research Center for Material Culture in Amsterdam, November 2018, https://www.youtube .com/watch?v=XXQqyzTP1zU.

33. Calvin L. Warren, *Ontological Terror: Blackness, Nihilism, and Emancipation* (Durham: Duke University Press, 2018), 2. The emphasis is in the original text.

34. Debra Walker King, *African Americans and the Culture of Pain* (Charlottesville: University of Virginia Press, 2008), 29.

35. I'd like to thank one of the reviewers of my manuscript for offering this language.

36. Courtney R. Baker, *Humane Insight: Looking at Images of African American Suffering and Death* (Urbana: University of Illinois Press, 2015), 4.

37. Chapman, *Prove It on Me.*

38. Ida B. Wells-Barnett, *Southern Horrors & The Red Record* (AmazonClassics, 2021).

39. Baker, *Humane Insight,* 94–95.

40.   https://en.oxforddictionaries.com/definition/regard.

41. Johnson and Lubin, *Futures of Black Radicalism.*

42. Sharpe, *In the Wake,* 10–11.

43. I would like to thank Deva Woodly for pushing me to think more systematically about how I apply the idea of a "regard" for Black pain to the specific examples I narrate.

44. Dionne Brand, *A Map to the Door of No Return: Notes to Belonging* (Toronto: Vintage Canada, 2002).

45. Hortense J. Spillers, "Mama's Baby, Papa's Maybe: An American Grammar Book," *Diacritics* 17, no. 2 (1987): 67, https://doi.org/10.2307/464747.

46. These quotes were drawn from two different Twitter users, both of whom posted on July 7, 2016, the day following Philando Castile's murder. His name was misspelled in both tweets.

47. The day after Castile was killed, during a march for police accountability in Dallas following these two murders, a Black gunman named Micah Xavier Johnson shot at a group of police officers, killing five. Johnson was not affiliated with any of the Black organizations active at the time, and his actions were condemned by them.

48. Before this there were individual, less coordinated attempts at such statements, including BYP100's "Agenda to Keep Us Safe," released in 2014, and the "Agenda to Build Black Futures," released in early 2016.

49. For the full, updated platform, see M4BL, "Policy Platforms," *M4BL* (blog), https://m4bl.org/policy-platforms/.

50. It is worth noting that the parameters of the platform were criticized by some members of BYP100 (in one instance explosively and in public) for appearing to take a reformist approach toward prisons and policing as opposed to clearly articulating an abolitionist stance. It was also criticized for being published with BYP100 as an author and endorser without sufficient input from members.

51. The "war" on poverty, initiated by the Johnson administration in 1964, began this trend. While that effort lacked the same discriminating and nefarious intent as the later examples, it still proved inadequate to the task of properly addressing the structural problems besieging Black and brown communities before being chipped away at by the overall rightward lurch in American politics since the 1980s.

52. Susan Sontag, *Regarding the Pain of Others* (New York: Picador, 2004), 5.

53. Hartman, *Scenes of Subjection*, 18.

54. Ibid.

55. Gray was the principal color among the variety of uniforms worn by Southern soldiers, largely because of its association with state sovereignty, and in contrast to the federal government's blue uniforms.

56. James M. Mayo, "War Memorials as Political Memory," *Geographical Review* 78, no. 1 (1988): 62–63, https://doi.org/10.2307/214306.

57. The spatial logic of such placement clearly indicates an attempt to make a notion of justice and law synonymous with a particular narration of history, one in which whiteness acts above all else as the baseline definition.

58. Hartman, *Scenes of Subjection*, 117. For more on this, see a regularly updated report compiled by the Southern Poverty Law Center: "Whose Heritage? Public Symbols of the Confederacy," https://www.splcenter.org/20190201/whose-heritage-public-symbols-confederacy.

59. Southern Poverty Law Center: "Whose Heritage?"

60. Mills, *The Racial Contract*, 1; the emphasis is mine.

61. The park had up to that point been named after Lee.

62. For the entire interview, see "Meet the College Student Who Pulled Down a Confederate Statue in Durham & Defied White Supremacy," *Democracy Now!* August 16, 2017, https://www.democracynow.org/2017/8/16/meet_the_college_student_who_pulled.

63. Lee A. McBride III, *Ethics and Insurrection: A Pragmatism for the Oppressed* (London: Bloomsbury, 2022).

64. Regarding her arrest, she explained: "The sheriff . . . and the establishment want to make a political prisoner of me, and they want to make an example of me. And they want to scare people and they want to scare Black people, and they want to scare people of color, and they want to scare people who are reclaiming their agency. And they can't."

65. Takiya Thompson has explicitly cited Newsome's actions as an influence, stating in the same interview, "I could not have—you know, she created a model of possibility for me. And I was thinking about her."

66. For the entire statement, see BYP100, "We Are Dismantling All Structures of White Supremacy," *Medium* (blog), August 20, 2017, https://byp100.medium.com/last-monday

-august-14th-the-byp100-durham-chapter-mobilized-in-solidarity-with-comrades -f285524561f0.

67. The emphasis is in the original.

68. Denise Ferreira da Silva, "The Scene of Nature," in *Searching for Contemporary Legal Thought*, ed. Christopher Tomlins and Justin Desautels-Stein (Cambridge: Cambridge University Press, 2017), 275–89, https://doi.org/10.1017/9781316584361.015.

69. Ain Raven Ealey, interview by the author, April 1, 2017, New York City. All of the Ealey quotes in this section are from this interview.

70. Threadcraft, "North American Necropolitics and Gender," 554.

71. "Say Her Name," https://www.aapf.org/sayhername.

72. Threadcraft, "North American Necropolitics and Gender," 554.

73. Autumn Robinson, interview by the author, April 25, 2018, New York City. All of Robinson's quotes are from this interview.

74. Some participants elected to have their response photographed without them present.

75. For me, this takes place by reading "in" as "I'm."

76. This example was echoed during the 2020 uprisings when the light projection artist Dustin Klein and his collaborators transformed the Robert E. Lee Monument in Richmond, Virginia, into a symbol of remembrance, healing, and celebration by projecting the faces of George Floyd, Breonna Taylor, and Black historical figures like Harriet Tubman, Martin Luther King Jr., and Frederick Douglass onto the statue.

Chapter 4. A Joyful Rebellion

1. Here we ought to consider culture in terms of behaviors, beliefs, and aesthetics in a broad sense, as well as how "the" as an article denotes a specific "Black" culture. At least in the United States, if not elsewhere, notions of "the culture" have become popular among Black youth, evidenced in phrases like "do it for the culture." In my reading, this is both an etic and emic position, insofar as it simultaneously articulates a shared, even if contested, understanding of what Black culture is, while it also names an action that would affirm and therefore constitute this culture. In the main, statements like this tend to represent how understandings of Blackness among Black people have expanded and become more flexible.

2. Rodriguez, "Abolition as a Praxis of Being Human," 1576.

3. Harris and Solomon, "Black Grammar," 3117.

4. While the precise origins of this chant are not known, it was taught to BYP100 members at the M4BL Convening in Cleveland, July 2015 (BYP100, *The Black Joy Experience Resource Guide*, 2017).

5. As Barbara Holmes notes, one way to think about the Black church is as "referring to a dynamic religious entity forged in oppression and sustained by practices that were often covert and intuitive." Barbara A. Holmes, *Joy Unspeakable: Contemplative Practices of the Black Church*, 2nd ed. (Minneapolis: Fortress Press, 2017).

6. Hesse, "White Sovereignty."

7. Crawley, *Blackpentecostal Breath*.

8. This chant plays on the song by gospel duo Mary Mary called "I Luh God" and was "remixed" by BYP100 in 2016 at the suggestion of Dr. Kai M. Green, who is also a BYP100 member (BYP100, *The Black Joy Experience Resource Guide*, 2017).

9. Ranciere, quoted in Hesse, "White Sovereignty," 600.

10. This chant came from Camp Akili in Oakland and was introduced to BYP100 in 2013 (BYP100, *The Black Joy Experience Resource Guide*, 2017).

11. I allude here to the hymn, repurposed time and again, but most commonly attributed to and popularized by the civil rights movement: "We Shall Overcome."

12. This quote was used to highlight the role of joy and culture in BYP100's strategic plan. I helped draft that document.

13. Sharpe, *In the Wake*, 17.

14. Javon Johnson, "Black Joy in the Time of Ferguson," *QED: A Journal in GLBTQ Worldmaking* 2, no. 2 (2015): 180, https://doi.org/10.14321/qed.2.2.0177. The emphasis in this quote is mine.

15. Deva Woodly, "The Joy of Us: Identity Work and the Movement for Black Lives," *In What Now? On Future Identities*, ed. Kristin Chappa and Anne Barlow (London: Black Dog Publishing, 2018).

16. This description was found on their website, which is no longer active.

17. For more on this, see King, *African Americans and the Culture of Pain*, chap. 6; Lawrence W. Levine, *Black Culture and Black Consciousness: Afro-American Folk Thought from Slavery to Freedom* (Oxford: Oxford University Press, 2007), chap. 5.

18. Levine, *Black Culture and Black Consciousness*, 359.

19. "Blueprint for the Black Joy Era | Jazmine 'Da K.O.S.' Walker & Amber Phillips | TEDxRVA," 2017, https://www.youtube.com/watch?v=ZzP3AxOmmjY.

20. This quote was drawn from a transcription of their TEDx Talk.

21. Wardell Julius Clark, *Kill Move Paradise*, TimeLine Theatre, https://timelinetheatre.com/events/kill-move-paradise/.

22. Olivia Clement, "National Black Theatre Launches 48th Season Today," *Playbill*, September 7, 2016, https://playbill.com/article/national-black-theatre-launches-48th-season-today.

23. To accompany and contextualize the performance, Christina Knight authored the short essay "Black Joy in the Hour of Chaos." While not explicitly cited here, this essay has been helpful in my thinking on the matter of Black joy and signals the congruous thinking around this subject that was taking place at the time and continues today. See Christina Knight, "Creative Time: Black Joy in the Hour of Chaos," https://www.academia.edu/21304271/CREATIVE_TIME_Black_Joy_in_the_Hour_of_Chaos. For more on the performance itself, see Ronald Bunn, "Black Joy in the Hour of Chaos," *Routes*, May 31, 2015, https://routes-mag.com/central-park-black-joy-in-the-hour-of-chaos/.

24. https://www.blackjoyparade.org.

25. http://www.thepartynoire.com.

26. BYP100, *The Black Joy Experience Resource Guide*, 2017.

27. Ibid.

28. One of the most telling examples of this ubiquity was a post by Lindsay Peoples for "The Cut," a vertical on *New York Magazine*'s digital platform. The post, titled "The 7 Best Black Joy

Moments at the Royal Wedding" (May 20, 2018, https://www.thecut.com/2018/05/royal-wedding-best-black-joy-moments.html), pointed out all the instances in which, according to Peoples, Black joy was present during the marriage ceremony of Prince Harry Windsor and actress Meghan Markle. As it was a "royal wedding," the event was a space traditionally absent Black people altogether.

29. Terrion L. Williamson, *Scandalize My Name: Black Feminist Practice and the Making of Black Social Life* (New York: American Literatures Initiative, 2016), 16.

30. Woodly, "The Joy of Us."

31. Da Silva, "Toward a Black Feminist Poethics," 81.

32. What does it mean that an event like the Black Joy Parade has a slew of corporate sponsors? Can figurations of Black joy sustain its emancipatory potential if it can be bought and sold?

33. This quote is drawn from the transcript of their TEDx Talk.

34. Ibid.

35. Camp, "The Pleasures of Resistance."

36. Lia T. Bascomb, "Productively Destabilized: Black Studies and Fantastic Modes of Being," *Souls* 16, no. 3–4 (2014): 149, https://doi.org/10.1080/10999949.2014.968957.

37. This view is relevant not simply because of the precision with which the quote captures the sentiment I'm sketching here but because the headline of the review itself features the phrase "Black joy" as a way of describing what Van Peebles captures with the play.

38. Williamson, *Scandalize My Name*, 15; Gina Dent, ed., *Black Popular Culture* (New York: New Press, 1998), 2.

39. Johnson, "Black Joy in the Time of Ferguson," 180.

40. Johnson elaborates on this point: "our bodies harbor knowledge, and in these moments every smile, head nod, hip shake, and high five is an *exchange of embodied truths* that black joy is phenomenally transformational" (ibid.).

41. Jonathan Judaken and Jennifer L. Geddes, "Black Intellectuals in America: A Conversation with Cornel West," *Hedgehog Review* 9, no. 1 (2007): 87.

42. I quote here from a conversation between West and other scholar as captured in Dent, *Black Popular Culture*, 86.

43. Hartman, *Scenes of Subjection*, 118.

44. I draw here from Cruz's words, captured on my phone, at an event in which he spoke.

45. See Joycelyn Hughes and Kofi LeNiles, "Voices from the Field: Uplifting and Amplifying: An Interview with Kleaver Cruz," *Journal of Negro Education* 86, no. 3 (2017): 341–44.

46. Several months before Cruz launched his project, Veronica Agard expressed a similar sentiment in an article published on the site *For Harriet*. According to Cruz, he was not aware of this article when he started TBJP but learned of it subsequently and ended up taking a portrait of Agard as part of the series.

47. Lucille Clifton, *The Book of Light* (Port Townsend, WA: Copper Canyon Press, 1992), 25.

48. Sarah Lewis, "Vision & Justice: Guest Editor Note," *Aperture*, February 23, 2016, https://aperture.org/editorial/vision-justice/.

49. Barnor Hesse and Juliet Hooker, "Introduction: On Black Political Thought inside Global Black Protest," *South Atlantic Quarterly* 116, no. 3 (2017): 444, https://doi.org/10.1215/00382876-3961428.

50. Ibid., 454.

51. Ibid., 444.

52. My account differs in that I attempt to read and theorize this origin story in order to deepen how we understand the role of Black joy in M4BL rather than as a mechanism to inform the reader that TBJP exists.

53. See Kleaver Cruz, "The Black Joy Project," https://kleavercruz.com/the-black-joy-project.

54. Joy James and João Costa Vargas, "Refusing Blackness-as-Victimization: Trayvon Martin and the Black Cyborgs," in *Pursuing Trayvon Martin: Historical Contexts and Contemporary Manifestations of Racial Dynamics*, ed. George Yancy and Janine Jones (Lanham, MD: Rowman and Littlefield, 2012), 193.

55. Spillers, "Mama's Baby, Papa's Maybe," 67.

56. Cruz, "The Black Joy Project."

57. Cruz was a founding member of the NYC chapter of the Black Lives Matter Global Network. Members of this chapter still meet, but they are no longer affiliated with BLM.

58. Kimberly Juanita Brown, "Regarding the Pain of the Other: Photography, Famine, and the Transference of Affect," in *Feeling Photograph*, ed. Elspeth H. Brown and Thy Phu (Durham: Duke University Press, 2014), 190, https://doi.org/10.1215/9780822377313-008.

59. Kleaver Cruz, interview by the author, April 20, 2018, New York City.

60. Brown, "Regarding the Pain of the Other," 190.

61. Sharpe, *In the Wake*, 20.

62. Spillers, "Mama's Baby, Papa's Maybe," 67.

63. Calvin Warren, "Black Care," *liquid blackness* 3, no. 6 (2016): 39.

64. Spillers, "Mama's Baby, Papa's Maybe," 67.

65. Warren, "Black Care," 37.

66. Spillers, "Mama's Baby, Papa's Maybe," 67; Warren, "Black Care," 37.

67. Spillers, "Mama's Baby, Papa's Maybe," 67.

68. Cruz, "The Black Joy Project."

69. I draw here from comments Cruz made at an event on Black archiving practices.

70. Spike Lee's Malcolm X (re)ignited an interest in Malcolm and was part of a broader revival of race-based thinking and aesthetics in the 1990s.

71. Each of these photos can be located on The Black Joy Project's Instagram page and are dated December 6, 2015. They are among the first images Cruz posted for the project. See "The Black Joy Project® (@theblackjoyproject) • Instagram Photos and Videos," https://www.instagram.com/theblackjoyproject/.

72. Cruz interview.

73. Nicole R. Fleetwood, *Troubling Vision: Performance, Visuality, and Blackness* (Chicago: University of Chicago Press, 2011).

74. Cruz, "The Black Joy Project."

75. Cruz used his personal page on Facebook to post pictures before launching TBJP.

76. bell hooks, *Black Looks: Race and Representation*, 2nd ed. (New York: Routledge, 2014), 10.

77. Though, as we shall see, it is not left out of the messaging that often is connected to those images.

78. Williamson, *Scandalize My Name*, 9.

79. I draw here from comments Cruz made at the same event on Black archiving practices.

80. Woodly, "The Joy of Us."

81. Moten, *In the Break*.

82. Cruz interview.

83. Elizabeth Currans, "Utopic Mappings: Performing Joy," *Obsidian* 41, no. 1/2 (2015): 92.

84. Paul Gilroy, *The Black Atlantic: Modernity and Double-Consciousness* (Cambridge, MA: Harvard University Press, 1993), 38; Currans, "Utopic Mappings," 92.

85. Hesse and Hooker, "Introduction: On Black Political Thought," 448.

86. Ibid., 449.

87. A recognition of this fact motivated, at least in part, the photo book and exhibition *Black Joy and Resistance* by Adrienne Waheed, which surveys and demonstrates the similarities between different scenes of Black joy, including beyond national boundaries. For more on the book, see "Black Joy and Resistance," http://blackjoyandresistance.com/.

88. Cruz interview.

89. Stuart Hall, "Cultural Identity and Diaspora," in *Colonial Discourse and Post-Colonial Theory* (New York: Routledge, 1994).

90. "A Luv Story Bar—Google Search," https://www.google.com/search?q=A+luv+story +bar&oq=A+luv+story+bar&aqs=chrome..69i57j0i22i30l9.5401j0j7&sourceid=chrome&ie =UTF-8.

91. Jewel Cadet, e-mail communication with the author.

92. Aliyyah I. Abdur-Rahman, "The Black Ecstatic," *GLQ: A Journal of Lesbian and Gay Studies* 24, no. 2–3 (2018): 344, https://doi.org/10.1215/10642684-4324849.

93. Kemi Adeyemi, Kareem Khubchandani, and Ramon Rivera-Servera, eds., *Queer Nightlife* (Ann Arbor: University of Michigan Press, 2021), 3.

94. Abdur-Rahman, "The Black Ecstatic," 345.

95. Eric A. Stanley, *Atmospheres of Violence: Structuring Antagonism and the Trans/Queer Ungovernable* (Durham: Duke University Press, 2021), 118.

96. Ibid., 121.

97. Ibid., 7.

98. Human Rights Campaign, "Fatal Violence against the Transgender and Gender Non-Conforming Community in 2021," https://www.hrc.org/resources/fatal-violence-against-the -transgender-and-gender-non-conforming-community-in-2021.

99. The language quoted here comes from the viral video, which is also the basis of the description.

100. Stanley, *Atmospheres of Violence*, 5–6.

101. Ibid., 17; Abdur-Rahman, "The Black Ecstatic," 345.

102. Adeyemi, Khubchandani, and Rivera-Servera, *Queer Nightlife*, 3.

103. https://www.bet.com/article/fwgl0a/celebrate-29-days-of-black-queer-excellence.

104. Cathy J. Cohen, "Punks, Bulldaggers, and Welfare Queens: The Radical Potential of Queer Politics?" *GLQ: A Journal of Lesbian and Gay Studies* 3, no. 4 (1997): 437–65, https://doi .org/10.1215/10642684-3-4-437.

105. Hartman, *Wayward Lives, Beautiful Experiments*, 227.

106. Ibid.

107. Ibid.

Chapter 5. The Operation(s) of Care

1. The following dialogue took place on BYP100 NYC's Group Me on the evening of Donald Trump's election in 2016. Because the names of the people involved in this discussion are not germane to its meaning and they play no further role in any other aspect of the narrative I will sketch, I have chosen to only include their first initial. In instances where the first initial repeats itself, I have elected to include an additional letter from their name.

2. While at this point the election had not been officially called for Trump, things were decidedly pointing in that direction. The AP did not officially announce Trump as the winner until 2:41 a.m.

3. Sage is often present in movement circles. It is understood to be both cleansing and grounding, especially prior to a ceremony or meeting, and its usage is derived from its historical place in slave medical treatments. BYP100 *Stay Woke, Stay Whole: A Black Activist Healing Manual* (2017), 15.

4. Solange Knowles, "Cranes in the Sky," *A Seat at the Table* (2016).

5. These quotes are drawn from the Group Me text exchange.

6. On this, Keeanga-Yamahtta Taylor's account remains instructive. In particular, see Taylor, "Barack Obama: The End of an Illusion," in *From #BlackLivesMatter to Black Liberation*.

7. Some of the phrasing and sentiment about care and material conditions are owed to Dr. Ashante M. Reese from the following Twitter post: Ashanté M. Reese [@AMReese07], "We'd Do Well to Refuse the Tendency to Render 'Care' as Metaphor Rather than a Set of Practices That Shape/Refuse/Inform/Speak Back to Material Conditions," January 29, 2021, https://twitter.com/AMReese07/status/1355192387035930628.

8. Lorde, *Sister Outsider*.

9. Sharpe, *In the Wake*, 5, 123.

10. Warren, "Black Care," 44.

11. Ibid., 44–45.

12. Assata Shakur, *Assata: An Autobiography* (Chicago: Lawrence Hill Books, 2001).

13. A "kick-back" is a planned social gathering that falls just sort of a full-fledged party.

14. "Packing the court" refers to galvanizing community support to be present in the courthouse during and after an arraignment. It also has often included care packages for the people who spend time in a holding cell while waiting to see a judge.

15. The idea of "principled struggle," most often attributed to the activist and community organizer NTanya Lee, has become a centerpiece of BYP100's culture. Principled struggle acknowledges that "to learn and to grow is to struggle," that "struggle is a condition for change and liberation," and that within and beyond the movement we must "work to foster and cultivate spaces . . . to move through conflict in a way that makes us better." Quoted from BYP100's Freedom Forecast distributed internally in 2018.

16. "Hidden abode" is a reference to Marx's description of the unseen dimensions of capitalism. Karl Marx, *Capital: Volume 1: A Critique of Political Economy*, trans. Ben Fowkes (London: Penguin Classics, 1992).

17. Ealey interview.

18. isysadmin, "It Is Time for Accountability," *Statement from the Frontlines of BLM* (blog), https://www.blmchapterstatement.com/no1/.

19. YahNé Ndgo, "Tell No Lies," *Statement from the Frontlines of BLM* (blog), https://www
.blmchapterstatement.com/no2/.

20. Very few members who were present that day would say that the kick-back was completely successful in this regard. In fact, some of the issues that helped motivate the gathering
persisted and continued to spill out into public view.

21. The word "ashe" is frequently used throughout the movement ecosystem, including online. Drawn from the West African Yoruba religion, it is meant in this context to harken back to
our collective African roots and to the power we collectively hold to produce change.

22. I discuss BYP100's Healing and Safety Council in more detail later in the chapter.

23. According to the *Black Joy Experience Resource Guide*, Je Naé led BYP100 DC chapter
members in a version of the "I Love Being Black" chant after a meeting during an "herbal healing
session." Upon hearing it BYP100 member Johnathan Lykes, who was hosting the session at his
house, put the chant to music. It has since circulated widely in movement spaces and is featured
on the album *The Black Joy Experience* released in 2018.

24. Ron Eyerman, *Cultural Trauma: Slavery and the Formation of African American Identity*
(Cambridge: Cambridge University Press, 2002).

25. Elizabeth Alexander, *The Trayvon Generation* (New York: Grand Central Publishing,
2022).

26. Lorde, *Sister Outsider*, 142.

27. Ibid., 135–36. The emphasis on "horizontally" is mine.

28. Ibid., 135, 138. The emphasis on "ourselves in each other" is mine.

29. Ibid., 136.

30. Ibid., 135.

31. Ibid., 139.

32. Ibid., 135, 138–39.

33. Fanon, *The Wretched of the Earth*, 145.

34. From an interview Lorde gave in *A Litany for Survival: The Life and Work of Audre Lorde*
(Third World Newsreel, 1996), https://video.alexanderstreet.com/watch/litany-for-survival
-the-life-and-work-of-audre-lorde-a-90-min.

35. Gwendolyn Brooks, *Blacks* (Chicago: Third World Press, 1994).

36. Ibid.

37. Brand, *A Map to the Door of No Return*.

38. Prentis Hemphill, "Healing Justice Is How We Can Sustain Black Lives," *HuffPost*, February 7, 2017, https://www.huffpost.com/entry/healing-justice_b_5899e8ade4b0c1284f282ffe.

39. King, *African Americans and the Culture of Pain*.

40. https://blacklivesmatter.com/healing-justice/.

41. Ibid.

42. Ibid.

43. As Lorde made clear, Black people have survived, and in the movement, Black survival
is viewed as debt that we owe; we walk the path that has been paved for us even as we grow by
making that path our own.

44. Hemphill, "Healing Justice Is How We Can Sustain Black Lives."

45. BYP100, *Stay Woke, Stay Whole: A Black Activist Healing Manual*, vol. 2 (2019), 21.

46. Ibid., 21–22.

47. Ibid., 21; Green et al., "#BlackHealingMatters," 912.

48. Green et al., "#BlackHealingMatters," 913.

49. BYP100, *Stay Woke, Stay Whole*, vol. 2.

50. Green et al., "#BlackHealingMatters," 912. The first BYP100 national convening—an annual event that brings all of the organization's chapters together—was held in Durham, NC, in 2016. The second was held in New Orleans in 2017. The third, which marked BYP100's fifth anniversary, was held in Chicago in 2018. I attended the convenings held in 2017 and 2018. I had just joined the organization when the first convening was held and did not feel comfortable going, though I was welcome to.

51. BYP100, *Stay Woke, Stay Whole*, 1:2.

52. Green et al., "#BlackHealingMatters," 916.

53. BYP100, *Stay Woke, Stay Whole*, 1:2.

54. Green et al., "#BlackHealingMatters," 922.

55. Ibid.

56. BYP100, *Stay Woke, Stay Whole*, 2:21.

57. Green et al., "#BlackHealingMatters," 922.

58. Ibid.

59. Williamson, *Scandalize My Name*, 10.

60. Zenzele Isoke, "Black Ethnography, Black(Female)Aesthetics: Thinking/Writing/Saying/Sounding Black Political Life," *Theory & Event* 21, no. 1 (2018): 149.

61. Ibid.

62. This is not to say that these types of gatherings are unique to Black people but that they instead hold symbolic importance that is distinct, a fact made clear enough by the countless number of relatively recent depictions of these very locations by Black filmmakers.

63. This fact has taken on additional light in recent years, helping to catalyze the phrase "while Black" as a way to describe the various instances in which Black being in public is policed and scrutinized.

64. Isoke, "Black Ethnography," 149. It should be noted that Isoke's invocation has a specific reference to and resonance with her own work as a "black [female] ethnographer" and the women she interviewed as part of that work.

65. Williamson, *Scandalize My Name*, 10. In this passage, Williamson thinks along with Ralph Ellison.

66. There are multiple descriptions available that define the aims of the Very Black Project.

67. "The Life of a Digital Immigrant | Episode 056 Ft. André Singleton," *Am I Allowed to Like Anything?* podcast, https://anchor.fm/darian.

68. "The Life of a Digital Immigrant."

69. Ibid.

70. During this portion of the interview, Singleton explains that he had been "speaking in hashtag" since 2007 when he was a student at the New School, by which he means he would conclude sentences with the add-on "hashtag xyz" as a way of adding emphasis to whatever point had just been made.

71. "The Life of a Digital Immigrant."

72. Ibid.

73. Ibid.

74. This figure does not include derivative hashtags like #theveryblackproject and #veryblackproject.

75. The source of this interview is no longer available but was accessed at https://ubuntubiographyproject.com/2017/12/23/andre-d-singleton/

76. See Katherine McKittrick, "Mathematics Black Life," *Black Scholar* 44, no. 2 (2014): 16–28, https://doi.org/10.1080/00064246.2014.11413684; Hartman, *Scenes of Subjection*.

77. The caption to the post and many others includes #soulfie, slang for a selfie that captures and projects emotion. Also note the use of the Yoruba word "ashe" (here spelled as "axe"), mentioned in the chapter.

78. It is explicit in the sense that there are numerous references to slavery, often accompanied by an evocation of the "ancestors," which, as I describe in the chapter, is prevalent within the movement.

79. My own recollection of Rolle comes from the movie *Rosewood*, a historical drama directed by John Singleton based on the Rosewood massacres that took place in Florida in 1923. In it, Rolle plays Aunt Sarah, who is killed as a result of anti-Black violence.

80. This was the case until the popularity of their eldest son JJ's (played by Jimi Walker) now-iconic phrase "DY-No-Mite" shifted the direction of the show toward JJ's antics.

81. Elizabeth Alexander, *The Black Interior: Essays* (Saint Paul, MN: Graywolf Press, 2004), 91–98.

82. Iton, *In Search of the Black Fantastic*, 20.

83. Ibid. In chapter 2, I use the same thread in Iton's thought to describe the emergence of spaces for Black feminist organizing in the 1960s and 1970s.

84. Alexander, *The Black Interior*, 91.

85. Notably, the image from Weems's portrayal of Black intimacy, largely from the perspective of Black women, is accompanied by a quote from Singleton that reads: "I think the word kitchen is very Black."

86. "THE VERY BLACK PROJECT on Instagram: '@rahielt Is the Truth! 🙏❤️💁🏾 If You Don't Know Who She Is Then You Really Need to Get into Her! She Is Really #boutitboutit! 🙌🏾 Axé! #thisaintyomamascivilrightsmovement #verytruthful #verycontemporary #veryblack,'" https://www.instagram.com/p/8HaXeUMsEf/.

87. Ibid.

88. Note the similarities between the language used here and that of Cyd Nichols of the Millions March, outlined in chapter 1.

89. McKittrick, *Dear Science and Other Stories*, 13.

Coda. Politics in (and of) the Wake

1. Aimé Césaire, *Discourse on Colonialism*, trans. Joan Pinkham (New York: Monthly Review Press, 2001), 1.

2. Fanon, *The Wretched of the Earth*, 235.

3. Ibid.

4. Ibid.

5. Hartman, *Lose Your Mother*, 1.

6. Tobi Haslett, "Magic Actions: Looking back on the George Floyd Rebellion," *n+1* (blog), July 21, 2021, https://www.nplusonemag.com/issue-40/politics/magic-actions-2/.

7. Sharpe, *In the Wake*, 131.

8. Ransby, *Making All Black Lives Matter*, 100–101.

9. Ibid.

10. Ibid.

11. Crawford, *Black Post-Blackness*.

12. McKittrick, *Dear Science and Other Stories*, 161; Gooding-Williams, *In the Shadow of Du Bois*, 16.

13. Hartman, *Lose Your Mother*, 170.

14. "The Mandate."

BIBLIOGRAPHY

Abdur-Rahman, Aliyyah I. "The Black Ecstatic." *GLQ: A Journal of Lesbian and Gay Studies* 24, no. 2–3 (2018): 343–65. https://doi.org/10.1215/10642684-4324849.

Adeyemi, Kemi, Kareem Khubchandani, and Ramon Rivera-Servera, eds. *Queer Nightlife*. Ann Arbor: University of Michigan Press, 2021.

Alexander, Elizabeth. *The Black Interior: Essays*. Saint Paul, MN: Graywolf Press, 2004.

———. "'Can You Be Black and Look at This?': Reading the Rodney King Video(s)." *Public Culture* 7, no. 1 (1994): 77–94. https://doi.org/10.1215/08992363-7-1-77.

———. *The Trayvon Generation*. New York: Grand Central Publishing, 2022.

Alexander, Michelle. *Faces at the Bottom of the Well*. Rev. ed. New York: Basic Books, 2018.

Allen, Ernest, Jr. "The New Negro: Explorations in Identity and Social Consciousness, 1910–1922." In *1915, the Cultural Moment: The New Politics, the New Woman, the New Psychology, the New Art & the New Theatre in America*, ed. Adele Heller and Lois Palken Rudnick, 48–68. New Brunswick, NJ: Rutgers University Press, 1991.

Aptheker, Herbert. *American Negro Slave Revolts*. 5th ed. New York: International Publishers, 1983.

Baker, Courtney R. *Humane Insight: Looking at Images of African American Suffering and Death*. Urbana: University of Illinois Press, 2015.

Baldwin, Davarian L., and Minkah Makalani, eds. *Escape from New York: The New Negro Renaissance beyond Harlem*. Minneapolis: University of Minnesota Press, 2013.

Bascomb, Lia T. "Productively Destabilized: Black Studies and Fantastic Modes of Being." *Souls* 16, no. 3–4 (2014): 148–65. https://doi.org/10.1080/10999949.2014.968957.

Baucom, Ian. *Specters of the Atlantic: Finance Capital, Slavery, and the Philosophy of History*. Durham: Duke University Press, 2005.

Berger, John. "The Nature of Mass Demonstrations." *International Socialism*, 1st ser., 34 (Autumn 1968): 11–12. https://www.marxists.org/history/etol/newspape/isj/1968/no034/berger .htm.

Beverly, Michele Prettyman. "No Medicine for Melancholy: Cinema of Loss and Mourning in the Era of #BlackLivesMatter." *Black Camera* 8, no. 2 (2017): 81–103. https://doi.org/10.2979 /blackcamera.8.2.05.

Bey, Marquis. *Anarcho-Blackness: Notes toward a Black Anarchism*. Chico, CA: AK Press, 2020.

"Black Lives Matter beyond America's Big Cities." *Washington Post*, July 8, 2020. https://www .washingtonpost.com/politics/2020/07/08/black-lives-matter-beyond-americas-big-cities/.

Black Youth Project (BYP100). "We Are Dismantling All Structures of White Supremacy." *Medium* (blog), August 20, 2017. https://byp100.medium.com/last-monday-august-14th-the-byp100-durham-chapter-mobilized-in-solidarity-with-comrades-f285524561f0.

Blain, Keisha N. *Set the World on Fire: Black Nationalist Women and the Global Struggle for Freedom.* Philadelphia: University of Pennsylvania Press, 2018.

"Blueprint for the Black Joy Era | Jazmine 'Da K.O.S.' Walker & Amber Phillips | TEDxRVA." 2017. https://www.youtube.com/watch?v=ZzP3AxOmmjY.

Brand, Dionne. *A Map to the Door of No Return: Notes to Belonging.* Toronto: Vintage Canada, 2002.

brown, adrienne maree. *Emergent Strategy: Shaping Change, Changing Worlds.* Reprint. Chico, CA: AK Press, 2017.

Brown, Kimberly Juanita. "Regarding the Pain of the Other: Photography, Famine, and the Transference of Affect." In *Feeling Photograph,* ed. Elspeth H. Brown and Thy Phu. Durham: Duke University Press, 2014. https://doi.org/10.1215/9780822377313-008.

Brown, Vincent. "Social Death and Political Life in the Study of Slavery." *American Historical Review* 114, no. 5 (December 1, 2009): 1231–49. https://doi.org/10.1086/ahr.114.5.1231.

Brown, Wendy. *In the Ruins of Neoliberalism: The Rise of Antidemocratic Politics in the West.* New York: Columbia University Press, 2019.

Bruce, La Marr Jurelle. "Mad Is a Place, or, The Slave Ship Tows the Ship of Fools." *American Quarterly* 69, no. 2 (2017): 303–8. https://doi.org/10.1353/aq.2017.0024.

Bunn, Ronald. "Black Joy in the Hour of Chaos." *Routes,* May 31, 2015. https://routes-mag.com/central-park-black-joy-in-the-hour-of-chaos/.

Camp, Stephanie M. H. *Closer to Freedom: Enslaved Women and Everyday Resistance in the Plantation South.* Chapel Hill: University of North Carolina Press, 2004.

———. "The Pleasures of Resistance: Enslaved Women and Body Politics in the Plantation South, 1830–1861." *Journal of Southern History* 68, no. 3 (2002): 533–72. https://doi.org/10.2307/3070158.

Campt, Tina Marie. "Black Visuality and the Practice of Refusal." *Women & Performance: A Journal of Feminist Theory* 29, no. 1 (2019): 79–87. https://doi.org/10.1080/0740770X.2019.1573625.

———. "Refusal and Radical Hope." Lecture, "Refusal and Radical Hope" symposium, Amsterdam, November 2018, Research Center for Material Culture. https://www.youtube.com/watch?v=XXQqyzTP1zU.

Carruthers, Charlene. *Unapologetic: A Black, Queer, and Feminist Mandate for Radical Movements.* Boston: Beacon Press, 2018.

Carty, Victoria. *Social Movements and New Technology.* New York: Routledge, 2019. https://doi.org/10.4324/9780429493119.

Castells, Manuel. *Networks of Outrage and Hope: Social Movements in the Internet Age.* Malden, MA: Polity Press, 2012.

Césaire, Aimé. *Discourse on Colonialism.* Trans. Joan Pinkham. New York: Monthly Review Press, 2001.

Chan, Melissa. "Philando Castile Was a Role Model to Hundreds of Kids." *Time,* July 7, 2016. https://time.com/4397086/minnesota-shooting-philando-castile-role-model-school/.

Chandler, Nahum D. "Of Exorbitance: The Problem of the Negro as a Problem for Thought." *Criticism* 50, no. 3 (2008): 345–410.

———. "Originary Displacement." *Boundary 2* 27, no. 3 (2000): 249–86.

Chapman, Erin D. *Prove It on Me: New Negroes, Sex, and Popular Culture in the 1920s*. New York: Oxford University Press, 2012.

Chatelain, Marcia. "#BlackLivesMatter: An Online Roundtable with Alicia Garza, Dante Barry, and Darsheel Kaur." *Dissent* (blog), January 19, 2015. https://www.dissentmagazine .org/blog/blacklivesmatter-an-online-roundtable-with-alicia-garza-dante-barry-and -darsheel-kaur.

Cineas, Fabiola. "Oluwatoyin Salau Found Dead in Tallahassee, Florida, after Sharing Story of Sexual Assault on Twitter." *Vox*, June 16, 2020. https://www.vox.com/2020/6/16/21292237 /oluwatoyin-salau-death.

Clark, Wardell Julius. *Kill Move Paradise*. TimeLine Theatre. https://timelinetheatre.com /events/kill-move-paradise/.

Clement, Olivia. "National Black Theatre Launches 48th Season Today." *Playbill*, September 7, 2016. https://playbill.com/article/national-black-theatre-launches-48th-season-today.

Cohen, Cathy J. *The Boundaries of Blackness: AIDS and the Breakdown of Black Politics*. Chicago: University of Chicago Press, 1999.

———. "Punks, Bulldaggers, and Welfare Queens: The Radical Potential of Queer Politics?" *GLQ: A Journal of Lesbian and Gay Studies* 3, no. 4 (1997): 437–65. https://doi.org/10.1215 /10642684-3-4-437.

Crawford, Margo Natalie. *Black Post-Blackness: The Black Arts Movement and Twenty-First-Century Aesthetics*. Urbana: University of Illinois Press, 2017.

Crawley, Ashon T. *Blackpentecostal Breath: The Aesthetics of Possibility*. New York: American Literatures Initiative, 2016.

Cruz, Kleaver. "The Black Joy Project." https://kleavercruz.com/the-black-joy-project.

Currans, Elizabeth. "Utopic Mappings: Performing Joy." *Obsidian* 41, no. 1/2 (2015): 90–102.

Da Silva, Denise Ferreira. "The Scene of Nature." In *Searching for Contemporary Legal Thought*, ed. Christopher Tomlins and Justin Desautels-Stein, 275–89. Cambridge: Cambridge University Press, 2017. https://doi.org/10.1017/9781316584361.015.

———. "Toward a Black Feminist Poethics: The Quest(ion) of Blackness toward the End of the World." *Black Scholar* 44, no. 2 (2014): 81–97. https://doi.org/10.1080/00064246.2014 .11413690.

"David Walker, 1785–1830. Walker's Appeal, in Four Articles; Together with a Preamble, to the Coloured Citizens of the World, but in Particular, and Very Expressly, to Those of the United States of America, Written in Boston, State of Massachusetts, September 28, 1829." https:// docsouth.unc.edu/nc/walker/walker.html.

Dawson, Michael C. "A Black Counterpublic?: Economic Earthquakes, Racial Agenda(s), and Black Politics." *Public Culture* 7, no. 1 (1994): 195–223. https://doi.org/10.1215/08992363-7 -1-195.

———. *Black Visions: The Roots of Contemporary African-American Political Ideologies*. Chicago: University of Chicago Press, 2003.

Dent, Gina, ed. *Black Popular Culture*. New York: New Press, 1998.

Douglass, Frederick, Peter J. Gomes, and Gregory Stephens. *Narrative of the Life of Frederick Douglass*. New York: Signet, 2005.

Douglass, Patrice D. "Black Feminist Theory for the Dead and Dying." *Theory & Event* 21, no. 1 (2018): 106–23.

Du Bois, W.E.B. *The Souls of Black Folk*. Unabridged ed. New York: Dover, 2016.

Edmunds, June, and Bryan S. Turner. *Generational Consciousness, Narrative, and Politics*. Lanham, MD: Rowman and Littlefield, 2002.

Eyerman, Ron. *Cultural Trauma: Slavery and the Formation of African American Identity*. Cambridge: Cambridge University Press, 2002.

Fanon, Frantz. *Black Skin, White Masks*. Trans. Richard Philcox. Rev. ed. New York: Grove Press, 2008.

———. *The Wretched of the Earth*. Trans. Richard Philcox. New York: Grove Press, 2005.

Faulkner, Neil. *A Radical History of the World*. London: Pluto Press, 2018.

"#FergusonFridays: Not All of the Black Freedom Fighters Are Men: An Interview with Black Women on the Front Line in Ferguson." *Feminist Wire*, October 3, 2014. https:// thefeministwire.com/2014/10/fergusonfridays-black-freedom-fighters-men-interview -black-women-front-line-ferguson/.

Fleetwood, Nicole R. *Troubling Vision: Performance, Visuality, and Blackness*. Chicago: University of Chicago Press, 2011.

Freeburg, Christopher. *Counterlife: Slavery after Resistance and Social Death*. Durham: Duke University Press, 2021.

Fry, Richard. "Millennials Overtake Baby Boomers as America's Largest Generation." *Pew Research Center* (blog), April 28, 2020. https://www.pewresearch.org/fact-tank/2020/04/28 /millennials-overtake-baby-boomers-as-americas-largest-generation/.

Garza, Alicia. "A Herstory of the #BlackLivesMatter Movement." *Feminist Wire*, October 7, 2014. https://thefeministwire.com/2014/10/blacklivesmatter-2/.

Gates, Henry Louis, Jr. "The Trope of a New Negro and the Reconstruction of the Image of the Black." *Representations* 24 (1988): 129–55. https://doi.org/10.2307/2928478.

Genovese, Eugene D. *Roll, Jordan, Roll: The World the Slaves Made*. New York: Vintage, 1976.

Getachew, Adom. *Worldmaking after Empire: The Rise and Fall of Self-Determination*. Princeton: Princeton University Press, 2020.

Gilbert, Jeremy. "This Conjuncture: For Stuart Hall." *New Formations*, no. 96–97 (March 2019): 5–37. https://doi.org/10.3898/NEWF:96/97.EDITORIAL.2019.

Gilroy, Paul. *The Black Atlantic: Modernity and Double-Consciousness*. Cambridge, MA: Harvard University Press, 1993.

Gooding-Williams, Robert. *In the Shadow of Du Bois: Afro-Modern Political Thought in America*. Reprint. Cambridge, MA: Harvard University Press, 2011.

Gordon, Lewis R. *Bad Faith and Antiblack Racism*. New York: Humanity Books, 1995.

Gould, Deborah B. *Moving Politics: Emotion and ACT UP's Fight against AIDS*. Chicago: University of Chicago Press, 2009.

Green, Kai M., Je Naé Taylor, Pascale Ifé Williams, and Christopher Roberts. "#BlackHealing-Matters in the Time of #BlackLivesMatter." *Biography* 41, no. 4 (2018): 909–41.

Guy-Sheftall, Beverly, ed. *Words of Fire: An Anthology of African-American Feminist Thought*. New York: New Press, 1995.

Hahn, Steven. *A Nation under Our Feet: Black Political Struggles in the Rural South from Slavery to the Great Migration.* Cambridge, MA: Belknap Press, 2005.

Hall, Joan Wylie, ed. *Conversations with Audre Lorde.* Jackson: University Press of Mississippi, 2004.

Hall, Stuart. "Black Diaspora Artists in Britain: Three 'Moments' in Post-War History." *History Workshop Journal*, no. 61 (2006): 1–24.

———. "Cultural Identity and Diaspora." In *Colonial Discourse and Post-Colonial Theory.* New York: Routledge, 1994.

Harding, Vincent. *There Is a River: The Black Struggle for Freedom in America.* San Diego: Mariner Books, 1993.

Harney, Stefano, and Fred Moten. *The Undercommons: Fugitive Planning & Black Study.* New York: Autonomedia, 2013.

Harris, Christopher Paul, and Marisa Solomon. "Black Grammar: Repertoires of Abolition's Future, Present, and Past." *Social Science Quarterly* 102, no. 7 (2021): 3114–19. https://doi.org/10.1111/ssqu.13070.

Harris, Fredrick C. "The Next Civil Rights Movement?" *Dissent*, Summer 2015. https://www.dissentmagazine.org/article/black-lives-matter-new-civil-rights-movement-fredrick-harris.

Harris, Laura. "What Happened to the Motley Crew?: C.L.R. James, Hélio Oiticica, and the Aesthetic Sociality of Blackness." *Social Text* 30, no. 3 (2012): 49–75. https://doi.org/10.1215/01642472-1597332.

Hartman, Saidiya V. *Lose Your Mother: A Journey along the Atlantic Slave Route.* New York: Farrar, Straus and Giroux, 2007.

———. *Scenes of Subjection: Terror, Slavery, and Self-Making in Nineteenth-Century America.* New York: Oxford University Press, 1997.

———. *Wayward Lives, Beautiful Experiments: Intimate Histories of Riotous Black Girls, Troublesome Women, and Queer Radicals.* New York: W. W. Norton, 2020.

Haslett, Tobi. "Magic Actions: Looking back on the George Floyd Rebellion." *n+1*, July 21, 2021. https://www.nplusonemag.com/issue-40/politics/magic-actions-2/.

Hemphill, Prentis. "Healing Justice Is How We Can Sustain Black Lives." *HuffPost*, February 7, 2017. https://www.huffpost.com/entry/healing-justice_b_5899e8ade4b0c1284f282ffe.

Hesse, Barnor. "White Sovereignty (. . .), Black Life Politics: 'The N****r They Couldn't Kill.'" *South Atlantic Quarterly* 116, no. 3 (2017): 581–604. https://doi.org/10.1215/00382876-3961494.

Hesse, Barnor, and Juliet Hooker. "Introduction: On Black Political Thought inside Global Black Protest." *South Atlantic Quarterly* 116, no. 3 (2017): 443–56. https://doi.org/10.1215/00382876-3961428.

Holmes, Barbara A. *Joy Unspeakable: Contemplative Practices of the Black Church.* 2nd ed. Minneapolis: Fortress Press, 2017.

hooks, bell. *Black Looks: Race and Representation.* 2nd ed. New York: Routledge, 2014.

Hughes, Joycelyn, and Kofi LeNiles. "Voices from the Field: Uplifting and Amplifying: An Interview with Kleaver Cruz." *Journal of Negro Education* 86, no. 3 (2017): 341–44.

Human Rights Campaign. "Fatal Violence against the Transgender and Gender Non-Conforming Community in 2021." https://www.hrc.org/resources/fatal-violence-against-the-transgender-and-gender-non-conforming-community-in-2021.

Isoke, Zenzele. "Black Ethnography, Black(Female)Aesthetics: Thinking/Writing/Saying/ Sounding Black Political Life." *Theory & Event* 21, no. 1 (2018): 148–68.

isysadmin. "It Is Time for Accountability." *Statement from the Frontlines of BLM* (blog). https:// www.blmchapterstatement.com/no1/.

Iton, Richard. *In Search of the Black Fantastic: Politics and Popular Culture in the Post–Civil Rights Era*. Oxford: Oxford University Press, 2008.

James, C.L.R. *The Black Jacobins: Toussaint L'Ouverture and the San Domingo Revolution*. 2nd ed. New York: Vintage, 1989.

James, Joy. "Afrarealism and the Black Matrix: Maroon Philosophy at Democracy's Border." *Black Scholar* 43, no. 4 (2013): 124–31. https://doi.org/10.5816/blackscholar.43.4.0124.

Jamieson, Amber. "The Man Accused of Killing Toyin Salau Allegedly Admitted It to Police and His Mother." *BuzzFeed News*, June 21, 2020. https://www.buzzfeednews.com/article /amberjamieson/toyin-salau-aaron-glee-confession.

Jarrett, Gene Andrew. *A Companion to African American Literature*. New York: John Wiley & Sons, 2013.

Jhally, Sut. "Stuart Hall: The Last Interview." *Cultural Studies* 30, no. 2 (2016): 332–45. https://doi .org/10.1080/09502386.2015.1089918.

Johnson, Gaye Theresa, and Alex Lubin, eds. *Futures of Black Radicalism*. London: Verso, 2017.

Johnson, Javon. "Black Joy in the Time of Ferguson." *QED: A Journal in GLBTQ Worldmaking* 2, no. 2 (2015): 177–83. https://doi.org/10.14321/qed.2.2.0177.

Jones, Dustin. "What Is the 'Great Replacement' and How Is It Tied to the Buffalo Shooting Suspect?" NPR, May 16, 2022, sec. Race. https://www.npr.org/2022/05/16/1099034094 /what-is-the-great-replacement-theory.

Jones, LeRoi. *Home: Social Essays*. New York: Akashic Books, 2009.

Judaken, Jonathan, and Jennifer L. Geddes. "Black Intellectuals in America: A Conversation with Cornel West." *Hedgehog Review* 9, no. 1 (2007): 81–92.

Katch, Danny. "#BlackLivesMatter Looks to the Future." *SocialistWorker.org*, February 4, 2015. http://socialistworker.org/2015/02/04/blacklivesmatter-looks-ahead.

King, Debra Walker. *African Americans and the Culture of Pain*. Charlottesville: University of Virginia Press, 2008.

King, Martin L., Jr. *Letter from Birmingham Jail*. New York: Penguin, 2018.

Kishi, Roudabeh. "A Year of Racial Justice Protests: Key Trends in Demonstrations Supporting the BLM Movement." *ACLED* (blog), May 25, 2021. https://acleddata.com/2021/05/25/a -year-of-racial-justice-protests-key-trends-in-demonstrations-supporting-the-blm -movement/.

Knight, Christina. "Creative Time: Black Joy in the Hour of Chaos." https://www.academia.edu /21304271/CREATIVE_TIME_Black_Joy_in_the_Hour_of_Chaos.

Levine, Lawrence W. *Black Culture and Black Consciousness: Afro-American Folk Thought from Slavery to Freedom*. Oxford: Oxford University Press, 2007.

Lewis, Sarah. "Vision & Justice: Guest Editor Note." *Aperture*, February 23, 2016. https:// aperture.org/editorial/vision-justice/.

"The Life of an Afro-Digital Immigrant | Episode 056 Ft. André Singleton." *Am I Allowed to Like Anything?* Podcast. https://anchor.fm/darian.

A Litany for Survival: The Life and Work of Audre Lorde. Third World Newsreel, 1996. https://video.alexanderstreet.com/watch/litany-for-survival-the-life-and-work-of-audre-lorde-a-90-min.

Locke, Alain. "Enter the New Negro." In *The New Negro: Voices of the Harlem Renaissance*, ed. Alain Locke. Reprint. New York: Touchstone, 1999.

Lorde, Audre. *Sister Outsider: Essays and Speeches.* Reprint. Berkeley, CA: Crossing Press, 2007.

Maher, Geo. *A World without Police: How Strong Communities Make Cops Obsolete.* London: Verso, 2021.

"The Mandate: A Call and Response from Black Lives Matter Atlanta." *Southerners on New Ground* (blog), July 14, 2016. https://southernersonnewground.org/themandate/.

Marable, Manning, and Leith Mullings, eds. *Let Nobody Turn Us Around: An African American Anthology.* 2nd ed. Lanham, MD: Rowman and Littlefield, 2009.

Marshall, Stephen H. "The Political Life of Fungibility." *Theory & Event* 15, no. 3 (2012). https://muse.jhu.edu/article/484457.

Marx, Karl. *Capital: Volume 1: A Critique of Political Economy.* Trans. Ben Fowkes. London: Penguin Classics, 1992.

———. *The Political Writings.* Ed. David Fernbach. London: Verso, 2019.

Mayo, James M. "War Memorials as Political Memory." *Geographical Review* 78, no. 1 (1988): 62–75. https://doi.org/10.2307/214306.

McBride, Lee A., III. *Ethics and Insurrection: A Pragmatism for the Oppressed.* London: Bloomsbury, 2022.

McDuffie, Erik S. *Sojourning for Freedom: Black Women, American Communism, and the Making of Black Left Feminism.* Durham: Duke University Press, 2011.

McKittrick, Katherine. *Dear Science and Other Stories.* Durham: Duke University Press, 2021.

———. "Mathematics Black Life." *Black Scholar* 44, no. 2 (2014): 16–28. https://doi.org/10.1080/00064246.2014.11413684.

"Meet the College Student Who Pulled Down a Confederate Statue in Durham & Defied White Supremacy." *Democracy Now!* August 16, 2017. https://www.democracynow.org/2017/8/16/meet_the_college_student_who_pulled.

Mills, Charles W. *The Racial Contract.* Ithaca: Cornell University Press, 2022.

Morgan, Jennifer L. *Reckoning with Slavery: Gender, Kinship, and Capitalism in the Early Black Atlantic.* Durham: Duke University Press, 2021.

Moten, Fred. *In the Break: The Aesthetics of the Black Radical Tradition.* Minneapolis: University of Minnesota Press, 2003.

Movement for Black Lives (M4BL). "Policy Platforms." *M4BL* (blog). https://m4bl.org/policy-platforms/.

Mueller, Benjamin, and Ashley Southall. "25,000 March in New York to Protest Police Violence." *New York Times*, December 14, 2014, sec. New York. https://www.nytimes.com/2014/12/14/nyregion/in-new-york-thousands-march-in-continuing-protests-over-garner-case.html.

Murch, Donna. *Assata Taught Me: State Violence, Racial Capitalism, and the Movement for Black Lives.* Chicago: Haymarket Books, 2022.

Ndgo, YahNé. "Tell No Lies." *Statement from the Frontlines of BLM* (blog). https://www.blmchapterstatement.com/no2/.

Neal, Larry. "And Shine Swam On." In *Black Fire: An Anthology of Afro-American Writing*, ed. Amiri Baraka and Larry Neal, 637–56. Baltimore: Black Classic Press, 2007.

———. "The Black Arts Movement (1968)." In *A Sourcebook on African-American Performance*. New York: Routledge, 1999.

"The Negro Artist and the Racial Mountain by Langston Hughes." Poetry Foundation. https://www.poetryfoundation.org/articles/69395/the-negro-artist-and-the-racial-mountain.

"(1977) The Combahee River Collective Statement." November 16, 2012. https://www.blackpast.org/african-american-history/combahee-river-collective-statement-1977/.

Osterweil, Vicky. *In Defense of Looting: A Riotous History of Uncivil Action*. New York: Bold Type Books, 2020.

Peoples, Lindsay. "The 7 Best Black Joy Moments at the Royal Wedding." *The Cut*, May 20, 2018. https://www.thecut.com/2018/05/royal-wedding-best-black-joy-moments.html.

Planas, Antonio. "Black Man Grabbing Tea from Car Shot by New Jersey Police and Paralyzed, Lawsuit Says." NBC News, March 18, 2022. https://www.nbcnews.com/news/us-news/unarmed-black-man-grabbing-tea-car-shot-new-jersey-police-paralyzed-la-rcna20640.

Purnell, Derecka. "If Even Beyoncé Had a Rough Pregnancy, What Hope Do Other Black Women Have?" *Guardian*, April 23, 2019, sec. Opinion. https://www.theguardian.com/commentisfree/2019/apr/23/beyonce-pregnancy-black-women.

Rael, Patrick. *Black Identity and Black Protest in the Antebellum North*. Chapel Hill: University of North Carolina Press, 2002.

Rankine, Claudia. "'The Condition of Black Life Is One of Mourning.'" *New York Times*, June 22, 2015, sec. Magazine. https://www.nytimes.com/2015/06/22/magazine/the-condition-of-black-life-is-one-of-mourning.html.

Ransby, Barbara. *Making All Black Lives Matter: Reimagining Freedom in the Twenty-First Century*. Oakland: University of California Press, 2018.

Reed, Anthony. "The Black Situation: Notes on Black Critical Theory Now." *American Literary History* 34, no. 1 (2022): 283–300. https://doi.org/10.1093/alh/ajac001.

Robinson, Cedric J. *Black Marxism: The Making of the Black Radical Tradition*. 2nd ed. Chapel Hill: University of North Carolina Press, 2000.

———. *Black Movements in America*. New York: Routledge, 1997.

Rodriguez, Dylan. "Abolition as Praxis of Human Being: A Foreword." *Harvard Law Review* 132, no. 6 (2019): 1575–1612.

Scott, David. "Introduction: On the Archaeologies of Black Memory." *Small Axe* 12, no. 2 (2008): v–xvi.

———. "The Temporality of Generations: Dialogue, Tradition, Criticism." *New Literary History* 45, no. 2 (2014): 157–81. https://doi.org/10.1353/nlh.2014.0017.

Sexton, Jared. "'The Curtain of the Sky': An Introduction." *Critical Sociology* 36, no. 1 (2010): 11–24. https://doi.org/10.1177/0896920509347136.

Shakur, Assata. *Assata: An Autobiography*. Chicago: Lawrence Hill Books, 2001.

Sharpe, Christina. *In the Wake: On Blackness and Being*. Durham: Duke University Press, 2016.

———. *Monstrous Intimacies: Making Post-Slavery Subjects*. Durham: Duke University Press, 2010.

Sinha, Manisha. *The Slave's Cause: A History of Abolition*. Reprint. New Haven: Yale University Press, 2017.

Smethurst, James Edward. *The Black Arts Movement: Literary Nationalism in the 1960s and 1970s.* New ed. Chapel Hill: University of North Carolina Press, 2005.

Smith, Neil. "Global Social Cleansing: Postliberal Revanchism and the Export of Zero Tolerance." *Social Justice* 28, no. 3 (2001): 68–74.

Solomon, Akiba. "Get on the Bus: Inside the Black Life Matters 'Freedom Ride' to Ferguson." *Colorlines*, September 5, 2014. https://www.colorlines.com/articles/get-bus-inside-black-life-matters-freedom-ride-ferguson.

Sontag, Susan. *Regarding the Pain of Others.* New York: Picador, 2004.

Southern Poverty Law Center. "Whose Heritage? Public Symbols of the Confederacy." https://www.splcenter.org/20190201/whose-heritage-public-symbols-confederacy.

Spillers, Hortense J. "The Idea of Black Culture." *CR: The New Centennial Review* 6, no. 3 (2006): 7–28.

———. "Mama's Baby, Papa's Maybe: An American Grammar Book." *Diacritics* 17, no. 2 (1987): 64–81. https://doi.org/10.2307/464747.

Spires, Derrick R. *The Practice of Citizenship: Black Politics and Print Culture in the Early United States.* Philadelphia: University of Pennsylvania Press, 2019.

Springer, Kimberly. *Living for the Revolution: Black Feminist Organizations, 1968–1980.* Durham: Duke University Press, 2005.

Stanley, Eric A. *Atmospheres of Violence: Structuring Antagonism and the Trans/Queer Ungovernable.* Durham: Duke University Press, 2021.

Stuckey, Sterling. *Slave Culture: Nationalist Theory and the Foundations of Black America.* 2nd ed. Oxford: Oxford University Press, 2013.

Taylor, Keeanga-Yamahtta. *From #BlackLivesMatter to Black Liberation.* Chicago: Haymarket Books, 2016.

Taylor, Paul C. *Black Is Beautiful: A Philosophy of Black Aesthetics.* Hoboken, NJ: Wiley-Blackwell, 2016.

Threadcraft, Shatema. "North American Necropolitics and Gender: On #BlackLivesMatter and Black Femicide." *South Atlantic Quarterly* 116, no. 3 (2017): 553–79. https://doi.org/10.1215/00382876-3961483.

Trouillot, Michel-Rolph. *Silencing the Past: Power and the Production of History.* 2nd rev. ed. Boston: Beacon Press, 2015.

Walcott, Rinaldo. *The Long Emancipation: Moving toward Black Freedom.* Durham: Duke University Press, 2021.

Walker, David. *David Walker's Appeal to the Coloured Citizens of the World.* Eastford, CT: Martino Fine Books, 2015.

Warren, Calvin L. "Black Care." *liquid blackness* 3, no. 6 (2016): 36–47.

———. "Black Nihilism and the Politics of Hope." *CR: The New Centennial Review* 15, no. 1 (2015): 215–48. https://doi.org/10.14321/crnewcentrevi.15.1.0215.

———. *Ontological Terror: Blackness, Nihilism, and Emancipation.* Durham: Duke University Press, 2018.

Wells-Barnett, Ida B. *Southern Horrors & The Red Record.* AmazonClassics, 2021.

Wilderson, Frank B., III. *Red, White & Black: Cinema and the Structure of U.S. Antagonisms.* Durham: Duke University Press, 2010.

Williams, Eric. *Capitalism & Slavery*. 3rd ed. Chapel Hill: University of North Carolina Press, 2021.

Williamson, Terrion L. *Scandalize My Name: Black Feminist Practice and the Making of Black Social Life*. New York: American Literatures Initiative, 2016.

Woodly, Deva R. *The Politics of Common Sense: How Social Movements Use Public Discourse to Change Politics and Win Acceptance*. New York: Oxford University Press, 2015.

———. *Reckoning: Black Lives Matter and the Democratic Necessity of Social Movements*. New York: Oxford University Press, 2021.

Wright, Richard. "Blueprint for Negro Writing (1937)." In *African American Literary Theory: A Reader*, ed. Winston Napier, 45–53. New York: New York University Press, 2000.

Wynter, Sylvia. "On How We Mistook the Map for the Territory, and Reimprisoned Ourselves in Our Unbearable Wrongness of Being, of Desêtre: Black Studies toward the Human Project." In *A Companion to African-American Studies*, 107–18. New York: John Wiley & Sons, 2006. https://doi.org/10.1002/9780470996645.ch9.

———. "Sambos and Minstrels." *Social Text*, no. 1 (1979): 149–56. https://doi.org/10.2307/466410.

———. "Unsettling the Coloniality of Being/Power/Truth/Freedom: Towards the Human, After Man, Its Overrepresentation—An Argument." *CR: The New Centennial Review* 3, no. 3 (2003): 257–337.

INDEX

Page numbers in *italics* denote figures.

Abdur-Rahman, Aliyyah I., 153, 157

abled bodies/the differently abled, 29, 39

abolitionism (abolition of world system), 12, 20, 27–29, 35–40, 46–49, 75–79, 95, 201–5; an abolitionist way of life, 153–54, 157, 193, 198–99; Black grammar of, 53, 140–42, 145–46; and Black joy, 133–34, 138–42, 145–46, 153–54, 157, 205; and care, ethics/operations of, 166, 177, 179, 193, 198–99; praxis of, 179, 204; and reconstruction of society, 34, 36, 46–47, 75, 204; vs. reformist approach, 14–15, 53–58, 216n65, 226n50

abolitionism (movement to end slavery), 54–56

activism, 4, 32, 39, 61, 104, 140, 202; Black, 23–25, 34–35, 94, 99, 177–78; multiracial, 4, 11–12, 20–21, 32. *See also by name/movement*

advocacy, 25

Afrarealism, 41

Africa: independence in, 201; Negritude movement of, 29, 59; Pan-Africanism, 63–65, 72. *See also* diaspora, Black; Middle Passage

African Americans. *See entries beginning with* Black; *specific topics*

African Blood Brotherhood, 65

Afropunk festival, 109–10, 127

agency, Black and Brown, 41, 49, 104–5, 201, 226n64

Agnew, Phillip, 22

Alexander, Elizabeth, 83, 89, 170, 191, 224nn25 and 30

alienation, 56, 105, 145, 152, 223n6

Alkalimat, Abdul, 19, 27

Allen, Ernest, Jr., 64

allies, 56, 123

ancestors, 3, 40, 149, 169, 176, 194–99, 205, 235n78

anger, 11, 84, 165, 171; day of, 5, 213n4. *See also* rage

anti-Blackness, 4–6, 11–13, 19–23, 37–47, 60–65, 75, 78, 202–4 and passim; Black counterpublic as providing counternarratives to, 191; Black joy in spite of/rejection of, 123–25, 130–32, 149–50, 154–56, 189; and Black pain, 87–96, 102–6, 113–14; and care, ethics/operations of, 161, 170–75, 179, 191, 194, 198; as global, 150; and impossibility of justice, 96; legacies of, 98; and "origin of the subject," 84; and property as superordinate to Black life, 31–32, 49, 204; rage forced upon us by, 124–25; total climate of, 30, 38. *See also under* racism: anti-Black; white supremacy; *specific topics, e.g.,* terror; violence

anticipation, power of, 29, 204

Arab uprisings, 8, 16

Arbery, Ahmaud, 88, 214n20

archives/Black archiving practices, 51, 85–86, 94, 117, 209, 223n7, 230n69, 231n79; of Black diaspora, 197–98; and Black joy, 132–34; and counterarchival practice, 187–95, 197; social media and, 144

art, 43, 59, 61–62, 70–71, 74, 110, 143

arts, Black, 66–75; Black Arts Movement
(BAM), 47, 66–75, 123, 171. *See also* art;
dance; Harlem Renaissance; music; New
Negro movement; theater
ashe, 168, 204, 233n21, 235n77
Assata chant, 163, 165
Assata's Daughters, 27
assimilation, 33, 74, 76, 223n3
authority, 44, 62–63, 69, 76–77, 104, 120.
See also government; leadership; police;
power
autonomy, 18, 27, 30, 63

baby boomers, 15. *See also* generations
Baker, Courtney, 94
Baker, Ella, 73, 104, 166
Baldwin, Davarian L., 59
Baldwin, James, 192
Baltimore, MD, 11
Bandung Conference, 72
Baraka, Amiri, 67, 69–70, 73
Barry, Dante, 20, 22
BARTS (Black Arts Repertory Theater and
School), 73
Bascomb, Lia, 132
BeatKing, 11
beauty, 62, 67–68, 71, 75, 78, 129, *148*, 185;
"Black is beautiful," 29, 47, 135
"beloved community," 147–51
Berger, John, 11
Bey, Marquis, 79, 210
Beyoncé, 11, 135
"Beyond November," 25. *See also* Black
Youth Project 100 (BYP100)
Black Arts Movement (BAM), 47, 66–75,
123, 171
Black Arts Repertory Theater and School
(BARTS), 73
Black counterpublic. *See* counterpublic,
Black
Black death. *See* death, Black
Black experience, 25, 27–28, 38, 42, 58–59,
70, 78; and Black joy, 121, 131, 145; and

care, ethics/operations of, 184, 191. *See
also* Black life; Black livingness; quotid-
ian experience
#blackgirlmagic, 125, 127
Black grammar. *See* grammar, Black
"Black is beautiful," 29, 47, 135
Black joy. *See* joy, Black
Black Joy Experience (BJE), 128–29, 147
Black Joy Experience Resource Guide, The,
179, 233n23
Black Joy Mixtape, 126, 147
The Black Joy Project (TBJP), 133–35, 138–
51, *144, 146, 148,* 181–82, 230n71. *See also*
Cruz, Kleaver; joy, Black
Black-led social movements, 5–6, 39. *See also
by name/description*
Black life: attending to full expanse of,
198–99; Black joy in and as, 131–34; and
Black livingness, 53, 123, 199, 234n63; core
and soul of, 46; dignity of, 135; everyday,
46, 59, 67–68, 70, 74–75, 78, 89 (*see also*
quotidian experience); honoring all,
109; the "largeness that is Black life," 38,
124; multivalent nature of, 70; non-
pathologized, 89; property as superordinate to, 31–32, 49, 204; resilience of, 40,
121, 191; in the wake, 131 (*see also* wake,
living in). *See also* Black experience;
Blackness; survival, Black; *specific topics,*
e.g., liberation
Black Life Matters Ride, 23–25, 216n64
#BlackLivesMatter, 5–8, 10, 16, 18–29, 124–
27, 170; political culture of, 6–8, 19–20;
time of, 7–8, 12, 26–29, 35, 37, 40–43, 47,
94, 105, 124, 153, 161–63, 174, 179, 182, 186,
202–4. *See also* Black Lives Matter
Movement
Black Lives Matter Global Network
(BLMGN), 16–17, 166–67, 174–75, 230n57
Black Lives Matter Movement, 4–43 passim,
92–94, 166, 202–4, 224n29; two births of
(*see* #BlackLivesMatter; Movement for
Black Lives [M4BL])

Black livingness, 53, 123, 199

Blackness, 12–13, 18–24, 28–33, 37–47, 59–62, 68–78 and passim; author's relationship with, 208; and being Pro Black, 194, 195; "Coming to Blackness," 208; concept of, 19; criminalization of, 22, 33, 94, 97, 175, 222n3; definition of, 43; embodiment of, 170, 187–88; honoring, 169–73; loving/embracing, 69–76, 168–69, 194, 233n23; meaning of, 202–3; nature of, 43; "poethics of," 130; political mobilizations of, 136; primacy of, 191; problem spaces of, 23, 78; reimagining, 61–62, 182–83; unapologetic, 37, 61, 68, 79, 114, 125, 157, 182, 186–87, 198, 202; understanding of, among Black people, 227n1. See also Black life; specific topics, e.g., identities; joy, Black

Black pain. See pain, Black

Black Panther Party, 8, 74

Black performance, 127

Black performativity, 123

Black Power, 8, 29, 35, 47, 69–70, 72–76, 97, 123, 171, 191

Black self: collective, 47, 58. See also entries beginning with self

Black Situation, 7, 28, 30, 47; and Black political development, 30–31, 37–38, 42, 48–49, 56, 58, 70, 106, 129, 170–71, 173, 182, 203

Black Visions Collective, 27, 216n75

Black Youth Project 100 (BYP100), 16–17, 25–26, 37, 103–25, 128–29, 152, 207–8, 228n8, 228n10, 228n12, 232n 1, 232n 3, 232n15, 233n23, 234n50; "Agenda to Build Black Futures," 225n48; "Agenda to Keep Us Safe," 225n48; and care, ethics/operations of, 163–70, 173, 177–80, 194–98; emergence of, 25–26; Healing and Safety Council (HSC), 168, 177–80; M4BL, relationship with, 166, 226n50, 227n4; mission and lens of, 25–26; Our Streets, Our Bodies, Our Voices (OS/OB/OV),

95, 107–9, 111–13, 112, 117, 118–19, 120, 165; political culture of, 106

Blain, Keisha, 65

Blake, Jacob, 31–32

BLM. See Black Lives Matter Movement

BLMGN. See Black Lives Matter Global Network

blues music, 69

bodies, Black, 4, 89–93, 135, 161; moving while captive, 46, 52–53 (see also chanting; dancing; shouting; singing); as site of resistance, 52. See also embodiment; specific topics, e.g., death, Black

Bolshevik Revolution, 64

Bonner, Marita, 67

Booker, Muhlaysia, 155–56

boundaries, 44, 95, 109, 133, 135, 139, 231n87; of Blackness/Black life, 95, 141; gender-based drawing of, 60

boycotts, 73, 102

Boyd, Rekia, 31

Braithwaite, Kwame, 135

Brand, Dionne, 174

Brazil, 49, 150–51

Briggs, Cyril, 65, 69

Brooks, Gwendolyn, 159, 173

Brooks, Rayshard, 88

Brown, Michael, 3–4, 23, 125, 141, 186, 213n1. See also Ferguson, Missouri/Ferguson uprisings

Brown people. See marginalized people and groups; people of color (POC); specific topics

Brown v. Board of Education, 73

Brown, Wendy, 8

Buffalo, NY shooting, 6, 9

BYP100. See Black Youth Project

Cadet, Jewel, 152–53, 158, 167

cadre development, 27

Camp Akili (Oakland), 228n10

Camp, Stephanie, 49, 52, 132

Campt, Tina Marie, 92, 225n32

capitalism/capitalist world system, 15–16, 18, 39–40, 62, 78–79, 98 and passim; abolitionism as aiming to undo/remake, 201–5 (*see also* abolitionism); atomized alienation produced by, 152; Black, 65; and Black joy, 130, 133–34, 151–54; corrupt social relations in, 49; current crisis in, 202; extractive/exploitative agenda of, 162, 201; as feeding off Black pain, 121, 157, 162, 174, 181, 188, 197–98; "freedom" under, 57; property as superordinate to Black life in, 31–32, 49, 204; racial, 14, 48, 161, 173; reformist approach to, 14–15, 53–58, 216n65, 226n50; rejection of, 49, 65; and the state, 174; violence of, 162, 201. *See also* abolitionism; neoliberalism; *specific topics, e.g.,* carceral power

captivity, shifting states of, 31, 48, 94, 175; the Covid-19 pandemic, 8–9, 152

and moving while captive, 46, 52–53 (*see also* chanting; dancing; shouting; singing); staging, 107–20. *See also* carceral power; slavery

carceral power, 12, 173–75, 177, 180, 198, 203; and criminalization of Black/Brown people, 22, 33, 94, 97, 131, 175, 222n3; enclosures of, 36, 161; law and order, everyday language of, 14; and property as superordinate to Black life, 31–32, 49, 204. *See also* captivity; police

care, ethics/operations of, 159–203; "Black care," 162; Black radical, 177, 180; ethics of, 6, 14, 26, 38–39, 79, 134, 161–62, 173–78, 186, 200–203; as form of study, 203; and healing justice, 174–80; and inclusion/inclusivity, 6, 26, 38, 173, 177, 182, 193–94, 202–3; mutual-aid societies/parties, 63–64, 157; as political act, 175; practice of, 157, 169; responding to racial hurt with, 175; self-care, 129, 169; spaces of, 178, 181–82

Caribbean, 49, 64; Negritude movement of, 29, 59. *See also* Wynter, Sylvia

"car ramming," 32

Carr, Julian S., 100

Carruthers, Charlene, 26

Castells, Manuel, 18

Castile, Philando, 83–88, 90, 93–98, 127, 223n7, 225nn46–47; "Philando Castile Was a Role Model to Hundreds of Kids" (Chan), 223n9

Castile, Valerie, 96–98

celebration, 12, 39–40, 78, 101, 118, 123–32, 138, 169, 227n76; Blackness as worthy of, 147; despite oppression, 23. *See also* joy, Black; *specific topics/descriptions, e.g.,* Very Black Project; Ratchet Realm

centering the marginalized, 26, 39, 133, 147, 192

Césaire, Aimé, 59, 200

Césaire, Suzanne, 59

change, 21; continuity despite, 42, 58–69; transformative justice, 178. *See also* abolitionism; reformism

chants/chanting, 3, 53, 100, 176, 179, 227n4, 228n8, 228n10; Assata's chant, 163, 165; and Black joy, 121–24, 129, 133, 151, 158; "I Love Being Black," 69–76, 168–69, 233n23

Chapman, Erin, 60–61

Charlottesville, VA, "Unite the Right" rally in, 101, 105

Chauvin, Derek, 10

Chief Keef, 11

Chinese Revolution, 72

church, Black, 43, 123, 227n5

cis heteropatriarchy. *See under* patriarchy: heteronormative

citations, Black, 187–94

citizenship, 44–58, 61, 69, 74–75, 78, 85, 91

civil disobedience, nonviolent, 21

Civil Rights Act, 73, 76

Civil Rights movement, 4–5, 29, 35, 69, 76, 90, 94, 99–100, 192, 228n11. *See also individual names; specific topics and events*

Civil War, U.S., 47, 49, 55, 57–58, 94, 99–100

class, 44, 76, 165; and classism, 62, 118. *See also by description, e.g.,* elites; middle class; underclass

Clifton, Lucille, 134
climate change/catastrophe, 9, 201
club movement, Black women's, 60–61
codes, racial, 60, 84
Cohen, Cathy, 25, 44, 158
Cold War, 35, 72
colonialism, 9–10, 62–63, 65, 72, 169–71, 187, 200–203; gendered racial-colonial dominance, 121; and slavery, 6, 29–30, 33, 42, 46–47, 50–53, 170; and white sense, enclosures of, 14. *See also* wake, living in
colonization, 36, 103; and decolonization, 150 and radicalism of the colonized/enslaved, 36, 51–53, 79, 123, 204. *See also* plantation politics
Combahee River Collective, 9, 26, 29, 77
communism, 59, 65–66, 72
community: being in, 147, 178, 208; "beloved," 147–51; Black communal living, 54, 63; Black communities, 18, 26–27, 33, 41, 107–10, 116, 137, 169, 194, 216n75, 226n51; the Black community, 18, 28–30, 34, 44, 108–9, 124, 126–27, 135, 165, 170–71, 184, 192–94, 203; feeling of, 127–28; and interdependence, 157, 160–61, 197, 201; "we have each other," 160–61
Confederacy: gray uniforms of, 99, 226n55; monuments of, 10, 95, 99–106, 227n76
Confederate Soldiers Monument (Durham, NC), 95, 99–103, 105–6
conflict resolution, 174, 178
Congolese Independence, 72
Congress of Racial Equality, 24
conjunctural analysis, 30
Constitution, U.S., 54
Cooke, Sam, 69
Cooper, Anna Julia, 60–62
Cooper, Peter, 127
counterpublic, Black, 18–19, 27, 43, 53, 61, 76–78, 180, 197; as counternarrative to anti-Blackness and white supremacy, 191
Covid-19 pandemic, 8–10, 152
Cox, Albert, 99–100

"Cranes in the Sky" (Solange Knowles), 160
Crawford, Margo Natalie, 29, 68, 71, 75, 204
Crawley, Ashon, 38
criminalization of Black and Brown people, 22, 33, 94, 97, 131, 175, 222n3
cruelty, 47–48, 86, 171
Cruz, Kleaver, 134–35, 138–51, 144, 146, 148, 181–82, 229nn44–46, 230n57, 230n71. *See also* Black Joy Project, The (TBJP)
Cuban Revolution, 72
Cullen, Countee, 68
Cullors, Patrisse, 22–24
culture: multiculturalism, 139; neoliberalism and, 33; "our history/our culture" paradigm, 101, 105
culture, Black, 43, 227n1; Black folk culture, 35–36, 46, 52–54, 126, 169, and radicalism of the colonized/enslaved, 36, 79, 123, 204; Black popular culture, 44, 191–92; and cultural expression, 29, 58–59, 74, 78–79; political (*see under specific topics, e.g.,* Movement for Black Lives: political culture of)
Currans, Elizabeth, 149–50

dancing, 7, 11, 205; and Black joy, 121, 123–24, 127–29, 132–33, 148; and care, ethics/operations of, 160, 190; of the disposable, 152–58; moving while captive, 46, 52–53; twerking, 152–53, 158
Dash, Julie, 192
Da Silva, Denise Ferreira, 104–5; and "poethics of Blackness," 130
Davis, Miles, 192
Dawson, Michael, 18, 76–77. *See also* counterpublic, Black
death, Black: Black joy as refusing the repetition of, 154–55; Black protest as resulting from (*see* protest, Black); extrajudicial killings of Black and Brown people, 103–4; honoring the dead and dying, 36,

death, Black (*continued*)
131–32, 204; premature, 34, 39, 42, 73, 85, 89, 129, 153, 156, 165, 168, 222n3, 224n24; recorded on social media, 27, 78, 83–88, 90, 97, 140, 202; repetition of, 27, 31, 78, 90, 96–98, 154–55, 202, 223n3. *See also* lynching; murder; pain, Black

debates, intramural, 18, 43

decolonization, 150

defacement. *See under* property: defacement of

"defund the police," 10, 92

dehumanization, 134, 150

Delany, Martin, 56, 65

democracy, 14, 68, 104, 106, 139, 150, 201, 224n29; American, 9, 28

Dent, Gina, 132

Depression, Great, 59

deviance, politics of, 158

dialogues, 182; within the Black intramural, 18, 43, 116–17, 120, 192–93

diaspora, Black, 7–8, 74, 92, 150–51, 169, 182, 186–87, 201; archives of, 197–98. *See also* Middle Passage

dignity, 23, 37, 135

direct action, 12, 21–22, 25, 39, 110; the Black Joy Experience (BJE), 128–29, 147; nonviolent, 94, 102

disability/the differently abled, 26, 39

disposability, Black, 39, 152, 156, 177

dispossession, 11, 33, 46, 49, 66, 98, 104, 141; and struggle waged against domination, 36–39

diversity, 13, 74; multiracial activism, 4, 11–12, 20–21, 32

Dixon, Ejeris, 23

domination, 52–53, 100, 121, 171, 174; struggle waged by dispossessed against, 36–39. *See also by description, e.g.,* colonialism

Domingo, W. A., 65–66

double-consciousness, 70–71

Douglass, Frederick, 54, 84, 135, 227n76

Dream Defenders, 21–22, 24–25

Dred Scott v. Sandford, 56, 91

drugs, "war on," 97

Du Bois, W.E.B., 48, 62, 64, 67–68, 192

Durham, NC, Confederate Soldiers Monument in, 95, 99–103, 105–6

Ealey, Ain Raven, 107–8, 114–18, 165, 227n69

economics: economic freedom, 26; economic justice, 97; and the 2008 financial collapse, 8, 77. *See also specific topics/systems, e.g.,* capitalism

education, 25–26, 45, 58, 61, 66; *Brown v. Board of Education,* 73; political, 25–26, 129

Electoral College, U.S., 9

elites, Black, 44, 46, 53, 56–57, 67, 74, 191–92; the "Reconstruction Generation," 60

Ellington, Duke, 69

Elliott, Missy, 11

Elzie, Johnetta, 17–18

emancipation, 43, 67, 121, 133, 136, 217n93, 229n32. *See also* abolitionism; freedom; liberation

"Emancipation Park" memorial, 101

embodiment, 10–11, 33, 46, 63, 67, 79, 109; and Black joy/Black joy as, 37, 122, 149–50, 154, 157; of Blackness, 170, 187–88. *See also* bodies, Black

emigration: Black, 56–58; and immigrants, 39

empathy, 94, 98, 108, 140

enclosures, 14, 36, 74, 133, 158, 161. *See also* property

engagement, 78, 95

Enlightenment, 54, 90; and post-Enlightenment political thought, 90

enslavement. *See* slavery

equality, 28, 54–56, 62, 75, 91, 134, 150. Congress of Racial Equality, 24. *See also* inequality; solidarity

erasure, 6–7, 101, 103, 139–40

ethics of care. *See under* care: ethics/operations of

ethnography, 181, 208, 234n64

Evers, Medgar, 73

excellence, Black, 127, 135

experience, Black. *See* Black experience

exploitation, 9, 57, 62–63, 74, 84, 162, 201. *See also specific topics, e.g.,* slavery

Facebook. *See* social media

family, Black, 75, 191

Fanon, Frantz, 15, 17, 41, 71, 173, 192, 200–201, 205, 220n56

Farrakhan, Louis, 35

fascism, 9, 20

Faulkner, Neil, 8

fear, 112, 115–17, 188

feminism, Black, 9–10, 13, 35, 37, 39, 77, 126, 203, 235n83; and care, ethics/operations of, 166, 170–73, 181, 186; queer, 26, 166; radical, 41, 170–71; "Victorian," 60–62. *See also individual names*

femmes, Black, 128, 153, 165

Ferguson, Missouri/Ferguson uprisings, 4–5, 11, 17, 23–24, 186

Ferrell, Brittany, 24

financial collapse of 2008, 8, 77

fire, 10, 31, 34, 36, 50, 53, 73, 162, 202

First Indochina War, 72

Fleetwood, Nicole R., 145

Florida, 20–22, 34, 235n79. *See also* Martin, Trayvon

Floyd, George, 10–11, 88, 93, 227n76

folk culture, Black, 35–36, 46, 52–54, 126, 169; and radicalism of the colonized/enslaved, 36, 79, 123, 204

"For the Gworls" collective, 157

Frankie and Maze, 11

Freeburg, Christopher, 36

freedom, 25–26, 28, 36, 52–53, 79; Black struggle for, 52–53; BYP100, as envisioned by, 25–26; under capitalism, 57; experiments with, 63; solidarities around, 48–49; spaces of, 200; "yet to come," 34, 48–49, 124. *See also* abolition; emancipation; liberation

Freedom Rides, 23–24, 73

Fugitive Slave Act, 56

Fulton, Justin, 182–87, 189, 197. *See also* Very Black Project

future, Black, 37, 41, 121, 124, 163, 176, 199–205; "Agenda to Build Black Futures" (BYP100), 225n48; and anticipation, power of, 29, 204; and Black grammar, 53, 140–42, 145–46; prefiguration of, 79; reimagining, 14, 34; "yet to come," 34, 48–49, 52, 79, 105, 122, 124, 153, 169, 217n93. *See also* abolitionism; liberation

Garner, Eric, 3–4, 213n1

Garrison, William Lloyd, 55

Garvey, Marcus, 64–65, 69

Garza, Alicia, 18, 22–23, 26, 28

Gates, Henry Louis, Jr., 60, 68

gender, 4, 12, 16, 44, 60, 75–77, 202–3; and Black joy, 135, 142; and Black pain, 91–92, 109, 120; and care, ethics/operations of, 164–65, 170; gendered racial-colonial dominance, 121. *See also specific topics, e.g.,* heteronormativity; masculinity

gender nonconforming people, 27, 29, 34, 39, 77, 113, 128, 155, 157. *See also* transgender and gender nonconforming (TGNC) people

generations, 14–16, 19–20, 27–28; and politics, generational, 14–16, 28; the Reconstruction Generation, 60; and trauma, generational, 5, 173–75, 188; the Trayvon generation, 170. *See also by description, e.g.,* millennials

Generation X, 15

Generation Z, 15

genocide, 33, 55, 103

Genovese, Eugene, 48, 50–51

gentrification, 33

geographies, 135; Black/of Blackness, 120, 181–82; of Black suffering, 56, 105–6; of containment/confinement, 49, 56; of the marginalized, 112. *See also by description, e.g.,* kitchens/the kitchen table

Georgia, 100

Ghanaian Independence, 72

'ghetto,' 152

Gilbert, Jeremy, 30

Gilroy, Paul, 150

Gooding-Williams, Robert, 43, 45, 52

Good Times (sitcom), 190–91

government, 77; loss of the white man's, 100; and self-governance, Black, 56–57. *See also* ungovernability; *specific institutions, e.g.,* Supreme Court, U.S.; *specific systems of government*

grammar, Black, 53, 140–42, 145–46

grassroots activities/organizations, 4, 24, 74

Great Depression, 59

"great replacement" theory, 9

group consciousness, 133, 147

guerrilla warfare, 49

Gurley, Akai, 3, 213n1

Hahn, Steven, 42

Haitian Revolution, 50

Hall, Stuart, 30, 46–47

Hands Up United, 24, 216n65

Hansberry, Lorraine, 66

happiness. *See* joy, Black

Harding, Vincent, 30

Harlem Renaissance, 59, 65–68. *See also* New Negro movement

harm, 11, 97, 124; and care, ethics/operations of, 162–67, 170–74, 177–70, 194, 203; intramural, 34–35

Harris, Kamala, 35

Harrison, Hubert, 64

Hartman, Saidiya, 3, 8, 15–16, 36, 40, 63–64, 84, 89, 121, 158, 187, 204

healing: in the aftermath/moving through grief, 18, 169–70, 173–80; healing justice, 174–80. *See also* care, ethics/operations of

Healing and Safety Council (HSC), 168, 177–80; Healing and Safety Community Care Circle, 177, 198

Hemphill, Prentis, 175–77

Henderson, Jajuan R., 31

Hesse, Barnor, 123, 136, 150, 210, 223n3, 224n29

heteronormativity, 14, 65, 75, 77, 156. *See also under* patriarchy: heteronormative

Heyer, Heather, 32

hierarchies, 13, 34, 45, 52, 165, 203; racial, 67, 99–100, 105–6, 224n19

history: Black, 49, 70, 188, 227n76; "our history/our culture" paradigm, 101, 105. *See also specific topics and events*

homophobia, 156

homosexuality, 75. *See also* LGBTQ+ people

Honeycutt, Sequoia, *112*, 112–14

Hooker, Juliet, 136, 150

hooks, bell, 39, 145, 192

Hooks, Mary, 3, 40, 205

hope, 3, 15; and anticipation, power of, 29, 204; diasporic, 8; misplaced, 56, 76. *See also* future, Black

Huber, Anthony, 32

Hughes, Langston, 56, 67–68

human rights, 21, 140

Human Rights Campaign (HRC), 154–55

Hurston, Zora Neale, 67

hypervisibility of Black pain, 27, 37, 39, 78, 202

identities, 15–16; Black, 40, 46, 54, 59, 70, 125, 130, 133, 136, 138, 171, 173; Blackness as more than, 40; collective/communal, 36, 52; dominant American, 64; and double-consciousness, 70–71; generational, 16; and identity work, 133, 138; intersecting, 24, 26, 108; and power, 171; southern, 99

"I Love Being Black," 69–76, 168–69, 233n23

immigrants, 39; Black emigration, 56–58. *See also* marginalized people and groups

imperialism, 9

incarceration. *See* carceral power; prisons

inclusion/inclusivity, 14, 28, 44, 92, 106, 128, 139, 152–53, 156; and care, ethics/operations of, 6, 26, 38, 173, 177, 182, 193–94, 202–3; radical, 6, 26, 38, 173, 202–3

Indigenous people, 33–34, 130–31, 162

Indonesia, 72

inequality: economic, 42; growing, 8, 201; structural, 191. *See also* intersectionality

infrastructure, 19, 23–24, 27

injustice, 8, 17, 21–22, 24, 34, 94. *See also* justice

Instagram. *See* social media

insurrection, 50, 54, 102, 162, 193, 204. *See also* rebellion, Black

interdependence, 157, 161, 197, 201; "we have each other," 160–61

International Monetary Fund, 72

internet. *See* social media; *specific movements, e.g.,* Black Joy Project

intersectionality, 9, 24, 26, 108

Isoke, Zenzele, 181–82, 234n64

Iton, Richard, 43–44, 65, 76–77, 192, 218, 235n83

Jackson, Esther Cooper, 66

James, C.L.R., 47–48, 192

James, Joy, 41, 57

jazz music, 69, 188, 192

Jemmont, Zakiya, 24

Jet magazine, 189–92, *190*

Jim Crow, 58, 64, 99

Johnson, Javon, 125, 128, 132, 229n40

Johnson, John H., 191

Jones, Claudia, 66

Joseph, Marc Bamuthi, 127–28

joy, Black, 37, 121–58, 167, 229n28; the Black ecstatic, 153, 157; the Black Joy Experience (BJE), 128–29, 147; *The Black Joy Experience Resource Guide,* 179, 233n23; *The Black Joy Experience* (album), 233n23; *Black Joy Mixtape,* 126, 147; The Black Joy Project (TBJP), 133–35, 138–51, *144, 146, 148,* 181–82, 230n71 (*see also* Cruz, Kleaver); in and as Black life, 131–34; "Blueprint for the Black Joy Era"(TEDx Talk, Phillips and Walker), 126–27; era of, 125–31; expressions of, 43, 132, 142; as

honoring the dead and dying, 131–32; as how liberation might look and feel, 158; from love embodied in face of oppression, 149; M4BL's insistence on, 76; and moving while captive, 46, 52–53 (*see also* chanting; dancing; shouting; singing); necessity of, 124, 131, 138, 142, 147, 150–51, 158; as political act, 134–36; power of, 147, 151, 202–3; as practice, 133, 154; as rebellion, 121–58; as refusing the repetition of Black death, 154–55; unapologetic, 11, 37, 39; in the wake, 124, 131, 138, 142, 147, 149–51, 158. *See also* celebration

justice, 28, 39, 62, 96–97, 102, 139; anti-Blackness and impossibility of, 96; economic, 97; healing, 174–80; punitive (*see* carceral power); racial, 2, 16, 22, 28, 96, 150; redefining/reimagining, 13, 177; struggle for, 132–33; transformative, 178. *See also* injustice

Kaba, Mariame, 180

Karenga, Maulana, 73

Karenga, Ron, 197

Kenosha, WI, 31–33

kick-back, 163, 167, 169, 232n13, 233n20

Kindred Southern Healing Collective, 175

King, Martin Luther, Jr., 73, 102, 150

"Da King of the South" (K.O.S.) (Walker), 126

King, Rodney, 89

kitchens/the kitchen table, 180–84, 186, 192, 197, 235n85

Knowles, Beyoncé, 11, 135

Knowles, Solange, 160

Ku Klux Klan (KKK), 131

Kwanzaa, 197

language: of law and order, 14; of the oppressed/of the oppressor, 66; of rights and liberty, 54; of slavery's afterlife, 87. *See also* dialogue; grammar, Black; storytelling

laughter, 126, 132–33, 167

law and order, 14. *See also* carceral power; police

leadership, 21, 25, 28, 35, 62–63, 72; and care, ethics/operations of, 164–65; development, 25; heroic, 49

Lee, Robert E., 101, 226n61, 227n76

Lee, Spike, 143, 230n70

lesbian women, Black and Brown, 77. *See also* LGBTQ+ people

Levine, Lawrence, 126

Lewis, Sarah, 135

LGBTQ+ people, 26, 75, 153, 156–57, 193, 223n10; and queer nightlife, 153, 157. *See also by description, e.g.,* transgender and gender nonconforming (TGNC) people

liberalism, 49, 61, 91, 161, 166–67. *See also* neoliberalism; *specific topics, e.g.,* assimilation

liberation/Black liberation, 10, 12, 65, 75, 94–95, 106, 166–67, 173; a Black future premised on, 199; Black grammar as prefiguring, 53, 140–42, 145–46; Black liberation movements, 26, 167; how it might look and feel, 158 (*see also* joy, Black); as practice, 175–77. *See also* abolitionism; freedom

Liberator, The (anti-slavery newspaper), 55

life, Black. *See* Black life

livingness, Black, 53, 123, 199; "living while Black," 6, 234n63

Livingston, Jennie, 192

Locke, Alain, 66–68

looting, 49, 219n27

Lorde, Audre, 13, 54, 91, 159, 162, 170–73, 192, 233n43

love, 129, 132, 145; and Black joy, 149; for Blackness/being Black, 69–76, 168–69, 194, 233n23; embodied, despite oppression, 149; for ourselves and each other, 163–69, 186

Lumumba, Patrice, 73

Luv Story bar, 152; "A Ratchet Realm," 133, 152–54, *154,* 157–58, 167, 193–94

lynching, 10, 62, 89, 94, 114; legal, 96. *See also* murder

Maher, Geo, 10

Malcolm X, 17, 73, 143, 171, 230n70

March on Washington (1963), 25, 73

marginalization/marginalized people and groups, 6, 33–34, 44–45, 76–77, 91–92, 95, 120, 135; and care, ethics/operations of, 162, 176, 192–93; and centering the marginalized, 26, 39, 133, 147, 192; extrajudicial killing of, 103–4; geographies of, 112; the historically marginalized, 26–27, 39, 109, 126, 130, 133, 138, 147, 176, 192, 203; within the intramural, 77; and secondary marginalization, 44, 165, 192–93. *See also by description, e.g.,* LGBTQ+ people; people of color

Maroons, 49–50, 56–57, 63

Martin, Trayvon, 4, 20–22, 25, 31, 161, 170; and the Trayvon generation, 170

Marxism, 11, 30, 59

Marx, Karl, 7, 37, 41, 69

masculinity, 75, 164–65, 208

MAU (Millennial Activists United), 24, 216n65

Mayfield, Curtis, 49

Mayo, James, 99

McBride, Lee, 102

McDade, Tony, 31

McDuffie, Erik S., 66

McKay, Claude, 65

McKittrick, Katherine, 46, 53, 187, 199

men, Black, 26, 34, 77, 107, 127, 155–56; cis heterosexual, 10; extrajudicial murders of (*see individual names*); and sexism, 29, 61. *See also* masculinity

mental health, 169. *See also* care, operations of

Messenger, The (magazine), 66

M4BL. *See* Movement for Black Lives

middle class, Black, 54–55, 61, 70, 76, 135

Middle Passage, 28–29, 47–48, 52–53, 95–96, 131; slave ships, 42, 47–48, 52–53, 66, 83–84, 90, 182. *See also* diaspora, Black

Millennial Activists United (MAU), 24, 216n65

millennials, 14–16, 19–20, 23–24, 27. *See also* generations; *specific movements, e.g.,* Black Youth Project 100 (BYP100)

Million Hoodies, 20–22, 24, 216n53

Millions March, 4–5, 14, 16–17, 27, 93, 213n1, 235n88

Mills, Charles, 100

Minneapolis, MN, 10, 27, 31, 162

mobilization, Black/Black-led, 5, 16, 40, 77, 123, 136, 150–51, 192; and Black joy, 182; the first "wave of mass struggle," 19; mass, 12, 19; political, 138, 202; power of, 171; social media and, 18–20

Montgomery Bus Boycott, 73

monuments, Confederate. *See under* Confederacy: monuments of

Moore, Audley "Queen Mother," 66

Moore, Darnell, 23–24

Morgan, Jennifer, 48

Morrison, Toni, 192

Moten, Fred, 11–12, 32–33, 89, 95

mothers, Black, 96, 224n24

mourning. *See* death, Black; pain, Black

Movement for Black Lives (M4BL), 4, 8–10, 12–14, 27–43, 78, 133, 203, 208, 227n4; abolitionism of, 76; and Black joy, insistence on, 76, 133, 230n52; BYP100, relationship with, 166, 226n50, 227n4; and care, ethics/operations of, 173–74, 176, 180, 186; central platform of, 97–98; criticisms surrounding, 24, 226n50; evolution of, 12–14; generational character of, 20; and philosophical return to the source, 35–36; political and cultural zeitgeist triggered by, 13; political culture of, 9–10, 13–14, 20, 27–29, 35–40, 92, 202; rhizomatic nature of, 18; "Vision for Black Lives" statement, 42–43, 97. *See also* Black Lives Matter Movement

movements, social. *See* social movements

moving while captive, 46, 52–53. *See also* chanting; dancing; shouting; singing

Muhammad, Saladin, 19, 27

multiculturalism, 139

Murch, Donna, 20

murder: extrajudicial killings of Black and Brown people, 103–4; #SayHerName, 108; state-sanctioned, 3, 93, 96. *See also* lynching; *individual names*

music, 11, 14, 43, 61, 109–10, 127–29, 152–53, 192; the Black musical tradition, 69–71. *See also by description, e.g.,* blues; singing; *individual musicans/groups*

mutual-aid societies/parties, 63–64, 157

mutuality. *See* interdependence

National Association for Colored Women (NACW), 60–61, 65, 94

National Association for the Advancement of Colored People (NAACP), 61, 64, 94

nationalism: Black, 26, 52, 57–58, 61–62, 64–66, 73–76; racist, 160–61; white, 101, 103

National Urban League (NUL), 61

Neal, Larry, 67–71, 73

Negritude movement, 29, 59, 196

Negro World, The (Garvey), 65

neoliberalism, 33, 76; "neoliberal rationality," 8, 39

neo-Nazism, 32

New Negro movement, 29, 47, 58–68, 75. *See also* Harlem Renaissance

Newsome, Bree, 102–3, 226n65

Nichols, Synead (Cyd), 4–5, 16–17, 93, 213n3

"no-knock warrants," 108

Non-Aligned Movement, 72

nonviolence: civil disobedience, 21; direct action, 94, 102; Student Nonviolent Coordinating Committee (SNCC), 73, 166. *See also* protest

North Carolina, 100. *See also* Durham

North, U.S., 45, 53–58, 60, 64

Oakland, CA, 128, 130–31

Obama, Barack, 35, 135, 161

Occupy Wall Street, 8, 16

October Revolution, 64

oppression, 145–46; and anti-oppression work, 129; Black joy despite, 23, 149; interlocking systems of, 9, 24, 26, 108; language of the oppressed/language of the oppressor, 66; legacies of, 149; love embodied in face of, 149; as naturalized, 89, 224n20; structures of, 39; "triple," 66. *See also* intersectionality; violence

Organization for Black Struggle, 24

Organization of Afro-American Unity, 73

organizing/organizers, Black, 5, 23, 90, 105, 129, 205; "hidden abode" of, 165

Othering, 105

"our history/our culture" paradigm, 101, 105

Our Streets, Our Bodies, Our Voices (OS/OB/OV), 95, 107–9, *111–13*, 112, 117, *118–19*, 120, 165

Page, Cara, 175

pain, Black, 78, 83–120; capitalist system as feeding off, 15, 37–38, 121, 157, 162, 174, 181, 188, 197–98 and care, responding with, 174–75, 181, 188, 197–98; hypervisibility of, 27, 37, 39, 78, 202; as naturalized, 89; as not universal, 139; rebellion fueled by, 92 (*see also* rebellion); structural nature of, 133, 172, 178. *See also* death, Black; suffering, Black

Painter, Nell Irvin, 52, 63

Pan-Africanism, 63–65, 72

pandemic, Covid-19, 8–10, 152

Pantaleo, Daniel, 4

Paris Is Burning (Livingston), 192

Party Noire, 128–29, 147

paternalism, 45, 55, 64

patriarchy, 14, 35, 156–57; heteronormative, 79, 161, 173, 203; and violence, 34–35

people of color (POC), 3, 21, 124, 213n1, 226n64. *See also entries beginning with* Black; marginalized people and groups; *specific topics*

performance, Black, 127

performativity, Black, 123

personhood, 140, 172

Phillips, Amber J., 126, 128, 130

philosophy, Black, 41, 57; Afrarealism, 41. *See also by description, e.g.,* Movement for Black Lives

plantation politics, 36, 44–45, 49–54, 63, 66, 79, 106, 204; and Black joy, 122, 132; and care, ethics/operations of, 165–69, 183

"poethics of Blackness," 130

poetry, 7, 11, 37, 65–68, 71, 89–90, 125, 127

police: abolitionist vs. reformist approach to, 10, 92, 226n50; money spent on, 10, 92; and "no knock warrants," 108; and property as superordinate to Black life, 31–32, 49, 204; and racialized violence/brutality, 10, 24, 107–8, 213n1; and racial policing, 222n3; state-sanctioned murder by, 3, 93, 96 (*see also individual names*); surveillance and militarized policing of Black communities, 33, 118. *See also* carceral power

political culture. *See under specific topics, e.g.,* Movement for Black Lives: political culture of

politics: Electoral College, U.S., 9; generational, 14–16, 28. *See also by description, e.g.,* transfiguration, politics of

politics, Black, 76–79; and the Black counterpublic, 18–19, 27, 43, 53, 61, 76–78, 180, 191, 197; and Black joy as political act, 134–36; "Black life politics," 123; and Black political action, 13, 27, 142, 145–46, 151; and Black political development, 30–31, 37–38, 42, 48–49, 56, 58, 70, 106,

129, 170–71, 173, 182, 203; and care as political act, 175; and political education,
25–26, 129; and political freedom, 26;
a "politics without rule," 52, 204; "the
Black regime," 77; in the wake (*see under*
wake, living in: politics in/of). *See also*
mobilization, Black; *specific topics/
descriptions, e.g.,* Movement for Black
Lives (M4BL); plantation politics
popular culture, Black, 44, 191–92
poverty, 39, 77, 190; Black underclasses, 36,
63; "war on," 226n51
power: of anticipation, 29, 204; Black empowerment, 182; of Black joy, 147, 151,
202–3; of Black mobilization, 171; dynamics within Black community, 44; layers
of, 91–92; power relations, 30. *See also*
authority; Black Power; *by description,
e.g.,* carceral power; white supremacy
"Power" chant, 122–23
prefiguration, Black, 79
pregnancy, 224n24
presidency, U.S., 72, 161. *See also individual
names*
pride, 61, 103, 124, 172
prisons, 12, 23, 33, 131; abolitionist vs. reformist approach to, 226n50. *See also*
abolitionism; carceral power
private property. *See* property
privilege, 44, 60, 149–50
property: Black ownership of, 53–54, 56;
defacement of, 10, 50, 95, 99–106, 227n76;
protection of/as superordinate to Black
life, 31–32, 49, 204. *See also specific topics,
e.g.,* slavery
Prosser, Gabriel, 50
protest, Black, 5, 30–33, 41–42, 49, 123, 150,
219n27; described as "looting," 49,
219n27; modes of, 53; as resulting from
Black death (*see* death, Black); street
protests, 12. *See also by name/description,
e.g.,* Black Lives Matter Movement;
uprisings

public space, 99, 103–4, 107, 143; "social
cleansing of," 33
public sphere, 55, 62, 70, 138; Black, 44,
76–77 (*see also* counterpublic, Black);
plantation, 45–46, 52

queer people, 153; and queer nightlife, 153,
157. *See also* LGBTQ+ people
quotidian experience/quotidian spaces, 86,
145, 148, 173–74, 181; kitchens/the kitchen
table, 180–84, 186, 192, 197, 235n85. *See also*
Black experience; Black life: everyday

race: gendered racial-colonial dominance,
121; multiracial activism, 4, 11–12, 20–21.
See also specific topics
racial capitalism. *See under* capitalism:
racial
racial codes, 60, 84
racial justice, 2, 16, 22, 28, 96, 150
racial regimes, 29, 204
racial violence. *See under* violence: racial
racism: anti-Black, 11, 21–23, 28, 54–55. *See
also* anti-Blackness; intersectionality
radicalism, Black, 12, 14, 44–45, 48, 66, 70,
72, 77, 186, 202–4, 208; and anticipation,
power of, 29, 204; and Black joy, 150–51;
and Black radical feminism, 41, 170–71;
the Black radical tradition, 29–30, 36–37,
128–30, 150–51; of the colonized and enslaved, 36, 51–53, 79, 123, 204; as emerging
from Black pain, 95, 98. *See also specific
topics, e.g.,* ungovernability
Rael, Patrick, 54
rage: in aftermath of George Floyd's lynching, 10; Black mothers and, 96; for
change, 172; forced upon us by anti-
Blackness, 124–25; generational, 16; of
individuals with murderous intentions,
32. *See also* anger
Rainey, Gertrude "Ma," 67, 69
Randall, Dudley, 68
Randolph, A. Philip, 65–67, 69

Rankine, Claudia, 90

Ransby, Barbara, 18, 25

Ransby-Sporn, Asha, 19–20

rape, 34–35, 48

rap music, 11

"A Ratchet Realm," 133, 152–54, 154, 157–58, 167, 193–94

ratchet, the term, 153–54, 158, 193–94

rebellion, Black, 7, 33, 42, 46, 48, 57, 73; and Black grammar, 53, 140–42, 145–46; Black pain as fueling, 92; joyful, 121–58; slavery and/beginning of, 48; techniques of, 63, 79; in time of #BlackLivesMatter, 7–8, 12, 26–29, 35, 37, 40–43, 47, 94, 105, 124, 153, 161–63, 174, 179, 182, 186, 202–4. See also insurrection

reconstruction of society, 34, 36, 46–47, 75, 204

Reconstruction, the, 58–64 passim, 99; the "Reconstruction Generation," 60

redistributive policies, 71

Red Scare, 72

"red summers," 64

Reed, Adolph, 77

Reed, Anthony, 7, 28

reforms/reformism, 14–15, 53–58, 216n65, 226n50

refusal, practice of, 92

regard, 94–95, 98

reggae music, 153

reinvention, process of, 46, 52–53

reparations, 97

repetition of Black death, 27, 31, 78, 90, 96–98, 202, 223n3; Black joy as refusing, 154–55

"replacement" theory, 9

republicans, classical, 52, 54

Republicans/GOP, present-day. See right-wing movements; Trump, Donald

resilience: of Afrarealism, 41; of Black life, 40, 121, 191

resistance: armed, 65–66; Black joy as form of, 134; body as site of, 52; civil disobedience, nonviolent, 21; as core/soul of Black life, 46; and nondominated action,

52; by slaves, techniques and modes of, 50–53. See also grammar, Black; protest

respectability, 28, 45, 55–56, 58, 66–67, 74, 76, 89, 171; Black joy and, 135, 153, 156, 158; rejection of, 63, 67, 193; respectability politics, 114

revival, 21, 123

revolt, techniques of, 46, 51

revolution, 7, 16, 36–37, 44, 50–51, 54, 64, 72; Black joy and "revolutionary practice," 150; Black slave as revolutionary subject, 36, 79, 162, 204; and care, ethics/operations of, 163, 167, 173, 179, 181; "rehearsals of," 11; violent, 50, 56–57, 220n56

Revolutionary Action Movement, 73

Reynolds, Diamond, 83–88, 93, 223n7

rhythm and blues (R&B) music, 11, 152–53

Riggs, Marlon, 43, 192

rights, 139–40; equal, 150, 154; human, 21, 140; natural, 47–48. See also Civil Rights movement

right-wing movements, 9, 31–32; Charlottesville, VA, "Unite the Right" rally in, 101, 105; "us and them" mentality of, 101, 105. See also fascism; Trump, Donald

Riley, Clayton, 132

Rittenhouse, Kyle, 32

rituals, 46, 123–24, 129, 167–69, 176, 225n30

Roberts, Christopher, 178–80

Robeson, Paul, 66

Robinson, Autumn, 107–11, 114–17

Robinson, Cedric, 36–37, 46, 49–50, 55, 57–58, 72

Rodriguez, Dylan, 33, 121

Rolle, Esther, 190, 190–92, 235n79

Roof, Dylann, 102–3

Rosenbaum, Joseph, 32

Roye, Radcliffe "Ruddy," 135

safety, 21, 39, 49, 107, 109–14; "Agenda to Keep Us Safe" (BYP100), 225n48; and care, ethics/operations of, 177, 198

sage-burning, 160, 173–74, 232n3

Salau, Oluwatoyin, 34

Sambo, 60

sanctuary, 157, 178, 181. *See also* care, ethics/
operations of

San Domingo Revolution, 50

Sankofa, *196*

#SayHerName, 108

Scott, David, 15, 225n30

Scott, Dred. See *Dred Scott v. Sandford*

Scott, Rick, 22

secondary marginalization, 44, 165, 192–93

segregation, 42, 58

self-care, 129, 169. *See also* care, ethics/
operations of

self-defense, 20, 65

self-determination: Black, 56–57, 63–65, 68,
73–74, 103, 176; liberal, 92

self-fashioning: Black, 61, 78, 171; collective,
29, 31, 45–47, 54, 75, 203

self-help, 45, 58, 65

self-reflection, 172

Senghor, Léopold, 59

Sense, Britt, 135

separatism, Black, 57, 63

sexism, 24; of Black men, 61; Black men
against, 29; cissexism, 79

sexual assault/violence, 34–35, 48

sexuality, 4, 16, 26, 44, 76, 91, 120, 165, 170,
202, 208

sexual orientation, 107–8

sex workers, 73

Shakur, Assata, 163

Sharpe, Christina, 91, 124, 188–89; on an
ethics of care, 161–62, 177, 200, 202–3;
on largeness that is Black life, 38, 124; on
total climate of anti-Blackness, 30, 38

Simone, Nina, 69

Sims, Vicky, 34

singing, 53, 121, 123–24, 129, 132, 168, 190, 205.
See also chants/chanting; music

Singleton, Andre, 182–87, *185*, 189–93, 197,
234n70. *See also* Very Black Project

Sinha, Manisha, 28

sitcoms, Black, 190–91

sit-ins, 73, 102

slavery, 36, 42–58, 83, 197; abolition of, 54–56;
and Black radicalism, invention of, 51–53;
and Black rebellion, 48; Maroons, 49–50,
56–57, 63; and modern-day slave narratives, 90; and politics of the enslaved, 69,
75–76, 79, 204 (*see also* plantation politics); and radicalism of the enslaved, 36,
51–53, 79, 123, 204; and reframing Black
slave as revolutionary subject, 36, 79, 162,
204; and resistance, techniques and
modes of, 50–53; slave ships/the Middle
Passage, 28, 42, 47–48, 52–53, 66, 83–84,
90, 95, 131, 182; and violence against enslaved women, 48, 100. *See also* captivity;
plantation politics; wake, living in

Smethurst, James Edward, 69

Smith, Bessie, 67, 69

Smith, Neil, 33

socialism, 15, 64–66, 72

social media, 4, 17–20, 77–78, 166, 213n1,
230n71; Black death recorded on, 27, 78,
83–88, 90, 97, 140, 202; and Black joy,
125–27, 134–38, 143–46, *146*, *148*, *154*; and
hypervisibility of Black pain, 27, 37, 39,
78, 202; as public square, 18–20, 202;
and social movements, 13. *See also*
#BlackLivesMatter; Very Black Project

social movements, 6, 12–13, 28, 94, 133, 176;
Black-led, 5–6, 39; global, 202. *See also by
name/description*

social order, 11, 15, 34, 164, 201

solidarity/solidarities, 13, 52, 126, 137, 164,
176, 204; antebellum, 55; around freedom
yet to come, 48–49; Black intramural,
26–28, 194; international/transnational,
9, 62–63, 72

Solomon, Marisa, 14, 122, 210–11. *See also*
grammar, Black

song. *See* music; singing

Sontag, Susan, 98

soul music, 69

South Africa, 150–51

South Carolina, 102–3

Southern Christian Leadership Conference, 73

South, U.S., 51, 53, 57, 63–64, 75, 94, 99–100, 105. *See also specific locations; specific topics, e.g.,* Confederacy

sovereignty: Black, 56; performance of, 65; white, 123, 136, 150, 210, 223n3, 224n29

Soviet Union, 72

space/spaces: of care, 178, 181–82; racing of/ racialized battle over, 100–101, 105. *See also* public space; quotidian spaces

Spillers, Hortense, 96, 140–42

Springer, Kimberly, 77

Stand Your Ground laws, 4, 20

Stanley, Eric, 153–54, 156

Stay Woke, Stay Whole: A Black Activist Healing Manual (BYP100), 178–80, 232n3

Steez, Fresco, 34–35, 125

stereotypes, Black, 60

Sterling, Alton, 97

Stewart, Maria, 55

storytelling, 181, 191; modern-day slave narratives, 90

street harassment, 116–17

street protests, 12

strikes, 36

struggle, Black, 7, 22, 24, 58, 61, 173; dual mode of address, 28, 55–56; for freedom, 52–53; and intramural struggles, 122; principled, 232n15; role of leadership in, 63; waged by dispossessed against domination, 36–39

Stuckey, Sterling, 47, 52

Student Nonviolent Coordinating Committee (SNCC), 73, 166

subjection, 6, 10, 48, 51, 89, 95–98, 125, 156, 202; refusal of, 36

subjugation, 38–40, 64, 85–86, 90, 172

submissiveness, performative, 85

suffering, Black, 133; geographies of, 56, 105–6; spectacle of, 89. *See also* pain, Black; trauma; vulnerability

Supreme Court, U.S., 9, 56, 73; *Brown v. Board of Education,* 73; *Dred Scott v. Sandford,* 56, 91

survival, Black, 123, 134; as core/soul of Black life, 46; everyday heroism of, 5, 40; "frontiers of survival," 96; trying to live when you were not meant to survive, 73. *See also* care, ethics/operations of

"talented tenth," 62

Taylor, Breonna, 31, 88, 108, 214n20, 227n76; #SayHerName, 108

Taylor, Je Naé, 168, 179–80

TBJP. *See* Black Joy Project, The

Terrell, Mary Church, 60–62

terror/terrorism: anti-Black, 20, 31, 114, 155, 202–3; "car ramming," 32; "war on," 97

Tesfamariam, Rahiel, 193

Texas, 100, 155

theater, 71, 73, 127–28, 132

Third World Women's Alliance, 77

Thomas, Edward, 155

Thompson, Takiya, 99–104, 106, 226n65

Threadcraft, Shatema, 88–89, 107–8, 223n10, 224n17

Till, Emmett, 93–94

Till-Mobley, Mamie, 94

Tometi, Opal, 22

Tongues Untied (Riggs), 192

Toomer, Jean, 68

transfiguration, politics of, 150

transformative justice, 178

transgender and gender nonconforming (TGNC) people, 112–14, 153, 155–56, 165. *See also* gender nonconforming people; LGBTQ+ people; transgender people

transphobia, 156

trauma, 84, 108–9, 143, 186; collective, 126, 131–32, 169–70; generational, 5, 173–75, 188; grief and healing in aftermath/

moving through, 18, 169–70, 173–80; historical, 174; of secondary marginalization, 165; of state violence, 31, 174. *See also specific events and descriptions, e.g.,* sexual assault

Trenton, New Jersey, 31

Trouillot, Michel-Rolph, 6

Trump, Donald, 9, 101, 105, 159–61, 169, 197, 232nn1–2

Tubman, Harriet, 46, 227n76

Turner, Nat, 50, 57

TV sitcoms, Black, 190–91

2020 uprisings, 27, 31–34, 41, 49, 53, 78, 88, 97, 102, 105, 108, 227n76 (*See also* Floyd, George; Taylor, Breonna)

twerking, 152–53, 158

Twitter. *See* social media

Ujima, 197–98

unapologetic Blackness, 37, 61, 68, 79, 114, 125, 157, 182, 186–87, 198, 202

underclasses, Black, 36, 63

Underground Railroad, 49

ungovernability, 63, 122, 153–54, 157, 193

United Nations, 72

United States: Black experience in, 25 (*see also* Black experience); Constitution of, 54; and the 2008 financial collapse, 8, 77; as "leader of the free world," 72; mainstream life in, 74; presidency of, 72, 161 (*see also individual presidents*); rightward lurch in politics of, 226n51; and "us/them" mentality, 101, 105. *See also specific locations; specific topics and events, e.g.,* Civil War, U.S.

unity, 13, 46, 52–53, 74

universalism, 54, 139

Universal Negro Improvement Association (UNIA), 64–66

uplift, 45, 56, 58, 64–65, 76, 89, 168, 191; Black joy and, 123, 126, 128, 134–35, 144

uprisings: of 2020, 27, 31–34, 41, 49, 53, 78, 88, 97, 102, 105, 108, 227n76 (*See also* Floyd, George; Taylor, Breonna); *See also by description, e.g.,* Arab uprisings; Ferguson uprisings

"us and them" mentality, 101, 105

utopia, 8, 132, 149

Van Peebles, Melvin, 132

Very Black Project, 180, 182–98, 234n66, 234n70, 235nn74–88; as call to action, 186, 193; as ongoing conversation, 196. *See also* Fulton, Justin; Singleton, Andre

Vesey, Denmark, 50

"Victorian Black feminism," 60–62

Victorian ideals, 60, 67

Vietnam, 72

vigilante violence, 4, 20–22, 25–26, 31–32, 90

violence: anti-Black, 19, 33, 62, 64, 90, 103, 125, 142, 235n79; anti-trans, 155–56; and armed resistance, 65–66; Blackness and, 224n25; of capitalist world system, 162, 201; intramural, 165, 170; patriarchal, 34–35; physical, against enslaved women, 48, 100; racial, 14, 42, 46, 53, 73, 95, 102, 131, 139, 181; revolutionary, 50, 56–57, 220n56; sexual, 34–35, 48; state-sanctioned, 3, 94, 107; structural, 162; systems of, 21, 216n75; white, 56, 94. *See also by description, e.g.,* murder; vigilante violence

Virginia, 100, 227n76. *See also* Charlottesville

visibility: hypervisibility of Black pain, 27, 37, 39, 78, 202; politics of, 94

Voting Rights Act, 73, 76

vulnerability, 26, 39, 90, 95, 97, 122, 157. *See also* interdependence

wake/living in the wake, 6, 38, 200–205; and care, need for, 161, 169, 174, 181–82; necessity of Black joy in, 124, 131, 138, 142, 147, 149–51, 158; politics in/of, 38–40, 47, 76, 95, 124, 138, 150, 161, 174, 182, 200–205

Walker, David, 42–43, 57, 126, 128, 130–31

Walker, Jazmine, 126

war: on Black people/forever war waged against Black life, 97–98; guerilla warfare, 49; metaphors of, 97, 226n51. *See also specific wars*

War for Independence, 53

Warren, Calvin, 90, 142, 162

Washington, Booker T., 62

Washington, Kerry James, 192

Washington, March on (1963), 25, 73

Watts uprising, 73

Weems, Carrie Mae, 192, 235n85

"we have each other," 160–61

welfare state regimes, 72

Wells, Ida B., 62, 94

"We Ready, We Coming" chant, 124

West, Cornel, 132–33

Western civilization, 78, 205

"What's Wrong with You" chant, 123

"while Black," the phrase, 6, 234n63

white abolitionists, 55–56

white domination, 53, 100

white forms, 74–75

white nationalism, 101, 103

whiteness, 60, 90–91, 101, 226n57. *See also specific topics, e.g.,* property

white sense, 14, 36–38, 42, 79, 203

white sovereignty, 123, 136, 150, 210, 223n3, 224n29

white supremacy, 6, 9–13, 29–33, 42–47, 53–55, 60–65, 79; Black counterpublic as providing counternarratives to, 191; and Black joy, 123, 130–31, 135, 149–50; and Black pain, 86, 91, 101–6; calling out, 123; and care, ethics/operations of, 170–71, 191; Charlottesville, VA, "Unite the Right" rally in, 101, 105; global, 150; neo-Nazism, 32; self-defense and armed resistance against, 65–66; structural nature of, 54, 58. *See also* anti-Blackness

Williamson, Terrion, 121, 129, 146, 180–82, 234n65

Withers, Bill, 11

women, Black, 22, 24, 27, 60–66, 77, 125–27, 192, 213n3, 235n85; Black mothers, 96, 224n24; club movement of, 60–61; enslaved, physical violence against, 48, 100; as "hidden abode" of Black organizing, 165; lived experience of Black working-class, 66; murders of, 108, 165 (*see also individual names*); National Association for Colored Women (NACW), 60–61, 65, 94; and pregnancy/birth, 224n24; "unruly," 153; "wayward lives" of turn-of-the-century young, 63–64. *See also specific topics, e.g.,* feminism; kitchens; sexism

working class, Black, 59, 64, 66–67

world-making, 39, 46, 79, 132, 181, 203–5

World War I, 59, 64, 66

World War II, 66–67

Wright, Richard, 59, 66–67

Wynter, Sylvia, 12, 36, 53, 60, 93, 204, 224n20

Yanez, Jeronimo, 83–88, 90, 93–96

"yet to come," 52, 79, 105, 122, 153, 169, 217n93; freedom as, 34, 48–49, 124

York, Asanni, 157

Yoruba religion, 233n21, 235n77

youth-led organizations, 24, 166

Zimmerman, George, 4, 20–22; acquittal of, 4, 22, 25